Researching Play from a Playwork Perspective

Play is of critical importance to the well-being of children across the globe, a fact reflected in Article 31 of the United Nations Convention on the Rights of the Child (UNCRC). Yet, existing literature on the subject is largely confined to discussing play from a developmental, educational or psychological perspective. *Researching Play from a Playwork Perspective* offers a new and exciting angle from which to view play, drawing on the authors' own experience of conducting research into various aspects of this all-important and pervasive phenomenon.

This innovative work will act as a compass for those looking to undertake research into different aspects of play and child welfare. Each chapter explores how the author has combined established and new research methodologies with their individual playwork approaches to arrive at emergent understandings of playwork research. The overall conclusion discusses directions for future research and develops a new model of playwork research from the four common themes that emerge from the contributions of individual authors: children's rights, process, critical reflection and playfulness. Examples from the United Kingdom, Nicaragua and Sweden give this unique work international relevance.

Researching Play from a Playwork Perspective will appeal to researchers and students around the world working in the fields of playwork, childcare, early years, education, psychology and children's rights. It should also be of interest to practitioners in a wide variety of professional contexts, including childcare and therapy.

Pete King is a senior lecturer in Childhood Studies at Swansea University, and his current research has been published in both national and international journals, including *Journal of Playwork Practice* and the *American Journal of Play*. Pete currently lectures on Children's Rights, Developmental and Therapeutic Play, Perspectives on Play and Research Methods.

Shelly Newstead is a doctoral candidate at the UCL Institute of Education, London, and has worked in the playwork field for over 25 years as a practitioner, trainer, author, editor and publisher. Shelly is the founding editor of the *Journal of Playwork Practice* and the Vice-President of ICCP (International Council for Children's Play).

Advances in Playwork Research
Series Editor: Shelly Newstead, UCL, UK

Advances in Playwork Research features original international scholarship from the emerging discipline of playwork, bringing together cutting-edge research by those working in the playwork field and studies on playwork from other disciplines. The series explores a wide range of topics related to the theory and practice of playwork, from empirical research on playwork practices, to conceptual studies on playwork theory and research. *Advances in Playwork Research* encompasses a variety of methodological approaches, including qualitative, quantitative, mixed methods and historical studies.

https://www.routledge.com/Advances-in-Playwork-Research/book-series/APR

Books in this series:

Researching Play from a Playwork Perspective
Edited by Pete King and Shelly Newstead

Researching Play from a Playwork Perspective

Edited by Pete King and
Shelly Newstead

LONDON AND NEW YORK

First published 2018
by Routledge
2 Park Square, Milton Park, Abingdon, Oxon OX14 4RN

and by Routledge
711 Third Avenue, New York, NY 10017

Routledge is an imprint of the Taylor & Francis Group, an informa business

© 2018 selection and editorial matter, Pete King and Shelly Newstead; individual chapters, the contributors

The right of the editors to be identified as the authors of the editorial material, and of the authors for their individual chapters, has been asserted in accordance with sections 77 and 78 of the Copyright, Designs and Patents Act 1988.

All rights reserved. No part of this book may be reprinted or reproduced or utilised in any form or by any electronic, mechanical, or other means, now known or hereafter invented, including photocopying and recording, or in any information storage or retrieval system, without permission in writing from the publishers.

Trademark notice: Product or corporate names may be trademarks or registered trademarks, and are used only for identification and explanation without intent to infringe.

British Library Cataloguing-in-Publication Data
A catalogue record for this book is available from the British Library

Library of Congress Cataloging-in-Publication Data
A catalog record for this book has been requested

ISBN: 978-1-138-65607-9 (hbk)
ISBN: 978-1-315-62214-9 (ebk)

Typeset in Galliard
by Apex CoVantage, LLC

To all the past, present and future playworkers who push the boundaries of playwork.

Contents

List of figures ix
Acknowledgements x
List of contributors xi
Abbreviations xiv
Foreword by Peter K. Smith xv

Introduction 1
PETE KING AND SHELLY NEWSTEAD

1 **Why the playworker's mind-set is ideal for research with children: child researchers investigate education rights in Nicaragua** 8
HARRY SHIER

2 **Playwork research as the art of 'mirroring'** 25
SHELLY NEWSTEAD

3 **Nomadic wonderings on playwork research: putting a dialectical and ethnographic methodology to work again** 39
WENDY RUSSELL

4 **Researching children's play as a playworker-ethnographer** 56
HANNAH SMITH BRENNAN

5 **Playing at research: playfulness as a form of knowing and being in research with children** 73
PHILIP WATERS

6 Process, participation and reflection: how playwork practice influenced a mixed-methods approach to researching children's perception of choice in their play 90
PETE KING

7 Using action research to explore play facilitation in school-based school-age childcare settings 109
EVA KANE

Conclusion 123
PETE KING AND SHELLY NEWSTEAD

Index 129

Figures

3.1	Second-generation model of an activity system	46
6.1	Research design map	99
6.2	Play Detective Diary sheet	100
6.3	The Play Choice Scale	101
8.1	Researching play from a playwork perspective	126

Acknowledgements

We would like to thank all the contributors to this monograph for sharing their playwork and PhD experiences, and Gordon Sturrock and the late Professor Perry Else, who encouraged us both on our own research journeys. We would also like to thank the staff at Routledge for their support and each other for such an interesting project!

Contributors

Eva Kane works as senior lecturer in pedagogy at Jönköping University, where she teaches at the teacher training program for school-age childcare. Her PhD was an action research project that explored staffs' play practices at school-age childcare. She lived for 19 years in Northern Ireland, where she spent the last six years working for PlayBoard NI developing the 'Fit for Play' quality award for out of school clubs. When she returned to Sweden in 2007, she started working in school-age childcare in a school in Sollentuna, before moving on to Stockholm University. Eva has made several contributions to books in Swedish used in the teacher training for school-age childcare staff. She has also written some articles in English: for example, "'What If? As If', an approach to action research practice: becoming-different in school-age childcare", published in *Educational Action Research 2015*.

Pete King is a senior lecturer at Swansea University and teaches across a range of undergraduate and postgraduate programmes, including Therapeutic and Developmental Play and Research Methods. Pete's professional practice in play and playwork began in 1996 by setting up and running an out of school club within a primary school in Oxford and then moved on to be responsible for a DfEE-funded project (Wokingham Out of School Demonstration Club Project), which was used as a pilot study for the publication *Best Play*. Pete has worked as a play development officer, playwork trainer and playwork lecturer and has developed play and playwork strategically in both England and Wales. Pete was responsible for the first open access play project in Pembrokeshire and then co-ran the successful BIG Lottery-funded Purple Routes project.

Shelly Newstead is a doctoral candidate at the UCL Institute of Education, London, and has worked in the playwork field for over 25 years as a practitioner, trainer, author, editor and publisher. Shelly is the founding editor of the *Journal of Playwork Practice* and the Vice-President of ICCP (International Council for Children's Play). Her current research interests include the history of playwork, and she has recently republished several rare adventure playground publications through www.commonthreads.org.uk. Shelly is also the Series Editor for the Routledge Advances in Playwork Research series.

Wendy Russell currently works as a Senior Lecturer in Play and Playwork at the University of Gloucestershire and as a consultant on children's play and playwork. She has worked in the playwork sector in the UK for over 40 years, first as a playworker on adventure playgrounds in London, then in a number of roles, including development work, research and education and training. Her freelance work has included working on a range of training, development, strategic, evaluation and research projects for local authorities, the private sector and local and national voluntary organisations. Her key publications include co-editing two volumes of *Philosophy of Play* (Routledge, 2013, 2015, with Malcolm MacLean and Emily Ryall), plus (with Stuart Lester) *Children's Right to Play: An Examination of the Importance of Play in the Lives of Children Worldwide* (Bernard van Leer, 2010) and *Play for a Change: Play, Policy and Practice – a Review of Contemporary Perspectives* (Play England, 2008).

Harry Shier was born in Belfast, Ireland, in 1954. He worked in England for many years, initially on adventure playgrounds, then in playwork training. In 1988 he founded Playtrain, an independent training agency specialising in children's rights, play and creativity. In the 1990s he worked and wrote extensively on children's participation rights, most notably developing the "Article 31 Children's Consultancy Scheme", which enables children to act as consultants to the management of cultural institutions, helping them make facilities and programmes child-friendly. This experience was crystallised in his 2001 paper "Pathways to Participation", which introduced a tool for analysing children's participation in decision-making that is now widely used throughout the world.

In 2001 he moved to Nicaragua, Central America, where he worked with a local community education organisation, CESESMA, supporting child workers on the region's coffee plantations in defending their rights – including the right to play. His published work from this period includes "Children as public actors: Navigating the tensions" (2010), "How children and young people influence policy-makers: Lessons from Nicaragua" (2014) and "Children as researchers in Nicaragua: Children's consultancy to transformative research" (2015), as well as significant work in Spanish. In 2009, on behalf of the International Play Association, he drew up the final report of the Global Consultation on Children's Right to Play, which helped convince the UN Committee on the Rights of the Child of the need for a General Comment on Article 31.

He is currently based in Ireland, where he has just completed a PhD at the Queen's University Belfast Centre for Children's Rights on Nicaraguan children's perceptions of human rights in school. His published writing, in English and Spanish, is available at www.harryshier.net.

Hannah Smith Brennan (née Hannah Henry Smith) currently teaches Sociology of Childhood in the Department of Sociology and Anthropology at James Madison University, Virginia. Since the 1990s, Dr. Henry Smith's work with children and youth has focused on professional practice that supports social, physical, intellectual, creative and emotional development. Her current academic and professional interests include informal education, children's rights, play, health and well-being, social and cultural identity and social constructions of children and childhood. As a consultant and social market researcher, Dr. Henry Smith has worked on access to play spaces, youth health and well-being, programme evaluation and national behaviour change initiatives. Dr. Henry Smith brings an engaged, dynamic and insightful approach to working with diverse young people, youth-serving organisations and university students to promote meaningful exchanges between professional practice and academic knowledge. Dr. Henry Smith is a member of the *Journal of Playwork Practice* editorial advisory board.

Philip Waters is the Creative Director for I Love Nature (ilovenature.org.uk), an activities, training and consultancy company in Cornwall, UK, and a researcher at the European Centre for Environment and Human Health, University of Exeter Medical School, UK. With an interest in children's fiction and a career of over 20 years working in various children's environments, Phil's research brings together play, narrative and nature within a visual methodological framework that aims to critically develop a form of praxis called 'narrative journey'. He is a keen writer, filmmaker and story-maker and enjoys bringing these elements together in his research with children.

Abbreviations

CESESMA	Centro de Servicios educativos en Salud y Medio Ambiente
CHAT	Cultural Historical Activity Theory
CPC	Children's Play Council (now called Play England)
IPA	International Playgrounds Association (now called International Play Association)
JNCTP	Joint National Committee on Training for Playwork
MAST	Manipulation of Affordances Scenarios Tasks
NOS	National Occupational Standards
NPFA	National Playing Fields Association (now called Fields in Trust)
NTOSRAO	National Training Organisation for Sport Recreation and Allied Occupations
NVQ	National Vocational Qualifications
Ofsted	Office for Standards in Education
PPSG	Playwork Principles Scrutiny Group
SNAE	Swedish National Agency for Education
TCCAAPC	The Crawley Community Association Adventure Playground Committee
TCRA	Transformative Research by Children and Adolescents
UK	United Kingdom
UN	United Nations
UNCRC	United Nations Convention on the Rights of the Child
UNICEF	United Nations International Children's Emergency Fund

Foreword

I enjoyed reading this intriguing collection of reflections on researching by playworkers. The authors are, or have been, in various ways carrying out research on the playwork experience. It is interesting to read the accounts of their own backgrounds and experiences. As is pointed out, this can considerably influence the kinds of research that one is interested in, the aims and the methods and philosophical approach that is taken.

The methods and approaches described are indeed very varied, although on the whole rather different from the more quantitative methods traditionally used in psychological research on play. I am very much in favour of using different methods, or combining methods, as appropriate to fit the aims of the study. Despite some commonalities, the variety of approaches presented in this book will be stimulating for the reader to assimilate, and there is a challenging set of distinctions made in many chapters, and at times quite philosophical discussions, to think about.

Many of the contributors grapple with the issue of the extent to which play can really be entirely a free choice of the child, and whether the 'adulteration' of play – intrusive adult guidance – is something to be avoided as destroying the benefits of free play. I see some force in the argument that the concept of an individual child freely choosing a play activity independent of any social and cultural context is rather meaningless. There are always constraints (or affordances) in the physical and social environment. Having said that, there are probably different benefits depending on the extent to which adults guide children's play. Minimal adult involvement can be beneficial for a child's own sense of empowerment and experiential learning. However, children are growing up in a larger society, and Vygotsky's notion of the ZPD (zone of proximal development), or Bruner's similar notion of scaffolding, suggest how sensitive adult involvement, which is attuned to the child's present state of development, can be beneficial in helping them cope with new challenges (Smith, Cowie, & Blades, 2015).

Another major theme in this book relates to the rights of children, and relatedly, the role of children and young people in the research process. Hart (1992), revised by Treseder (1997), designated five levels of this, in which young people are (i) Assigned but informed, or (ii) Consulted and informed, through to

(iii) Adult-initiated shared decisions with young people, (iv) Young people-initiated shared decisions with adults and (v) Young people-initiated and directed. Many chapters provide interesting consideration around how this set of issues was approached. The ages of children and their understanding of relevant issues are an important consideration. There should clearly always be respect for the rights of children in terms of research ethics and safety. Beyond just that, the potential for greater involvement of young people in the research process, and the harnessing of 'pupil voice', is becoming realised more in other areas of psychology, including, for example, experiences of young people with the internet (Spears, Kofoed, Bartolo, Palermiti, & Costabile, 2012). Indeed, the use of online tools (for example in design of playground environments) could be another way of involving young people in a productive way.

Of course, the experiences of children in playground environments go beyond play, embracing many facets of peer relationships, including more negative aspects, such as discrimination and violence (see also Hughes, 2012). These too are touched on in some of the contributions. Altogether there is much in this collection to interest not only playworkers but all involved in children's lives, their rights and their well-being.

Peter K. Smith
Goldsmiths, University of London, UK

References

Hart, R. (1992). *Children's participation: From tokenism to citizenship*. Issue 4 of Innocenti Essays, UNICEF International Child Development Centre.

Hughes, B. (2012). *Evolutionary playwork: Reflective analytic practice* (2nd ed.). London: Routledge.

Smith, P. K., Cowie, H., & Blades, M. (2015). *Understanding children's development* (6th ed.). Chichester: Wiley-Blackwell.

Spears, B. A., Kofoed, J., Bartolo, M. G., Palermiti, A. L., & Costabile, A. (2012). Positive uses of social networking sites: Youth voice perspectives. In A. Costabile & B. A. Spears (Eds.), *The impact of technology on relationships in educational settings* (pp. 7–12). London: Routledge.

Treseder, P. (1997). *Empowering children and young people: Promoting involvement in decision making*. London: Save the Children.

Introduction

Pete King and Shelly Newstead

Why *Researching Play from a Playwork Perspective*? Before attempting to explain what this book is about, two other questions need to be addressed; why another book on researching play, and what is playwork?

So, why another book on researching play? The recognition of play as an activity children engaged in was recorded in *The Laws* (Plato, 348BC) and was clearly a topic felt to be worthy of study. Play in Ancient Greece was linked to education and seen as something that children practice in relation to skills for later life, a theory later developed by Karl Groos in the 19th century and published at the turn of the 20th century (Groos, 1901). From Ancient Greece through to the 16th- and 17th-century writings of Locke, Rousseau and Froebel, it is clear that "play was recognised for centuries by many great philosophers as being essential for children's development" (Frost, 2009, p. 18). As a result, the study of play was incorporated into philosophical and theoretical writing.

The current interest in play as a subject to be studied and researched can arguably be traced back to Darwin's *The Origin of Species* (1859). During the 19th century, the philosophical theories of play emerged, although these theories often conflicted with each other (Howard & McInnes, 2013). The theories of play proposed were: play as surplus energy (Spencer, 1873), play as relaxation (Lazarus, 1883) and play as the practice of skills (Groos, 1901). During the early 1900s, children became more the focus of study (Hendrick, 1997), and one early researcher was Granville Stanley Hall, whose anthropological studies of children and indigenous peoples developed a theory of play as 'recapitulation' (Hall, 1904).

All these emerging theories provided the scope to study play from a biological, psychological and social perspective. During the 20th century, the study of children's play has been undertaken across many diverse disciplines, such as education (Montessori, 1914), anthropology (Schwartzman, 1978), social sciences (Parten, 1933; Corsaro, 1997; Broadhead, 2001), child development (Piaget, 1951) and the therapeutic benefits of play (Smilansky, 1968; Jennings, 1999). The study of play was predominately with pre-school children, as they were accessible participants in pre-school and primary school provision.

In the 1980s, Smith's (1986) review of play research acknowledged that the majority of play research was to support cognitive and creative outcomes and often focused on studying children's pretend play, as it was easy to observe, code and analyse.

Researching play has thus been taking place since 348 BC, so why now *from a playwork perspective*? The roots of playwork can arguably be traced back to the mid-Victorian era (Cranwell, 2006; Manwaring & Taylor, 2008). However, playwork as we know it today began in the adventure playgrounds set up after the Second World War and is now a regulated profession of over 50,000 people in the UK (Office for National Statistics (ONS), 2011). Although adults on the first adventure playgrounds were known as 'wardens', this term was replaced by 'playleader' at an early stage (Newstead, 2016) and defined by Abernethy as:

> A combination of father, mother, policeman and Robin Hood to the youngsters, helping them to find something that they like to do. They must be a person who really loves children, though not in a sentimental way. They must be able to impose discipline by his own personality, rather than by rules. They should understand that their aim is to teach them to use their leisure time properly, and to behave as civilised beings. They are not just 'occupying kiddies'. The leader must try to instil the habit of working and playing as freely as possible. But this freedom must in no way interfere with any other group of children or older people using the parks or open spaces. They must be able to stimulate their imagination and ideals: this is the best form of citizenship training.
>
> (Holme & Massie, 1970, p. x)

In 1975, the term 'playwork' was officially adopted to describe the work of adults on adventure playgrounds (International Playgrounds Association (IPA), 1975). Playwork as it is practiced today focuses on the whole on school aged children (Play England, 2009), although there are exceptions (Fisher, 2008). This developing playwork profession needed a theoretical basis for its application and practitioners turned to the scientific literature to underpin their practice, which was understood as "facilitate the play for children" (Hughes, 2001, p. 5). Bob Hughes, a practicing playworker himself, undertook an original literature-based study on different play types, initially identifying 15 in the literature, and later updated this work to include a sixteenth play type (Hughes, 1996a, 2002). This taxonomy of play types still influences the practice of playworkers. Hughes's (1996b) other influential publication, *Play Environments A Question of Quality*, can arguably be considered to be the start of a playwork perspective, in that it provided a rationale and some methodology to assess the quality of play provided by playwork environments.

During the next 20 years, playwork was developing as a profession but still lacked any evidence of its worth. This was brought to head at the 1998 Institute of Leisure and Amenity Management (ILAM) conference in Bournemouth, where the Rt. Hon. Chris Smith (Play*words*, 1998), then Secretary of State for Culture, Media and Sport, set out a direct challenge to the playwork field to demonstrate the benefits which are derived from play and play provision. This resulted in three research-based documents, "*Making the Case for Play*" (Cole-Hamilton, Harrop, & Street, 2002), "*Making the Case for Play: Building Policies and Strategies for School-Aged Children*" (Cole-Hamilton & Gill, 2002), which provided an analysis of research undertaken by statutory and third sector play services, and "*Best Play*" (Children's Play Council (CPC), National Playing Fields Association (NPFA) & PlayLink, 2000), which was supported by the developing playwork theories of Hughes (1996a, 2001), Sturrock and Else (1998) and Brown (2002).

Russell (2013) provides a good overall summary of the foundational theories that have supported the theoretical development of playwork:

> An evolutionary standpoint (Hughes, 2012) asserts that playing has evolved in order to provide children with the mechanism by which they develop adaptive capabilities, yielding both ontogenetic and phylogenetic benefits. A psychotherapeutic perspective (Sturrock & Else, 1998) claims that playing is healing or that it can prevent the development of neuroses or psychosis originating in childhood. A developmental approach (Brown, 2008) sees a rich environment for play as fundamental to children's development.
>
> (p. 4)

This evolving playwork theory underpinned the original Assumptions and Values of Playwork (Bonel & Lindon, 1996) and the review of the Assumptions and Values offered a "*New Playwork Perspective*" (Conway, Sturrock, & Hughes, 2004), resulting in the eight Playwork Principles:

> These principles establish the professional and ethical framework for playwork, describe what is unique about play and playwork, and provide the playwork perspective for working with children and young people.
>
> (Playwork Principles Scrutiny Group (PPSG), 2005)

Whether the Playwork Principles (2005) represent a playwork perspective on professional practice is debatable (Brown, 2008). However, they have underpinned professional playwork practice for over ten years and have three primary functions: provide a focus on the process of play, which is considered to be one aspect of the uniqueness of playwork (King, 2015; King & Waibel, 2016); being an advocate for play and facilitating spaces for children to play (CPC et al., 2000); and reflective practice (Kilvington & Wood, 2010). As Wragg (2011) stated, playwork is "the only discipline to work exclusively with the child's agenda" (p. 71). Wragg (2011) lists six assumptions of a playwork perspective on children's right to play: intrinsic perspective of play, the 'being child', the minority group child, the individual child, voluntary involvement, and non-coercion and anti-paternalism. Although the intrinsic perspective of play is reflected in the Playwork Principles (PPSG, 2005), the child's right to play is not specifically mentioned in them, a point discussed in more depth in Shier's chapter in this monograph.

Since the research-based publication of "Best Play" (CPC et al., 2000), play-focused research to support playwork practice has been undertaken, and this has ranged from literature-based studies critiquing other research to small-scale data collection and analysis (Armitage, 2001; Lester & Maudsley, 2006; Lester & Russell, 2008; Mannello & Statham, 2000). Manwaring and Taylor's (2008) play and playwork review revealed gaps in play and playwork knowledge and identified the need for more research into the nature and benefits of play from a playwork perspective. Since 2008, there has been a significant increase in research in the playwork field, in terms of playworkers being involved in research as postgraduate researchers and as practitioners (Cartmel et al., 2015) with both undergraduate and postgraduate research studies published in playwork textbooks (Brown, 2002; Brown & Taylor, 2008; Handscomb, Russell, & Fitzpatrick, 2007). However, there is still a lack of rigorous quantitative and qualitative research on play from a playwork perspective.

This monograph is not bold enough to challenge existing ontological (understanding of reality) and epistemological (understanding of knowledge) approaches to studying play. Rather, it poses the question, 'What is a playwork perspective when researching children's play?' All the authors within this book have been, or are still, playwork practitioners but have also now completed, or are in the process of undertaking, a PhD. The aim of this monograph is to explore whether coming from a playwork background has any influence on the way that doctoral researchers from the playwork field have approached the study of play.

The monograph is structured in a way that starts with what Shier identifies as a 'playworker mind-set' developed from professional practice "The Transformative Research by Children and Adolescents" (TRCA). The TRCA describes how children help design and analyse the research. Shier's chapter identifies many factors using TRCA which are also discussed in the other chapters (children's rights, power, participation, critical reflection). This 'playworker mind-set' is also reflected in Newstead's chapter around Playwork Mirror Theory, which was developed from her historical analysis of the playwork literature from the early adventure playgrounds. Russell's chapter discusses the diffractive nature of playwork and their ethnographic study, using Cultural Historical Activity Theory (CHAT) to research the dialectics of playwork. This is discussed with play being considered as both a political and ethical endeavour. Ethnography is also the focus of Smith Brennan's chapter. Smith Brennan used ethnography as her research method in her chapter. Smith Brennan's chapter also considers the political and ethical aspects in her research on the power relations and advocacy of marginalised people (children) as the importance of the critical ethnographer.

With reference to ethnography, playful research forms the main focus of Water's chapter. Waters argues that playfulness provides a context for child-friendly research using a story-based experience termed as Narrative Journey. The Narrative Journey is an approach towards and as a method in research with children. A playful approach is taken in King's mixed-methods study, where children were involved in data collection as both active and passive participants. King's chapter describes his mixed-methods study and compares these three key aspects from his professional practice (process, participation and reflection), which are considered within critical realism and critical theory and using Bronfenbrenner's (1995, 1999) process-people-context-time concept. The final chapter by Kane describes second-order action research on childcare and playwork environments in the UK and Sweden. Kane argues that playwork practice and action research are natural partners, as they both are involved in practice-changing, balancing practice, action and research. Kane considers power and social position, discussed through the playful setup of the 'upside-down' play session.

The concluding chapter pulls together the main points from each of the chapters and examines how a playwork perspective on researching children's play might be further explored.

References

Armitage, M. (2001). The ins and outs of school playground play: Children's use of 'play places'. In J. Bishop & M. Curtis (Eds.), *Play today in the primary school playground* (pp. 37–57). Maidenhead: Open University Press.

Bonel, P. & Lindon, J. (1996). *Good practice in playwork*. Cheltenham: Nelson Thornes Ltd.

Broadhead, P. (2001). Investigating sociability and cooperation in four and five year olds in reception class settings. *International Journal of Early Years Education*, 9(1), 23–35.

Bronfenbrenner, U. (1995). Developmental ecology through space and time: A future perspective. In P. Moen, G. H. Elder Jr, & K Luscher (Eds.), *Examining lives in context: Perspectives on the ecology of human development* (pp. 619–647). Washington, DC: American Psychological Association.

Bronfenbrenner, U. (1999). Environments in developmental perspective: Theoretical and operational models. In S. L. Friedman & T. D. Wachs (Eds.), *Measuring environment across the life span: Emerging methods and concepts* (pp. 3–28). Washington, DC: American Psychological Association Press.

Brown, F. (2002). Compound flexibility: The role of playwork in child development. In F. Brown (Ed.), *Playwork: Theory and practice* (pp. 51–65). Buckingham: Open University Press.

Brown, F. (2008). Fundamentals of playwork. In F. Brown & C. Taylor (Eds.), *Foundations of playwork* (pp. 7–13). Maidenhead: Open University Press.

Brown, F & Taylor, C. (Eds.) (2008). *Foundations of playwork*. Buckinghamshire: Open University Press.

Cartmel, J., Fitzpatrick, J., Handscomb, B., Podyma, R., Barclay, M., Tawil, B., & Clarke, T. (2015). Practice: Searching and re/searching. *Journal of Playwork Practice*, 2(2), 173–204.

Children's Play Council, National Playing Fields Association & PlayLink. (2000). *Best play what play provision should do for children*. London: National Playing Fields Association.

Cole-Hamilton, I. & Gill, T. (2002). *Making the case for play: Building policies and strategies for school-aged children*. London: National Children's Bureau Enterprises Ltd.

Cole-Hamilton, I., Harrop, A., & Street, C. (2002). *Making the case for play Gathering the Evidence*. London: National Children's Bureau Enterprises Ltd.

Conway, M., Sturrock, G., & Hughes, B. (2004). *A new playwork perspective*. Accessed July 8, 2016 from www.fairplayforchildren.org/pdf/1308498073.pdf.

Corsaro, W. A. (1997). *The sociology of childhood*. Thousand Oaks, CA: Pine Forge Press.

Cranwell, K. A. (2006). *Play organisations and the out-of-school child in London 1860–1914*. Unpublished doctoral dissertation, Institute of Education, University of London.

Darwin, C. (1859). *The origin of species by means of natural selection or the preservation of favoured races in the struggle of life*. New York: D. Appleton and Company.

Fisher, K. (2008). Playwork in the early years: Working in a parellel profession. In F. Brown & C. Taylor (Eds.), *Foundations of playwork* (pp. 174–178). Maidenhead: Open University Press.

Frost, J. L. (2009). *A history of children's play and play environments: Toward a contemporary child-saving movement*. New York & London: Routledge.

Groos, K. (1901). *The play of man*. London: William Heindemann.

Hall, G. S. (1904). *Adolescence* (Vol. 1). New York: Appleton Press.

Handscomb, B., Russell, W., & Fitzpatrick, J. (Eds.). (2007). *Playwork voices: In celebration of Bob Hughes and Gordon Sturrock*. London: London Centre for Playwork Education.

Hendrick, H. (1997). Constructions and reconstructions of British childhood: An intepretive survey 1800 to present. In A. James & A. Prout (Eds.), *Constructing and reconstructing childhood: Contemporary issues in the sociological study of childhood* (2nd ed., pp. 34–62). London: RoutledgeFalmer.

Holme, A. & Massie, P. (1970). *Children's play: A study of needs and opportunities*. London: Michael Joseph.

Howard, J. & McInnes, K. (2013). *The essence of play: A practice companion for professionals working with children and young people*. London: Routledge.

Hughes, B. (1996a). *A playworker's taxonomy of play types*. London: PlayLink.

Hughes, B. (1996b). *Play environments – A question of quality: A process for creating and assessing quality children's play environments*. London: PlayLink.

Hughes, B. (2001). *Evolutionary playwork and reflective analytical practice*. London: Routledge.

Hughes, B. (2002). *A playworker's taxonomy of play types* (2nd ed.). London: Playlink.

Hughes, B. (2012). *Evolutionary playwork and reflective analytic practice* (2nd ed.). London: Routledge.

International Playgrounds Association. (1975 August–September). *Adventure playgrounds and children's creativity*. International Playground Association 6th International Conference, University Bucconi, Milan, Italy.

Jennings, S. (1999). *Introduction to developmental playtherapy: Playing and health*. London, UK: Jessica Kingsley Publishers Ltd.

Kilvington, J. & Wood, A. (2010). *Reflective playwork: For all who work with children*. London: Bloomsbury.

King, P. (2015). The possible futures for playwork project: A thematic analysis. *Journal of Playwork Practice, 2*(2), 143–156.

King, P. & Waibel, A. (2016). Playwork practitioners' views on play provision in a South Wales local authority. *Journal of Playwork Practice, 3*(1), 35–48.

Lazarus, M. (1883). *Die Reize Des Spiels*. Berlin: Fred dummlersVerlagsbuch-handlung.

Lester, S. & Maudsley, M. (2006). *Play, naturally: A review of children's natural play*. London: Children's Play Council.

Lester, S. & Russell. W. (2008). *Play for a change: Play, policy and practice: A review of contemporary perspectives*. London: Play England/National Children's Bureau.

Mannello, M. & Statham, J. (2000). *The state of play: A review of open access play provision in Wales and the Play 2000 Grant Scheme*. Wales: National Assembly for Wales. Retrieved December 5, 2015, from www.assembly.wales/Committee%20Documents/p4.%20Annex%201-07022001-35051/3a7841ef0007dde800004be400000000-English.pdf.

Manwaring, B. & Taylor, C. (2008). *The benefits of play and playwork: Recent evidence-based research (2001–2006) demonstrating the impact and benefits of play and playwork*. London: SkillsActive.

Montessori, M. (1914). *Dr. Montessori's own handbook*. Shocker Books: Inc.

Newstead, S. (2016). *Deconstructing and reconstructing the unorthodox recipe of playwork*. Unpublished doctoral thesis, UCL Institute of Education, London, UK.

Office for National Statistics. (2011). *Statistical data from 2011 UK National Census* (Government document). London: Office for National Statistics. http://www.ons.gov.uk/ons/guide-method/census/2011/census-data/2011-census-ad-hoc-tables/ct0053-occupation-4-digits-.xls

Parten, M. (1933). Social play among preschool children. *Journal of Abnormal and Social Psychology*, 23, 136–147.

Piaget, J. (1951). *Play, dreams and imitation in childhood*. London: Routledge and Keegan Paul.

Plato. (2005). *348 BC LAW Plato* (translated by Benjamin Jowet). Retrieved from http://pinkmonkey.com/dl/library1/laws.pdf

Play England. (2009). *Charter for children's play*. Retrieved from www.playengland.org.uk/media/71062/charter-for-childrens-play.pdf.

Playwords. (1998). 'A commitment to play'. Playwords, 2 (pp. 8–9). Eastleigh, Hampshire: Common Threads Publications Ltd.

Playwork Principles Scrutiny Group. (2005). *Playwork principles*. Retrieved from www.playwales.org.uk/login/uploaded/documents/Playwork%20Principles/playwork%20principles.pdf.

Russell, W. (2013). *The dialectics of playwork: A conceptual and ethnographic study of playwork using cultural historical activity theory*. Unpublished doctoral dissertation, Gloucester: University of Gloucestershire.

Schwartzman, H. B. (1978). *Transformations: The anthropology of children's play*. New York: Plenum Press.

Smilansky, S. (1968). *The effects of sociodramatic play on disadvantaged preschool children*. New York: Wiley.

Smith, P. K. (1986). Play research and its applications: A current perspective. In P. K. Smith (Ed.), *Special aspects of education: 6 children's play: Research and practical applications* (pp. 1–16). London: Gordon and Breach.

Spencer, H. (1873). *The principles of psychology*. NewYork: D. Appleton and Co.

Sturrock, G. & Else, P. (1998). 'The Colorado Paper' – The playground as therapeutic space: Playwork as healing. In G. Sturrock & P. Else (Eds.) (2007), *Therapeutic playwork reader one* 1995–2000 (pp. 73–104). Eastleigh, Hampshire: Common Threads Publications Ltd.

Wragg, M. (2011). The child's right to play: Rhetoric or reality? In P. Jones & G. Walker (Eds.), *Children's rights in practice* (pp. 71–81). London: SAGE.

1 Why the playworker's mind-set is ideal for research with children

Child researchers investigate education rights in Nicaragua

Harry Shier

Introduction

This chapter draws on my experience as a PhD researcher investigating children's perceptions of human rights in school in Nicaragua's coffee-growing zone to claim that, for a researcher such as myself, coming from a playwork background, the ability to hold on to a playworker mind-set offers a distinct advantage when it comes to doing research in partnership with children.

To develop this argument, following this introduction, the chapter is structured in four sections. The next section starts with a return to my playwork roots in England in the 1970s and tells how from those roots grew the Article 31 Children's Consultancy Scheme in the late 1990s, and then how in 2001, I took these ideas with me to Nicaragua, where they gradually developed into the research methodology now known as "Transformative Research by Children and Adolescents" or TRCA (Centro de Servicios Educativos en Salud y Medio Ambiente (CESESMA), 2012; Shier, 2015). The second section explains the TRCA approach in more detail, showing how its epistemology, values and methods reflect its playwork-inspired origins, and how it has subsequently developed through practice. This is followed by a section describing my 2012–15 doctoral research project where TCRA was used as the main research methodology, giving rise to striking (and unexpected) findings on children's perceptions about their right to play. The final section reflects on how the researcher's ability to hold on to a deeply rooted playworker mind-set may have contributed to the possibility of such findings and, more generally, how this playworker mind-set may be advantageous for other researchers seeking to cut through the preconceptions and prescriptions of the adult professional world to engage more fully with children's ways of thinking and so get closer to a real understanding of children's own experiences, perceptions and agendas.

In writing this chapter, I have inevitably drawn heavily on my PhD thesis "Children's Rights in School: The perception of children in Nicaragua" (Shier, 2016). To avoid multiple self-citing, therefore, it should be understood in what follows that in all mentions of my doctoral research, unless another source is cited, this work has been used as the main reference.

Playwork roots

I worked as an adventure playground worker in South London from 1976–79 and later in Birmingham from 1986–87. During my time in London, I participated in one of the UK's earliest professional playworker training programmes and received my London Adventure Playground Association Adventure Playground Worker's Certificate. Though not a long time in career terms, the seeds sown on London's adventure playgrounds grew into a perennial commitment that guided me through a 20-year career in playwork training, professional development and consultancy, including a number of key national roles in the UK.

When I started in the 1970s, the playwork literature that we know today did not exist; indeed, there was very little to read on the topic of playwork, and this is an important point to bear in mind in relation to what follows. As a playworker, my concept of playwork was not informed by literature and had no explicit theoretical base, evidence base or epistemology. It was formed through critical reflective practice (though this term, too, was unknown at the time), enriched by debate amongst peer practitioners and the politics of radical community action that were current at the time (Lees & Mayo, 1984). Thus, when, in the following sections, I go on to talk about how TRCA has its roots in playwork, it has to be understood that these roots are embedded in the playwork that I practised and reflected on and the discourses that I and my peers developed to explain and justify it, and not in today's 'playwork literature'. Where more recent playwork literature is cited below, these are post hoc explanations, and not in themselves the foundations of my later work.

Indeed, in the 1970s, the concept of playwork itself was only beginning to emerge, to some extent as a rethinking of an older concept of 'playleadership' (Abernethy, 1968). The gradual changeover from 'playleadership' to 'playwork' was more than just a change of nomenclature, but marked a fundamental shift in how we conceived our relationship with the children we worked with. We no longer considered ourselves charged with 'leading' their play activities. As play was understood to be an innate drive within all children (Joint National Committee on Training for Playwork (JNCTP), 1985), children at play had no need of adult leadership. Instead, the adult role was reconceived to incorporate a wide range of tasks that together helped enable, resource and make safe the myriad play activities that the children themselves sought to realise. Though the word 'facilitate' had not yet come into fashion, it could be said that we were there to facilitate play rather than to lead it. My first published work, *Adventure Playgrounds: An introduction* (Shier, 1984), can be seen as a discourse on playwork as I then understood it.

Crucial to this way of thinking was our understanding of the *purpose* of play. Though scientists have puzzled over this for centuries (Ellis, 1973), to me it became obvious, simply by reflecting on the question, 'Why do human beings take so long to grow up?', and coming to the conclusion that:

> The reason is that the human is a learning animal. Unlike other species, we need this time to learn all the things we need to learn in order to function as

adult human beings in the complex societies we have developed . . . In other words, children have evolved as natural learners. That is their sole function in life. And the important thing is that this evolution of children as natural learners took place over many thousands of years, during which there were *no* schools, *no* teachers, *no* education authorities, *no* . . . tests, in fact not even a word for 'education' (which was invented much later by the Greeks). Children learn all the time, regardless of whether we teach them or not. And what we nowadays call 'play' is one of the fundamental mechanisms that our species has evolved to enable that learning to take place. We don't have to make children learn. Indeed, I sometimes feel our clumsy adult interventions largely serve to get in the way or stop them learning. Our role as adults is not to *make* children learn, but simply to do the best we can to provide a fertile environment for that learning, and maybe to guide and facilitate it along its many pathways.

(Shier, 2001, p. 2)

This is important for the argument I hope to develop in the final section of this chapter about why playworkers make ideal researchers with children. As a playworker, I knew my work facilitated children's learning, but I also understood it was not for me to decide *what* they should be learning or how (and also, significantly, it was not up to me to test or measure such learning, and indeed, it would have been impossible, as I had not specified what was to be learnt). Although at the time, we did not have the concept of 'play cues' (Sturrock & Else, 1998), they were already part of our practice. We resisted all talk of a playwork curriculum and sought instead to respond to the cues provided by the children about what kinds of play experiences they had in mind on a particular day (taking it for granted that learning and development would be happening anyway and so did not need to be programmed in).

A fundamental shift in my thinking occurred in the mid-1990s, when I 'discovered' the United Nations Convention on the Rights of the Child (UNCRC) (United Nation (UN), 1989), and specifically Article 31, which establishes play as a human right of all children. I realised that for years my playwork practice had been all about defending children's right to play, though until that epiphany (which occurred at the World Play Summit in Melbourne, Australia in 1993), I had not been fully aware of it. The rights-based approach now became my new guiding paradigm, not replacing, but underpinning and so strengthening my earlier thinking about the importance of play in children's lives and the potential role of adults in facilitating it. The espousal of a rights-based approach brings with it a radical change in how adult roles are conceived in relation to the facilitation of children's play. Formerly, the law (in the UK) enabled authorities to provide for play, but did not oblige them to do so. With human rights treaties, such as the UNCRC, comes the role of *duty-bearer*, meaning that the state, as party to the treaty, and those who act for it such as local authorities, now have defined obligations in relation to the human rights guaranteed in the treaty. Asbjørn Eide (1987) notably defined three types of states' obligations: to respect rights, to protect rights and to fulfil rights. In the case of children's play and Article 31, this means that all public authorities are *legally obliged* to refrain from any activity that infringes children's right to play; to act decisively to prevent others from infringing children's right to play; and, where circumstances prevent the realisation of children's right to play, to ensure that this right is fulfilled either by direct provision (e.g., council-run playgrounds/playcentres) or by facilitating such provision by others (e.g., funding for community-run playgrounds/playcentres). Unfortunately, however, in the over 25 years since the ratification of the UNCRC, successive UK governments have failed to legislate to incorporate these treaty obligations into domestic law.[1] While this means compliance cannot be enforced directly through domestic courts, the state has obligations under international law which lend strong legal and moral force to demands for the realisation of the right to play, particularly for children whose equal access to play is limited through social exclusion, discrimination or disadvantage.

In anticipation of what follows, it is worth noting here that, while in my professional life the 'discovery' of children's rights was a permanent paradigm shift leading to a change of direction, this was not true of playwork in general. Though modern playwork literature repeatedly refers to Article 31 and the right to play, the rights-based approach as outlined above has not become 'mainstream' as a guiding paradigm for playwork. Whilst I have come to see playwork as part of a broad range of adult responses to the realisation of every child's right to play (a small part in global terms, but still important), a more common view in the playwork literature is to see the right to play as part of a broader argument for the importance of playwork (see, for example, Beunderman, 2010; Wragg, 2011).

On returning to the UK from Australia, I founded the 'Article 31 Action Network' as a vehicle to make the UK playwork scene aware of the child's right to play embodied in Article 31 (Shier, 1995). As Article 31 also includes the right to participate freely in cultural life and the arts, we joined forces with like-minded professionals in the children's arts and media sector so that the new network could embrace all aspects of Article 31 (and attract arts funding). Promoting awareness of Article 31, however, required it to be understood in the context of the UNCRC as a whole, particularly its guiding principles: rights without discrimination (Article 2); decision-making in the child's best interests (Article 3); and the child's right to be heard and for her or his views to be given due weight by decision-makers (Article 12). This last was seen as particularly radical at the time (Lansdown, 2011) and was taken on board by the Network as an essential corollary of the child's right to play.

In launching the Article 31 Action Network, we needed to demonstrate in a concrete and attention-grabbing way what this might mean in practice; in other words, what difference would a child-rights-based approach make in play and the arts? Our answer was a pilot project that went on to become the 'Article 31 Children's Consultancy Scheme'. The initial idea was that teams of children (aged around 8–12) would be supported in taking on the role of expert consultants to the senior management of cultural and recreational institutions, and, after investigating their current provision, advise them on how to make projects, programmes and facilities more child-friendly. The pilots were run in 1997 at the Victoria and Albert Museum in London and Walsall Museum and Art Gallery in the English West Midlands. The approach was seen to be effective and was then further developed, tested and replicated over 30 times throughout the UK, with child consultants offering expert advice to some of the most prestigious cultural institutions in the land. For example: in 1998, child consultants were commissioned by the British Waterways Board to research the potential of the English canal network for children's recreation; in 1999, child consultants from the New-Age Traveller community were commissioned by the Children's Society to advise on play and recreation opportunities for Traveller children; and in 2000, child consultants advised the management of the Tower of London on how to make it less boring for younger visitors. This phase culminated in the UK Heritage Lottery Fund, providing funding for 20 further children's consultancy projects to be run in museums and art galleries throughout the UK. Although not written up in the academic literature at the time, some of these early experiences have been described in the practitioner literature (Shier, 1999a; 1999b; 2015).

Though the majority of these projects were in the arts and heritage sector, the thinking behind them was still rooted in playwork. This is not to say that the Children's Consultancy Scheme was an instance of playwork in practice, as it involved adult facilitators directing a series of carefully structured activities in order to ensure that specific outputs could be achieved within a given time-scale (which may occasionally occur in a playwork setting, but is not in keeping with its ethos). However, it treated children as the leading experts on what is child-friendly and what isn't, what's fun and what's boring, and what makes them feel included or excluded. What it drew from playwork was its belief in following the children's ideas (Playwork Principles Scrutiny Group (PPSG), 2005) and letting children present these ideas directly to decision-makers with minimal adult interference. Just as playworkers must learn to trust children's sense of the value of their chosen play activities, so managers and decision-makers were encouraged to trust children's sense of what worked for them and what didn't in a cultural or recreational facility.

Transformative Research by Children and Adolescents: a research methodology with roots in playwork

In 2001, I moved to Nicaragua, in Central America, where I worked with a local Non-Government Organisation (NGO) called CESESMA,[2] which supported child workers on coffee plantations in promoting and defending their rights, including, of course, the right to play (Shier, 2010; 2011).

Starting in 2007, CESESMA adapted the Children's Consultancy approach to a very different local context and began to apply it in its work with young coffee plantation workers. In that year, a team of child consultants from Santa Martha coffee plantation researched the problem of violence on the plantation and made the keynote presentation at a national forum on prevention of violence to children (Young Consultants of Santa Martha, 2009). Two years later, the same team was commissioned by Trócaire, the Irish Catholic Development Agency, to produce a report on the relationship between business and human rights in the coffee sector (Young Consultants of Santa Martha, 2011). These experiences shaped the development of the 'Children and Young People Defending our Right to Play' campaign, sponsored by the UK-based *PlayWords* magazine (Shier, 2011), in which three teams of child researchers carried out appraisals of play opportunities in their communities and assessed the factors that prevented them exercising their right to play. The children's research was published in the Mexican journal *Rayuela* (CESESMA, 2013) and also cited as evidence in the report 'Children's Right to Play' (Lester & Russell, 2010), which was influential in persuading the UNCRC to produce a General Comment on the right to play (Committee on the Rights of the Child, 2013).

In 2011, recognising the potential of the Children's Consultancy approach to contribute to the empowerment of children and adolescents, CESESMA tested a modified version, now renamed *'Transformative Research by Children and Adolescents'* (CESESMA, 2012). The term 'consultancy' (*consultoría* in Spanish) was dropped, and the young participants became 'researchers' rather than 'consultants'. While in the original UK context, the term 'consultant' gave weight to the children's advisory role and reflected their status as external experts, in Nicaragua their role became more that of *insider* investigators, researching and analysing aspects of their own reality, without the need for a commissioning client.

Influenced by the Latin American concept of popular education (*educación popular*) (Kane, 2001) and the work of Paolo Freire (2001), two aspects of the previous approach were seen as limiting the young consultants' empowerment. First, an adult always told them what topic they were going to research, instead of supporting them in deciding this for themselves. Second, once they handed in their report, there was no commitment to follow up or further action to support them in getting their recommendations implemented. To overcome these limitations, two changes were made to the original model. At the beginning of each project, the teams of young researchers decided for themselves what topics they wanted to research. They were encouraged to reflect on the problems that affected their communities and identify areas where they felt there were possibilities for change driven by research evidence. Through this process of reflection, they reached a consensus on the topics they wanted to research. The other new element was that, after completing their research reports, each team of young researchers was supported in developing an action plan to disseminate their findings and follow up their recommendations. These included actions that the young researchers could undertake without adult help, such as discussing their findings with other people in their villages, and also actions that required adult support, such as requesting a hearing before the Municipal Children and Youth Committee or contacting the media to undertake interviews. The supporting organisation made a commitment to accompany and facilitate the young researchers in implementing their action plans. It is in this phase that the children and adolescents start to contribute to the transformation of their lives and their communities. They do not do research for its own sake, but instead undertake 'transformative research' with a significant impact for themselves, their families and communities (Shier, 2015).

Although the TRCA approach grew out of earlier practice through a process of critical reflection and was not built on any existing methodological paradigm in the research literature, in retrospect, it has been found to have a good fit with Donna Mertens's *Transformational Paradigm* (Mertens, 2007), a conceptual fit that goes beyond the convenient synchronicity of names. A detailed account of the Transformative Paradigm as it relates to other paradigms in the literature and to TRCA as a methodology can be found in Shier (2016). In brief, however, Mertens (2010) describes its five defining characteristics as: (1) primacy of qualitative methods, (2) interactive link between researcher and participants, (3) accommodating cultural complexity, (4) explicitly addressing power issues and (5) acknowledging contextual and historical factors linked to discrimination and oppression.

Though it is unlikely that Mertens was thinking of playwork when she drew up this definition, it is an interesting exercise to identify the parallels. With very little editing, all five of Mertens's key factors can be applied to the practice of playwork as follows: (1) playwork relies on qualitative indicators rather than score-keeping to evaluate its effectiveness, (2) there is an interactive link between playworker and children, (3) good playwork recognises and embraces the (complex) cultural mix of the community in which it takes place, (4) reflective playwork explicitly addresses power issues: between playworker and children, amongst children and between both of these and society's decision-makers and (5) playwork not only acknowledges contextual factors leading to discrimination and oppression, but seeks to tackle them in striving to ensure equal play opportunities for all children.

To test the updated TCRA approach, four teams of child researchers were formed and supported in planning and carrying out research projects. For the first time in CESESMA's work, the children themselves chose their research topics. The team from El Plomo decided to look at the concept of 'Respect' and how lack of respect in families and communities leads to violence; the Yasica Sur team decided to research 'The violence that children suffer in the home'; the Samulalí team chose 'Parents who hit their children: Why do they do it and what are the alternatives?'; and, finally, the Yúcul team chose the topic of alcohol and its relation to violence in the community. As well as producing research findings and recommendations, the teams drew up action plans to publicise their research and push for the implementation of their recommendations from local community up to national level. They presented their reports first in their home villages and subsequently in municipal, and in some cases national, forums. The four reports were compiled and published in book form by CESESMA in Nicaragua in March 2012, and an English translation, 'Learn to live without violence', was published in the UK (CESESMA, 2012). All four teams used their research to advocate for change, but the team that made the most impact was the one from Yúcul. They presented their findings to the government's newly formed 'Family Life and Security Commission', which decided to make the alcohol problem a priority for local action. Local government and party officials admitted they had been aware of the issue for years, but it wasn't till the children came forward with their research that they felt forced to act on it. The local police also took action, confiscating illegal liquor and closing at least two unlicensed cantinas (bars). A popular national television channel then featured the young researchers on the evening news, and since then, the local authority and police have ensured no new liquor licenses are granted in the Yúcul area.

The TRCA research approach

Based on these experiences, CESESMA has set out the guiding principles that characterise its 'Transformative Research' approach:

1. It is founded on human rights.
2. It recognises that the foremost experts on children's everyday lives are children themselves, but also that, as researchers, they can learn more about a topic, expanding and deepening their existing knowledge.
3. CESESMA's experience suggests that children readily take on board and identify with the idea of themselves as researchers and understand what this role implies. The role of the adult is therefore seen as facilitating and accompanying the research process.
4. Children and adolescents are supported in planning, organising and carrying out their own research, and provided with technical support and resources similar to those which adult researchers would typically expect. The way in which this support is provided must be appropriate to the age and experience of the children and adolescents involved.
5. Children and adolescents produce their own research report in their own words, and also control how it will be designed and presented (for example, selecting drawings and photographs to illustrate their findings). If a formal report prepared by adults is required as part of a project, this is prepared and presented separately, and the two reports must not be confused.
6. The organisation that supports the young researchers must make a commitment to continue to accompany and support them in drawing up and carrying out an action plan to disseminate their findings, and promote the implementation of their recommendations.

(Summarised from CESESMA, 2012, p. 52)

Though the TCRA model has developed over the years, its roots in playwork, and more specifically in my own playwork practice, have underpinned this development and can still be seen behind these principles. As a playworker, I learned to recognise children as play experts who did not need to be led or instructed in playing. This was then extended in the Children's Consultancy model to recognise children as experts in what makes a facility or service child-friendly. TRCA now goes a step further by recognising them as experts in just about every area of their lived experience.

Although most of my own playwork experience was garnered decades before the advent of today's Playwork Principles (PPSG, 2005), the way these principles seek to distil the essence of playwork in a few words makes them an excellent point of comparison to highlight the similarities and differences between playwork and TRCA. Considering Point 2 above, for example, just as playworkers' interventions seek to enable children to extend their play and recognise the developmental benefit of doing so (PPSG, 2005, Playwork Principle no. 8), so TRCA supports children in expanding and deepening their existing knowledge on the issues that concern them. Point 3 above defines the adult role in TRCA as facilitating and accompanying the children's own research process, and Point 4 talks about how children are supported in planning, organising and carrying out their own research, and provided with the necessary resources. Again, there are obvious parallels with the Playwork Principles, which speak of how children determine and control the content and intent of their play (PPSG, 2005, Playwork Principle no. 2) and how the essential adult role is to support and facilitate the play process (PPSG, 2005, Playwork Principle no. 3). Similarly, Point 5 of the TCRA guidelines talks of children producing reports in their own words, where they also control the design and presentation, another parallel with Playwork Principle no. 2's insistence on children controlling both the content and intent of their play.

There are also, of course, differences. As discussed earlier, the rights-based approach that became my own guiding paradigm, though recognised by most playworkers, has not become essential to playwork in the same way. Playwork Principle no. 1 describes play as an 'impulse', a 'necessity', and 'fundamental . . . to wellbeing', but does not describe it as a human right. The first principle of TRCA, then, "[i]t is founded on human rights", while not inconsistent or at odds with a playwork approach, is not part of its essence either, though it is the essence of my own practice.

The other area of divergence is Point 6, which highlights the importance in TRCA of an action plan with objectives for the future. In children's play, a follow-up plan with set outcomes, while not impossible, would be the exception. This has to do with the definition of play as activity that is 'intrinsically motivated' (PPSG, 2005, Playwork Principle no. 1), meaning that whatever motivations the players have exist within the frame of the play itself and are not external to it. Children engaging in TRCA, on the other hand, are encouraged from the start to think of their research project not as an end in itself, but as a way to address problems in their schools or communities and push for change at different levels. Thus, while TRCA has its roots in playwork experience, and many parallels with playwork in concept, it is not, and never can be, an instance of playwork in practice.

Using TRCA in a doctoral research study: playwork roots influencing research practice

In writing a proposal for my own doctoral research, I took the unusual and risky step of proposing the 'Transformative Research by Children and Adolescents' approach as my main research methodology. It was risky in that I would be relinquishing control over much of the research process. If I was to be true to my own values and renounce all manipulation of the children, this meant trusting them to make important decisions for themselves, such as selection of the interview sample and the questions to be asked in child-to-child interviews. I would also have to accept whatever came back as the primary data for analysis. I was able to do this because, as an ex-playworker, I had no problem with trusting the children's thinking and following their ideas.

I therefore worked to support, facilitate and resource a research team consisting of eight boys and nine girls aged nine to 15, all of whom attended local primary schools in four neighbouring villages in the coffee-growing area of La Dalia. All were also involved in agricultural and/or domestic work after school. They travelled from their home villages to CESESMA's Community Learning Centre once a week for a total of six half-day workshops (their teachers and school heads having granted them time off school for this), and between the second and third workshops, they collectively interviewed 150 other children in their villages to gather data on their experiences and perceptions of, and opinions about, human rights in their schools.

The general principles of TRCA were set out in the previous section, where their close – but not too close – relationship to the Playwork Principles was discussed. Here, I want to look more closely at the specifics of my research project and again show how the playwork roots of my approach influenced the fieldwork practice and the findings. However, before looking at the ways I was able to bring a playwork approach to bear, it is important to recognise one significant way in which I could not do so. This is that when I approached the children to discuss their potential involvement, I had already chosen the research topic. Thus, rather than facilitating a process whereby they chose a topic to research, as the TRCA method requires, I was inviting them to engage in a research project on a topic I had already decided on, which could be seen as a backward step. The issue, however, is more complicated and nuanced. A first point to note is that adult researchers do not always get to choose their own research topics, as research agendas are often set by research funders and research projects developed accordingly. Should child researchers have a more privileged position, or might it be beneficial for them sometimes to work within this larger reality? Another factor to consider here is the potential research impact. Where research has been commissioned and paid for, this means that someone is interested in hearing the results, so an audience can be guaranteed for the presentation of the findings, thus increasing its likely influence (Lundy, 2007). Conversely, if research is motivated by child researchers' own concerns, it may be harder work to get the message across to those who can make a difference, although it is never impossible (see, for instance, the work by Manasa Patil on getting around as the child of a wheelchair user described by Kellett [2010, p. 201] and the work of the Young Researchers of Yúcul on alcohol and violence in Shier [2015, p. 212]). There are value and validity in both approaches.

The research topic having been thus established in advance, TRCA's playwork roots continued to be visible in the subsequent development of the project. As I worked with this team of child researchers, facilitating the development of their research project and putting together an interview format, I became aware that not only did they consider play and recreation to be rights to which they were entitled, but that they also gave a high priority to these rights. It was agreed to restrict their questionnaire to six or seven questions to keep the interviews and subsequent data analysis manageable and child-friendly. Most of the questions the team decided on were therefore about rights in general ("How does your teacher treat you?", "What rights have you learnt about in school?" "What rights are most violated in your school?" etc.). However, they also proposed a question on whether the right to play was respected or violated at school and how. It was striking that this was the only specific right they wished to address in this way: they did not, for example, propose equivalent questions on participation rights, the right to live without violence or the right to a quality education. Given the need to restrict the overall number of questions, I therefore asked them directly if they were sure they wanted to single out the right to play for this special treatment. They considered my question and confirmed their decision, so the question about the right to play stayed in.

The playwork roots of TRCA also helped to minimise the mediating effects of adult influence on the child interviewees and therefore ensure that their answers came as close as possible to representing their authentic perceptions and opinions. The following are some specific examples of how this approach sought to maximise the *trustworthiness* and in particular the *credibility* of the findings (Guba, 1981) and how this relates to playwork in theory or in practice:

- Although the topic of the research was children's rights in school, the entire research process took place away from school, in a purpose-built community learning centre that the children knew and felt comfortable in, thus creating a safe space where children were more likely to feel able to express themselves freely, which is typical of the spaces created through playwork practice.
- Child interview subjects were interviewed by child researchers (child-to-child interviewing). Unlike more typical data-gathering interviews which involve dialogue between a (usually adult) researcher and a research subject, the interview situation here was an unmediated (or minimally mediated) interaction between children, as in children's peer play.
- Child-to-child interviews also took place away from school premises, with no teachers or school staff anywhere near, once again creating a space where children could express themselves freely, as is typical of the best kind of playwork space.
- Adults (who were known to the children but not connected with the schools) were present at arm's length to ensure protection but did not interfere in data collection activities, another similarity with the best of playwork practice.
- Data analysis was carried out by the child researchers themselves. This process was done in small groups facilitated by adults whose role was to help the children's analyses and conclusions to emerge from discussion, rather than

pushing their own preferences. This point will be returned to in the concluding section, where it will be suggested that this is something it is often hard for adult professionals without a grounding in playwork to do.
- A report on the findings was written and designed by the young researchers themselves and subsequently published in an international journal under their own names (Niñas y Niños Investigadores, 2014). Another playwork parallel can be seen here: on those few occasions where playwork practice leads to specific products (such as a work of art or a construction), this would always be seen as belonging to the children and not presented as the achievement of the playworker.
- The adult facilitator returned to the young researchers' team on a second field trip to discuss issues arising from the initial data analysis. Although for logistical reasons, these final discussions took place on school premises, in every case, a separate space was found, and no teachers were present.
- A second, more detailed analysis of the young researchers' data was later carried out by the adult researcher (after the young researchers had given their express permission and approval). This second analysis was done in the original language (Spanish), and the data did not have to be translated into English. This meant that the analysis carried out by an adult researcher was also based on the children's actual words, thus avoiding the risk of misinterpretation of children's thinking and intentions by adults during translation. This sustained effort to be as true as possible to the children's own communicative intent relates to how effective playworkers strive to minimise the 'adulteration' of play (Sturrock & Else, 1998; Thomson, 2014); see also the concluding section for a fuller discussion of 'adulteration').

What the above account shows is that, while TRCA is not a form of playwork and in practice uses different mechanisms to achieve its ends, there are clear parallels to be seen, whose existence owes a lot to TRCA's evolution from its playwork roots.

A final question to ask, however, is: what effect did this have on the findings of the research? This chapter is not the place to set out the full findings, and these can be consulted in my thesis (Shier, 2016). However, it is relevant here to note certain aspects of the findings where the methodology used may have influenced what was found. Foremost of these was the unexpected primacy of the right to play, as both one of the rights children were most aware of and as one of the rights most violated in school, by both teachers and fellow students. Another relevant finding was that, in contrast, children's participation rights, in particular the rights to be heard and have a say in decision-making (Article 12 of the UNCRC), were almost invisible in the research data. Whilst the right to play was by a long way the right most frequently referred to by interviewees, the right to participate or have a say in decisions at school was barely mentioned; a finding strikingly at odds with previous reports of children's views on rights at school (e.g., the Get Ready for Geneva (GRFG) Drafting Committee, 2008, the Non-Government Organisation (NGO) Network for the Rights of the Child, 2004). Whilst the absence of data gives no clues as to possible explanations, my own hypothesis is that the findings of previous studies, where children appear to prioritise participation rights, may be more a reflection of a hidden agenda promoted (perhaps unconsciously) by adult researchers, than of the concerns of the children themselves. In other words, when research with children is guided by the interests of adult researchers, the resulting findings are likely to reflect those. When research is not guided by such an adult agenda – other that finding out what children really think – and a methodology such as TRCA is used that lets children foreground their own concerns, the findings are more likely to prioritise the right to play.

Why the playworker's mind-set is ideal for research with children

In this concluding section, I will argue that such findings were only possible because the children carried out the research themselves and in doing so were freed from any pressure to fulfil adult expectations regarding children's rights, and that, as well as being characteristic of the TRCA approach described in the previous sections, in a broader sense, this is also typical of the underlying 'playworker mind-set'. Even where a playwork-based approach is not made explicit in research methodology, the researcher who is able to maintain such a mind-set may be able to engage more fully with children's own experiences, perceptions and agendas.

The suggestion that there exists a single mid-set embraced by all playworkers is clearly an oversimplification, as can be seen, for example, in Russell's (2013) discussion of how playwork's central ideas have been formulated and reformulated over decades, all the while confronting and absorbing various inherent contradictions. However, the development, dissemination, broad acceptance and continuing discussion of the Playwork Principles (PPSG, 2005) provide a compass-bearing which points to some components that are widely accepted as making up such a mind-set (Brown, 2009). The Playwork Principles tell us that, "children and young people determine and control the content and intent of their play, by following their own instincts, ideas and interests in their own way for their own reasons" (Playwork Principle no. 2), and that, "For playworkers, the play process takes precedence" (Playwork Principle no. 4). Whilst it seems that only a small part of what is commonly described as 'play' (and indeed, what is described as 'playwork') fully meets these criteria, they stand for an ideal, or an aspiration, that many playworkers would endorse and as such are at the heart of my proposed 'playworker mind-set'.

Adherence to the playworker mind-set therefore means seeking to minimise the 'adulteration' of play. The term 'adulteration' is familiar in contemporary playwork literature (Sturrock & Else, 1998) but has different meanings for different authors. At its simplest, it is just the imposition of adult constraints, rules and limitations on children's play processes (Thomson, 2014), but it can also include the way a particular (adult-imposed) socio-political context limits or distorts play experience (Hughes, 2000) or the way that playworkers' own unresolved psychic needs get played out in their playwork practice, interfering with and corrupting the children's self-directed processes (Sturrock & Else, 1998). For any and all of these understandings, a fundamental task of playwork will always be to strive to minimise such adulterations in the way we work with children. These ideas together form the essence of what I am calling the 'playworker mind-set', as summed up here by Penny Wilson:

> One of the most basic underpinnings of the craft of the playworker is to understand that the play of children within the boundaries of a play setting must remain unadulterated by external agendas. This means that playworkers do not try to educate, train, tame, or therapeutically treat children in their time and space for play.
>
> (Wilson, 2010, p. 9)

My argument, then, is that (a) the playworker mind-set as described here differentiates playworkers from all the other kinds of professionals who work with children, (b) this difference gives us a clear advantage in conducting research with children in a way that is fully open to their way of understanding their world, and (c) this creates the possibility of different findings and new knowledge that cannot be accessed in other ways (not necessarily better or truer knowledge, but different and therefore valuable in itself).

As a rule, adult researchers, whether they approach their work from an academic or a practitioner standpoint, bring a wealth of professional knowledge and experience to bear on the problems they seek to investigate. This knowledge is organised in systems developed within the professions they belong to and, particularly in the case of academics, in the disciplines they identify with. Such professional knowledge systems tend to inculcate ways of thinking including pre-set lists of 'oughts', 'shoulds' and 'needs'. For example, educationalists have ideas about what children ought to learn, psychologists tend to impose professional concepts of 'normality' and childcare specialists often feel constrained in allowing children to experience risk etc.

This adult knowledge and experience fills our heads and determines our approach to every research question or issue. When adults set out to do research in partnership with children, these pre-set agendas cause problems. It is all but impossible for adult professionals to set aside, even for a minute, their strongly held professional self-belief founded in their professional knowledge and expertise.

Playworkers, by contrast, are the only professionals working with children who (if they are good at their job) seek to follow the children's agenda (PPSG, 2005) and do not impose their own professional programme. My experience as a doctoral researcher, and my critical reflection on that experience, has led me to believe that my background as a playworker gives me an advantage when it comes to working with children in a way that does not seek to control or manipulate their positions and purposes. Unless adult researchers can learn to leave aside their agendas and preconceptions and work with children in a way that goes beyond collecting data, seeking instead to understand children's way of thinking about the world they live in – in other words, become more like playworkers – we will never be able to access the valuable knowledge that children themselves can generate.

Transformative Research by Children and Adolescents, as practised by CESESMA in Nicaragua, is plainly not playwork. And yet, with its roots reaching back to the history and philosophy of playwork in the UK, it is firmly aligned with this playworker mind-set. In enabling us to clear away the remnants of adult professional agendas, positions and prescriptions, it helps us to hear and understand what children are concerned about and how they themselves experience and analyse these issues in their lives.

Notes

1 The Welsh Assembly has made significant progress in aligning law and policy in Wales with the provisions of the UNCRC, but its current devolved powers do not permit it to fully incorporate the Convention into Welsh law.
2 CESESMA stands for "Centro de Servicios Educativos en Salud y Medio Ambiente" (Centre for Education in Health and Environment).

References

Abernethy, W. D. (1968). *Playleadership.* London: National Playing Fields Association.
Beunderman, J. (2010). *People make play – The impact of staffed play provision on children, families and communities.* London: Play England.
Brown, F. (2009). *What is playwork?* (Children's Play Information Service Factsheet). London: National Children's Bureau.
Centro de Servicios Educativos en Salud y Medio Ambiente. (2012). *Learn to live without violence: Transformative research by children and young people* (H. Shier, Ed.). Preston: University of Central Lancashire and CESESMA. Retrieved from www.harryshier.net/docs/CESESMA-Learn_to_live_without_violence.pdf.
Centro de Servicios Educativos en Salud y Medio Ambiente. (2013). El juego infantil como derecho humano, de lo local a lo global. *Rayuela, 8,* 112–124.
Committee on the Rights of the Child. (2013). *General Comment No. 17: Article 31.* Geneva: United Nations.
Eide, A. (1987). *Report on the right to adequate food as a human right* (No. E/CN.4/Sub.2/1987/23). New York: United Nations.
Ellis, M. J. (1973). *Why people play.* Englewood Cliffs, NJ: Prentice-Hall.
Freire, P. (2001). *Pedagogy of the oppressed.* New York: Continuum (Original work published in 1968).
Get Ready For Geneva Drafting Committee. (2008). *Get ready for Geneva.* London: Children's Rights Alliance for England.
Guba, E. G. (1981). Criteria for assessing the trustworthiness of naturalistic inquiries. *Educational Communication and Technology, 29*(2), 75–91.
Hughes, B. (2000). *A dark and evil cul-de-sac: Has children's play in urban Belfast been adulterated by the troubles?* Unpublished master's thesis, Anglia Polytechnic University, Cambridge.
JNCTP Joint National Committee on Training for Playwork. (1985). *Recommendations on training for playwork* (The Salmon Book). London: Joint National Committee on Training for Playwork.

Kane, L. (2001). *Popular education and social change in Latin America*. London: Latin America Bureau.
Kellett, M. (2010). Small shoes, big steps! Empowering children as active researchers. *American Journal of Community Psychology, 46*(1), 195–203.
Lansdown, G. (2011). *Every child's right to be heard*. London: Save the Children.
Lees, R. & Mayo, M. (1984). *Community action for change*. Abingdon: Routledge.
Lester, S. & Russell, W. (2010). *Children's right to play: An examination of the importance of play in the lives of children worldwide*. The Hague: Bernard van Leer Foundation.
Lundy, L. (2007). 'Voice' is not enough: Conceptualising Article 12 of the United Nations Convention on the Rights of the Child. *British Educational Research Journal, 33*(6), 927–942.
Mertens, D. M. (2007). Transformative paradigm: Mixed methods and social justice. *Journal of Mixed Methods Research, 1*(3), 212–225.
Mertens, D. M. (2010). Philosophy in mixed methods teaching: The transformative paradigm as illustration. *International Journal of Multiple Research Approaches, 4*(1), 9–18.
Niñas y Niños Investigadores. (2014). Aprendiendo de niñas, niños y adolescentes investigadoras/es: Hacia una nueva pedagogía de derechos y deberes. *Rayuela (Mexico), 10*, 131–142.
Non-Government Organisation Network for the Rights of the Child. (2004). *Report by Swedish Children, young persons and adults to the UN committee on the Rights of the Child in Geneva 2004*. Stockholm: NGO Network for the Rights of the Child.
Playwork Principles Scrutiny Group. (2005). *The playwork principles*. Cardiff: Play Wales. Retrieved from www.playwales.org.uk/login/uploaded/documents/Playwork%20Principles/playwork%20principles.pdf.
Russell, W. (2013). *The dialectics of playwork: A conceptual and ethnographic study of playwork using cultural historical activity theory*. Unpublished doctoral dissertation. University of Gloucestershire, Cheltenham.
Shier, H. (1984). *Adventure playgrounds: An introduction*. London: National Playing Fields Association. Retrieved from www.harryshier.net/docs/Shier-AdventurePlaygrounds.pdf.
Shier, H. (Ed.). (1995). *Article 31 Action pack: Children's rights and children's play*. Birmingham: Play-Train.
Shier, H. (1999a). Letting children have their say. *Play Matters* (Autumn 1999), 10–11.
Shier, H. (1999b). What we really really want. *Playwords, 10*, 18–20.
Shier, H. (2001). Sailing the Seven Cs: A Child's Journey into the Future. Presented at the Network of Community Activities' biannual conference, Manly NSW, Australia, May 2001, Sydney: Network of Community Activities. Retrieved from http://www.harryshier.net/docs/Shier-Sailing_the_Seven_Cs.pdf
Shier, H. (2010). 'Pathways to participation' revisited: Learning from Nicaragua's child coffee workers. In N. Thomas & B. Percy-Smith (Eds.), *A handbook of children and young people's participation* (pp. 215–227). Abingdon: Routledge.
Shier, H. (2011). *The Nicaraguan children's 'defending our right to play' campaign as it happened, 2009–2011*. San Ramon, Nicaragua: CESESMA/Common Threads. Retrieved from www.harryshier.net/docs/Shier-Right_to_play_campaign.pdf.
Shier, H. (2015). Children as researchers in Nicaragua: Children's consultancy to transformative research. *Global Studies of Childhood, 5*(2), 206–219.

Shier, H. (2016). *Children's rights in school: The perception of children in Nicaragua*. Belfast: Queen's University Belfast. Retrieved from www.harryshier.net/docs/Shier-Children's_rights_in_school.pdf.

Sturrock, G. & Else, P. (1998). 'The Colorado Paper' – The playground as therapeutic space: Playwork as healing. In G. Sturrock & P. Else (Eds.) (2007), *Therapeutic playwork reader one* 1995–2000 (pp. 73–104). Eastleigh, Hampshire: Common Threads.

Thomson, S. (2014). 'Adulterated play': An empirical discussion surrounding adults' involvement with children's play in the primary school playground. *Journal of Playwork Practice*, 1(1), 5–21.

United Nations. (1989). *Convention on the rights of the child*. New York: United Nations.

Wilson, P. (2010). *The playwork primer*. College Park, MD: Alliance for Childhood.

Wragg, M. (2011). 'The child's right to play: Rhetoric or reality?' In P. Jones & G. Walker (Eds.), *Children's rights in practice* (pp. 71–81). Los Angeles: Sage Publications Ltd.

Young Consultants of Santa Martha. (2009). The young consultants of Santa Martha coffee plantation investigate the problem of violence. In B. Percy-Smith & N. Thomas (Eds.), *A handbook of children and young people's participation* (pp. 228–229). Abingdon: Routledge. Retrieved from www.cesesma.org/documentos/CESESMA-Young_Consultants_of_Santa_Martha.pdf.

Young Consultants of Santa Martha. (2011). *Rights and wrongs: Children and young people of santa Martha coffee plantation research the relationship between business and human rights on the plantation*. San Ramón, Nicaragua: CESESMA. Retrieved from www.cesesma.org/documentos/CESESMA-rights_and_wrongs.pdf.

2 Playwork research as the art of 'mirroring'

Shelly Newstead

Introduction

One of the features which distinguishes the practice of playwork from other approaches to working with children is that it takes place in the present tense (Nuttall, 2008). Playworkers shun adult concepts of planning and programming, timetables and themes, activities and outcomes in order to provide children with some time and space to follow their own instincts and determine their own agendas, rather than those of the adults around them (Hughes, 1996; Kilvington & Wood, 2010). As a playwork practitioner, I was always entirely comfortable with my role as a 'present tense professional', but I was also keenly aware that not all adults shared my enthusiasm for 'busking it' (not even all those who called themselves 'playworkers'). In my role as a playwork trainer, I became increasingly frustrated that some adults could not shift into what I regarded as a playwork way of thinking and being, firmly clinging instead to adult-centric notions of how best to 'keep children occupied'. Whilst I marvelled at my trainees' abilities to conjure up spectacular art and craft creations at the drop of a toilet roll, I struggled to find a way of articulating why I would really rather they didn't do it in the name of playwork (Newstead, 2011).

This question of how to explain the difference between 'us' and 'them' has vexed the playwork field ever since I started working in playwork in the late 1980s. However, as I discovered from my doctoral research, these debates date back to the early adventure playgrounds, where the practice of playwork originated. Unable to define what made the "right sort" (Bengtsson, 1970, p. 174) of adult, the adventure playground pioneers reluctantly concluded that adults suitable for the work were "born not made" (Lambert, 1974, p. 84; Allen and Nicholson, 1975, p. 245). What Francois (1969) described as "the fundamental qualities of heart, vocation and devotion" (p. 18) has often been put down to a personal and instinctive approach to working with children which cannot be taught (Russell, 1994), and internal debates and disagreements about the nature and purpose of playwork have taken place for the last 40 years (Benjamin & Welsh, 1992; Brown & Webb, 2002). Whilst playwork is often described as unique (Armitage, 2014; SkillsActive, 2008), playworkers have generally found it easier to describe what playwork is not, rather than articulate "what is it that playwork is" (Sturrock, 2007, p. iv).

It was the decapitation of a pink plastic hippo that eventually forced me to confront the issue of how to articulate the difference between a playwork approach and other ways of working with children. Whilst involved in a small-scale research project on playtimes in primary schools (Newstead, 2007), I observed a group of ten-year-old boys encircling a pink hippo-shaped plastic rubbish bin. Wielding the foam swords which I had put on the playground, the boys ceremoniously took the hippo's head clean off and then danced around gleefully as the absurd lump of pink plastic rolled down the playground at a rate of knots. I burst out laughing, sharing the children's delight in this new and surreal experience. It was only when I looked round and saw the faces of the other adults on the playground – most of them like thunder and not so much as a hint of a smile between them – that I stopped laughing and started to wonder why. Why had the children and I found the decapitation of a pink plastic hippo so hilarious? Why had the other adults not found it even remotely amusing? Why were they concerned about damage to school property, yet the thought had never crossed my mind? Did this make me an irresponsible adult, or were there other, subtler differences between me as a playwork practitioner and the other adults on the playground?

Not long after the 'hippo incident', I embarked on my doctoral studies. My original research design was an empirical study which set out to investigate whether adopting a playwork approach changed the way that children played. Based on my previous work on primary school playtimes, I wanted to explore the long-standing playwork assumption that there was something different about the way that playworkers worked with children and to measure whether this difference had any tangible effect on children's play. Whilst the measurement of children's play pre- and post-playwork intervention was a fairly straightforward exercise, this original research question stalled when it came to conceptualising 'a playwork approach' and constructing a model of playwork practice fit for the purposes of measurement. Existing models of playwork focused on the qualities of the spaces in which playwork took place (Hughes, 1996; Play England, 2008), rather than specifying precisely what playworkers did and how (and why) this was different to other ways of working with children. In a desperate attempt to find some sort of model of playwork as a practice (rather than a service), I went back to the literature from the days of the early adventure playgrounds to look for such a model.

Playwork history has generally been overlooked by contemporary playwork authors, who have traditionally produced accounts of their work based on their own personal experience or drawn on theories from other disciplines to make sense of their playwork experience (Cranwell, 1999; Heseltine, 1982). With only a (small and often inaccurate) handful of historical references in the contemporary playwork literature to work from, I embarked on an extensive search of international libraries and archives for literature produced by the adventure playground pioneers. This systematic search identified 482 rare and unknown historical playwork primary sources, defined as published and unpublished written materials authored by those with first-hand experience of doing or supporting the work of adventure playgrounds, as defined by Lady Allen of Hurtwood (Allen &

Nicholson, 1975). Playwork history was defined as 1946–1990 (see Newstead, 2016 for further discussion on this).

This fascinating and previously uncatalogued collection of primary sources included reports, reflective diaries, letters, books, pamphlets and magazine articles. However, one of the problems of working with this literature was that it was produced on a 'needs must' basis (Heseltine, 1982). Insights by the adventure playground pioneers about their unique approach to working with children are therefore strewn across all forms of literature. The advantages of children climbing trees can be found in committee minutes; funding applications reveal explanations of a distinct philosophical approach to the work, and the problems of working with sheep can be found in reports on playwork training. As a result, there is a distinct lack of a sequence and growth of knowledge in the literature, with small but highly significant clues about the unique nature and purpose of what became known as playwork practice repeated by different playwork authors across the decades.

Nearly three years into my doctoral study, it became clear that, instead of providing a model of practice, the historical playwork primary sources contained thousands of playwork tesserae – tiny fragments of knowledge – about what it meant to do playwork from a playwork perspective. At this point, my research question changed to address the question which has beset the playwork field since the days of the first adventure playgrounds: how to articulate the practice of playwork as a unique identity in its own right. Grounded Theory techniques were used to fracture the data (Corbin & Strauss, 1990) contained in the historical playwork literature, identifying the playwork tesserae which described what it means to do playwork from a playwork perspective. This deconstruction of the historical primary playwork sources identified a "core category" (Birks & Mills, 2011, p. 11) of "playwork philosophy": a distinct ontological perspective on children and childhood which has been lost in contemporary playwork. This lost philosophy of playwork created an operating theory, Playwork Mirror Theory (Newstead, 2016), which provides the unique playwork perspective to working with children in the playwork literature.

This chapter describes how this operating theory of 'mirroring' has been applied from its practical origins to other aspects of playwork infrastructure over the last 70 years. It explores the application of Playwork Mirror Theory to playwork research as a way of distinguishing research from a playwork perspective from other approaches to researching play.

Mirroring as playwork's operating theory

'Mirroring' is a trans-disciplinary concept which suggests that the replication of a behaviour will have a positive and/or desired effect on the subjects being imitated (see, for example: Jones, 2009; Pfeifer, Iacoboni, Mazziotta, & Dapretto, 2008). Mirroring the behaviours of others is understood to establish a connection and rapport between the person who is being 'mirrored' and the person who is 'mirroring' (Kohut, 1971). A miscellaneous collection of adults from diverse backgrounds and professions (Allen & Nicholson, 1975), the adventure playground pioneers intuitively adopted this idea as the operating theory for their work.

Playwork Mirror Theory (Newstead, 2016) derived from the adventure playground pioneers' distinct ontological perspective on the nature of children and childhood. They believed that children and adults were fundamentally different in nature. Children were understood to be creative, spontaneous, flexible and experimental, whereas adults were regarded as inherently organised and structured, preferring order, predictability and cleanliness in their day-to-day lives:

> Children like disorder or find some invisible other therein. Most adults hate it. Children do not in the least mind being dirty. Most adults abhor it. Children will find a source of enjoyment in the oddest and most unlikely play material: tin cans, milk bottle tops, broken slates, soil, cinders, firewood. The adult mind thinks of these things in terms of refuse and rubbish.
>
> (Mays, 1957, pp. 5–6)

The adult desire for order and structure conflicted with children's need to explore, test and experiment, and as a result, the adult world was "constantly finding itself at war" (Benjamin, 1961, p. 12) with children. It therefore came as no surprise to the adventure playground pioneers that children "rebelled against the hire-purchase-washing-machine culture with unfortunate results for the rosebushes" (Mygind, 1961, p. 203). Adventure playgrounds were conceived as "a children's republic" within an adult kingdom (Mygind, 1961, p. 202), so that children's creative, spontaneous and experimental natures could be accommodated within ordered and regulated adult society (Abernethy, 1968b; Benjamin, 1974; Cocken, 1976).

The "wide cleavage between youth and age, childhood and maturity" (Mays, 1957, p. 5) created a problem for the adventure playground pioneers, who recognised that their position in the adult camp could defeat their purpose for creating adventure playgrounds in the first place (Bertelsen, 1954). Children were understood to be "imitative members of our society" (Benjamin, 1974, p. 1), and therefore there was a danger that adult-designed and operated adventure playgrounds would encourage children to imitate adult ways of thinking and being, rather than following their own interests on their own terms. In an attempt to demonstrate to children that these were spaces in which they could do "what they need to do and not what adults think they ought to do" (Abernethy, 1968a, p. 17), the layout and operation of adventure playgrounds were deliberately designed to "mirror" (Lambert, 1974, p. 152) the creative and spontaneous nature of children. Land was left in a rough and uneven state (Abernethy, 1968b) and natural materials were supplemented by waste materials "scrounged" from local businesses and households (Balmforth & Nelson, 1978, p. 57). These "loose parts" (Nicholson, 1971) were a vital application of mirror theory, as they introduced new and changeable elements which encouraged children to explore and experiment (Grimsby Adventure Playground Association, 1957). Adventure playgrounds were developed on the hypothesis that if they mirrored children's creative, spontaneous and experimental natures, then children would be more likely to be creative, spontaneous and experiment. They pointed to children's use of waste ground as evidence for this theory:

> On summer evenings there were sometimes as many as sixty playing the rubbish and the rubble and broken bricks, and it was these children who first said, in the unmistakeable language of action, that they wanted a place of their own where they could find materials for games of their own invention.
> (Gutkind, 1952, n.p.)

The adventure playground pioneers believed that fixed equipment play spaces, designed by adults, produced uninspired and unimaginative behaviour in children because these were the types of behaviours suggested by the swings and slides. By contrast, the waste ground with its novel and unexpected finds and possibilities mirrored children's exploratory and experimental natures, thereby offering children an outlet for their spontaneous and creative behaviours (Allen, 1964; Benjamin, 1961). Adventure playgrounds were created as "an empirical science" (Bertelsen, 1953, p. 688), based on a working hypothesis that children were more likely to behave like children if the 'physical and psychical' (Bertelsen, 1972, p. 16) environment mirrored their creative, spontaneous and experimental natures:

> We should not forget that children spend a lot of their lives – at school, at home and elsewhere – in adult-dominated surroundings where they learn that there are definite limits to the way they use what is around them. Tables are for sitting at, not for overturning to make a fort or a pirate ship. Water is for drinking or washing in, not for playing with. The more an adventure playground feels like a different sort of place, the easier it is for children to believe that it really is somewhere where most of these restrictions do not apply, where they are free to experiment, to make a mess and to let their imaginations run riot. Waste materials play an important part in creating that different atmosphere, by making a playground's actual physical appearance different from that of school or home.
> (Sutherland & Soames, 1984, pp. 88–89)

Perhaps this was why Sørensen was so perturbed at the change of the English name for his invention from 'junk playgrounds' to 'adventure playgrounds' (Sørensen, 1968a). 'Junk' was the tangible manifestation of Sørensen's (1931) reason for inventing 'Skrammellegeplads'. The presence of 'junk' sent a signal to children that adventure playgrounds were "a different sort of place" (Sutherland & Soames, 1984, p. 88) and also provided a visual reminder to adults that within these different sort of spaces, it was the children's worldview that counted. Changing the name to 'adventure playgrounds' let adults off the hook of what the adventure playground pioneers saw as the disconcerting truth of the unfair treatment of children by adult-dominated society (Cocken, 1976; Benjamin, 1974).

Sørensen (1968b) was also originally doubtful that his 'Skrammellegeplads' should include adults, on the grounds that they might prevent children from acting according to their own natures. Some of the earliest adventure playgrounds in the UK were trialled without adult presence (Jackson, 1959). However, the adventure playground pioneers found that the right sort of adult proved useful to children in defending their space against the adult world, which was prone to see its need for firewood or garden ornaments as more important than the children's need for loose parts (Mays, 1957; Wills, 1988). The presence of adults also tricked those adults "who see only what their eyes show them" (Sandlands, 1955, p. 24) into believing that children were supervised and therefore 'under control' (Abernethy, 1968b).

In fact, the early playworkers went to great lengths to avoid supervising children. It was generally agreed that the best sort of adult on an adventure playground was 'unobtrusive' (Grimsby Adventure Playground Association, 1955; Buck, 1965, p. 13). Adults often made themselves invisible in plain sight by deliberately occupying themselves in ways which kept them out of the children's affairs, as described by Cocken (1976) "We had a phrase that if you saw anyone reading a comic – he's a leader" (p. 10). This strategy signalled to children that adults were minding their own business so that the children could get on with theirs (Turner, 1961).

However, children had other ideas about the role of adults, often requiring them "to provide materials, settle disputes, answer questions, take an interest and give first-aid to some very minor injuries" (Turner, 1961, p. 49). This level of engagement with children created a philosophical and practical dilemma for adults on adventure playgrounds. According to their own 'two cultures' philosophy, adult input into what they regarded as 'the affairs of children' (Abernethy, 1977, p. 14) could turn these children's republics (Mygind, 1961) into just another service for children where adult perspectives and priorities held sway:

> It can prove very difficult to help a child to nail two boards together without putting too much of one's own ideas into it. It does not require much of such 'help' before what was originally intended as an ice-cream kiosk ends up as a villa and thus a product of the adult fantasy.
> (Andersen, 1972, p. 86)

On the other hand, children often needed help or support, and denying this may lead to boredom and frustration (Turner, 1961; Lambert, 1974). The adventure playground pioneers turned once again to their operating theory of mirroring and applied it to their interactions with children whenever possible, as a way of avoiding making standard adult responses (National Playing Fields Association (NPFA), 1960). As Lambert (1974) observed, "When talking to children, it was important to avoid the kind of intervention that reminds him you are an adult, an outsider, one of Them" (p. 60). Adults first of all tried to see "through the eyes of a child" (Benjamin, 1974, p. 1) to understand about "what is going on at a child's level" (Lambert, 1974, p. 149). Then, wherever possible, they mirrored what they understood to be children's perspectives in order to demonstrate that these were the perspectives which mattered on adventure playgrounds (Jago, 1970).

Mirroring as a playwork meme

In the last 30 years, the rationale for the existence of playwork has shifted away from the original purpose of adventure playgrounds as a respite from adult-dominated society (Abernethy, 1968b; Allen, 1968), to providing and facilitating play for children (Play Principles Scrutiny Group (PPSG), 2005). Whilst this may appear to be an insignificant variation on a theme, this change from adult aims to outcomes for children has in effect reversed the original child-adult hierarchy of the adventure playgrounds. Within the dominant paradigm of playworkers as providers of play, children are dependent on adults to provide and enhance their play experiences (see, for example, Beunderman, 2010). In stark contrast to the early adventure playgrounds, where play was regarded as "the business of children themselves" (Lambert, 1974, p. 16), nowadays, "playwork makes children's play its core business" (Davy, 2007, p. 45).

Despite this ontological flit over the last 40 years, the adventure playground pioneer's operating theory of mirroring has survived and thrived throughout playwork practice and policy over the last 70 years. Although the operating theory of adventure playgrounds was never fully developed in the historical primary sources, this central theory of mirroring has been handed down meme-like from generation to generation of playwork practitioners. In the contemporary playwork literature, allusions to mirroring have been interpreted within the dominant paradigm of playworkers as providers and facilitators of play. It is generally understood that the practice of playwork should mirror the process of play, with several authors emphasising the need for playworkers to be playful themselves as a way of encouraging playfulness in children (Davy, 2007; Else, 2014; Russell, 2006). Heated debates about adults swearing in response to swearing by children can often be heard at playwork gatherings, with those from the adventure playground tradition arguing that reflecting back the child's mode of communication puts the adult on the child's level.

Mirror theory has also been extended to all aspects of playwork infrastructure as a form of playwork isopraxism. According to the original 'two cultures' theory of the adventure playground pioneers, adults are unlikely to be able to see things from a child's perspective. There is an assumption that mirroring a playwork approach in all aspects of policy and practice will enable adults to understand that a playwork perspective is different to other ways of working with children, where adult perspectives and priorities generally take precedence. For example, playworkers will gain understanding and respect from local communities if they mirror the way that people live and dress in these communities, and those attending a playwork conference will gain a better understanding of playwork if the event itself reflects the way that playworkers should behave (Hughes, 1975;

Meynell Games Group, 2016). This extension of the original mirror theory to playwork infrastructure is most consistent in the playwork training literature. Playwork education and training should mirror playwork (Handscomb & Virdi, 2007), in that playwork teaching and learning should reflect the conditions that would be created within a playwork setting (National Training Organisation for Sport Recreation and Allied Occupations (NTOSRAO), 2000; Lester & Russell, 2004; Taylor, 2008). The underlying assumption is that in modelling the sort of flexible, spontaneous behaviours required to be able to mirror children, playwork training (and trainers) provide a 'real-life' demonstration of the differences between the ordered and structured adult world and the 'here and now' culture of children.

Training has traditionally been regarded as the 'frontier territory' (Taylor, 1985) in the evolution of the playwork field from intuitive practical work to theory-based practice. However, in recent years, several playwork trainers and practitioners have undertaken studies at undergraduate and postgraduate levels, particularly in the area of play (McKendrick, Horton, Kraftl, & Else, 2014). These studies have drawn on theoretical and methodological approaches from a range of other disciplines which have brought many new insights into the playwork field. However, as the next section discusses, this interdisciplinary approach to researching play also has several drawbacks for the development of playwork research and the playwork field itself (Rennie, 1999).

The need for a playwork perspective to researching play

Research has played a key part in the development of playwork ever since the days of the first adventure playgrounds. When Lady Allen of Hurtwood brought back the idea of 'junk playgrounds' to the UK, there was no published literature and only one model in far-away Copenhagen to follow (Allen, 1946, 1953). Consistently described as an 'experiment' by the adventure playground pioneers (Burden, 1948; Gutkind, 1952; Benjamin, 1961), the UK adventure playgrounds pioneers had to find out how to set up and operate these "spaces filled with rubbish" (Bengtsson, 1970, p. 162) by trial and error (Turner, 1961; Herbert, 1968; Crowther, 1968). This informal research into what made adventure playgrounds successful was also supplemented by research carried out by scholars from a range of other disciplines (see, for example, Duggan, n.d.; Golcher, n.d.).

Echoing this early interdisciplinary approach (Abernethy, 1975), recent playwork studies have continued to draw on methodologies and theoretical perspectives from other disciplines. Furthermore, playwork research initiatives such as *Journal of Playwork Practice* have deliberately recruited scholars from other disciplines to support the development of theoretical and practical approaches to playwork. This interdisciplinary approach has introduced valuable insights to a traditionally isolated profession and has shed new light on what it means to do playwork. However, what an interdisciplinary approach cannot achieve is the definition of what it means to do playwork research from a playwork perspective. This term 'a playwork perspective' is frequently used in the contemporary playwork literature as a way of distinguishing playwork from other approaches to working with children (Hughes, 2012; Brown & Patte, 2013; PPSG, 2005). Although rarely defined, it is generally understood as "a playwork way of being, doing, thinking and learning" (Handscomb & Virdi, 2007, p. 17), or a playwork approach to working with children which is both unique to, and defined by, the experience of being a playworker. However, over the last 40 years, playwork has suffered a lack of credibility as a result of its inability to articulate its unique approach to working with children (Kingston, 2008; Williams, 1986). Without a defined playwork perspective with which to set playwork apart from others ways of working with children, playwork practitioners have found it difficult to resist being "outflanked" (Brown & Cheesman, 2003, p. 4) by other professions. There is a danger that continuing to pursue an interdisciplinary approach will result in the same indistinguishable fate for playwork research. Without a clear articulation of what it means to research play from a playwork perspective, playwork research, like playwork practice, may become all things to all people (Heseltine, 1982).

The question of identity is therefore as important for playwork as a developing discipline as it is for playwork as a developing profession. Without establishing solid ontological and epistemological foundations for playwork research, research carried out by those working in the playwork field is likely to be subsumed into other disciplines, in both a practical and a methodological sense. Researchers from the playwork field may become disempowered in their playwork-specific research interests by other disciplinary priorities, and unpublished research can fall between the cracks of other disciplines and become inaccessible to those working in the playwork field.

The next step in the evolution of playwork as a unique profession and a distinct discipline in its own right is to develop its body of knowledge which will inform the development of its practice and the development of the profession. Just as the adventure playground pioneers fortified the children's domains with fences against the incursion of the adult world (The Crawley Community Association Adventure Playground Committee (TCCAAPC), 1955), so playwork research needs to define its own disciplinary boundaries. Playwork Mirror Theory currently provides a theoretical foundation for playwork practice and infrastructure which distinguishes playwork from other approaches to working with children. In attempting to define a playwork approach to research, this founding operating theory of the adventure playground pioneers could also provide an ontological and epistemological foundation for the development of a playwork perspective to researching play.

The tradition of research within the Academy is focused on the development of new knowledge, which poses a considerable challenge for the development of Playwork Mirror Theory in relation to researching play. Playwork Mirror Theory separates out the adults from the child's world and prioritises, wherever possible, children's perspectives and knowledge over that of adults. At the core of this distinct approach lies the notion that in playwork, adults cannot know what is going on at a child's level and can therefore only hypothesise. The best that a playworker (either researcher or practitioner) can ever aim for is a form of epistemological equality, whereby the knowledge of the children and the knowledge of the adult stands side by side as equally valid within their own contexts, as illustrated by Jago (1970):

> I would sympathise with you if you felt that the towers and three storey huts appear very risky on the playground but in fact they appear as risks to us because we tend not to walk around ten or fifteen feet above the ground anymore, unless being paid as a builder, so we tend to be fearful and clumsy. These structures are not risky in a child's terms because he built them and knows their limits.
>
> (p. 2)

Clearly, such a radical departure from a traditional research approach of (adult) researchers as creators of new knowledge to adult/researchers as 'educated guessers of children's experience' challenges traditional notions of epistemological adult superiority and, from a playwork perspective, could lead to questionable 'findings'. An alternative application of Playwork Mirror Theory to research could be in the context of research design, where playwork research reflects the practice of playwork. Areas to explore might include the following;

- Does the research reflect a creative, experimental and flexible approach, not only with children involved in their study, but also in the methodological approach?
- How does the choice of methods reflect the (adult) researcher's lack of knowledge about children's experience and perspectives?
- How does the research reflect the theoretical foundation of playwork practice?
- What steps has the researcher taken to safeguard against the prioritisation of adult knowledge and perspectives over children's knowledge and perspectives in the analysis of the data?

Conclusion

This chapter has described how Playwork Mirror Theory was developed from the original ontological perspective on children and childhood of the adventure playground pioneers which was applied to the design and operation of adventure playgrounds. This fundamental operating theory – that children are more likely to behave like children if the 'physical and psychical' (Bertelsen, 1972, p. 16) environment mirrors their creative, spontaneous and experimental natures – has been handed down meme-like through subsequent generations of playworkers and has proved itself to be flexible and adaptable to a variety of situations of policy and practice. The next stage of the development of the playwork field as a profession and as an emerging academic discipline lies in the development of a unique body of knowledge about what it means to do playwork from a playwork perspective, which can only be produced by research which is carried out from a playwork perspective. Playwork Mirror Theory could serve as a credible theoretical foundation for developing playwork research as a unique approach to research which would remain faithful to its own professional and disciplinary principles. For, as Shier (1990) observed (perhaps with a nod to the notion of mirroring):

> Playwork has a different tradition – a different view of the world. Whatever comes out of this process, we must make sure it is true to our principles.
>
> (p. 33)

References

Abernethy, W. D. (1968a). *Playgrounds*. London: National Playing Fields Association.
Abernethy, W. D. (1968b). *Playleadership*. London: National Playing Fields Association.
Abernethy, W. D. (1975, August–September). *Training of workers for adventure play*. Paper presented at the Adventure Playground in Theory and Practice conference. Adventure Playgrounds and Children's Playgrounds; Report of the Sixth International Conference, University Bucconi, Milan, Italy.
Abernethy, W. D. (1977). *Notes and papers – A general survey on children's play provision*. London: NPFA National Playing Fields Association.
Allen, Lady Allen of Hurtwood. (1946). Why not use our bomb sites like this? *Picture Post*, 26–27.
Allen, Lady Allen of Hurtwood. (1953). *Proposed organisation for initiating adventure playgrounds*. (n.p.) (n.p.).
Allen, Lady Allen of Hurtwood. (1964). *New playgrounds*. London: The Housing Centre Trust.
Allen, Lady Allen of Hurtwood. (1968). *Planning for play*. London: Thames and Hudson.
Allen, M. & Nicholson, M. (1975). *Lady Allen of Hurtwood memoirs of an uneducated lady*. London: Thames and Hudson.
Andersen, R. (1972). From an educational point of view. In A. Bengtsson (Ed.), *Adventure playgrounds* (pp. 84–89). New York: Praeger.
Armitage, M. (2014). Playwork: The anarchy wing of sociology. In C. Burke & K. Jones (Eds.), *Education, childhood and anarchism: Talking Colin Ward* (pp. 113–122). Abingdon: Routledge.
Balmforth, N. & Nelson, W. (1978). *Jubilee Street – Pebble Mill's guide to adventure play*. Birmingham: BBC Books.
Bengtsson, A. (1970). *Environmental planning for children's play*. New York: Praeger.
Benjamin, J. (1961). *In search of adventure – A study of the junk playground*. Leicester: Blackfriars Press Ltd.
Benjamin, J. (1974). *Grounds for play*. London: National Council of Social Service.
Benjamin, J. & Welsh, R. (1992). Play and participation. *Streetwise*, 12, 2–8.
Bertelsen, J. (1953). The daily round on a junk playground. *Danish Outlook*, 6(6), 688–693.
Bertelsen, J. (1954). *Junk playgrounds*. [Letter to] Lady Allen of Hurtwood.
Bertelsen, J. (1972). Early experience from Emdrup. In A. Bengtsson (Ed.), *Adventure playground* (pp. 16–23). New York: Praeger.
Beunderman, J. (2010). *People make play – The impact of staffed play provision on children, families and communities*. London: Play England.

Birks, M. & Mills, J. (2011). *Grounded theory: A practical guide*. Los Angeles, CA and London: SAGE.
Brown, F. & Cheesman, B. (2003). Introduction: Childhood and play. In F. Brown (Ed.), *Playwork – Theory and practice* (pp. 1–5). Maidenhead: Open University Press.
Brown, F. & Patte, M. (2013). *Rethinking children's play*. London: Bloomsbury Academic.
Brown, F. & Webb, S. (2002). Playwork – An attempt at definition. *PlayAction*, 6–10.
Buck, D. (1965). *Adventure playgrounds as a countervailing agency to delinquency*.
Burden, G. (1948). The junk playground: An educational adjunct and an antidote to delinquency. *The Friend*, 4, 1029.
Cocken, D. (1976). *Child's play???': Memoirs of an adventure playground*. London: National Playing Fields Association.
Corbin, J. & Strauss, A. (1990). Grounded theory research: Procedures, canons, and evaluative criteria. *Zeitschrift Fur Soziologie*, 19(6), 418–427.
Cranwell, K. (1999, March). *The role of the study of history in the playwork profession*. Paper presented at the PlayEd 1999A – Theoretical Playwork and the Research Agenda Conference. Ely.
The Crawley Community Association Adventure Playground Committee. (1955). *Crawley adventure playground* [Pamphlet]. Crawley: The Crawley Community Association Adventure Playground Committee.
Crowther, S. (1968). *Play in London*. London: London Adventure Playground Association.
Davy, A. (2007). Playwork: Art, science, political movement or religion? In W. Russell, B. Handscomb, & J. Fitzpatrick (Eds.), *Playwork voices: In celebration of Bob Hughes and Gordon Sturrock* (pp. 41–46). London: London Centre for Playwork Education and Training.
Duggan, E. P. (n.d.). *A report to the Social Science Research Council on a feasibility study of the social and educational effects of adventure playgrounds*. (n.p.) (n.p.).
Else, P. (2014). *Making sense of play*. Maidenhead: Open University Press.
Francois, P. (1969, July). *Introducing the problem of leadership*. Paper presented at the Playgrounds: With or Without Leadership? 4th Conference Proceedings, Paris.
Golcher, W. J. (n.d.). *Adventure play*. (n.p.) (n.p.).
Grimsby Adventure Playground Association. (1955). *Joe Benjamin*. [Letter to] Lady Allen of Hurtwood. (n.p.) (n.p.).
Grimsby Adventure Playground Association. (Report 1957–58). *Adventure on the doorstep*. (n.p.) (n.p.).
Gutkind, P. C. W. (1952). *Report to Clydesdale Road playground committee – May 1952*. (n.p.) (n.p.).
Handscomb, B. & Virdi, M. (2007). Playwork learning – Sharing the journey. In W. Russell, B. Handscomb, & J. Fitzpatrick (Eds.), *Playwork voices: In celebration of Bob Hughes and Gordon Sturrock* (pp. 176–185). London: London Centre for Playwork Education and Training.
Herbert, J. A. M. (1968). *Venture into adventure*. Welwyn Garden City: The Broad-Water Press Ltd.
Heseltine, P. (1982). *Review of the current state of play*. Paper presented at the PlayEd 1982 – The Transcript Conference, Bolton. Ely: PlayEducation.
Hughes, B. (1975). *Notes for adventure playworkers*. London: Children and Youth Action Group.
Hughes, B. (1996). *Play environments: A question of quality*. London: PLAYLINK.

Hughes, B. (2012). *Evolutionary playwork* (2nd ed.). London: Routledge.
Jackson, M. (1959). *Thanks for 'very fine address at the Guildhall'*. [Letter to] Lady Allen of Hurtwood. (n.p.) (n.p.).
Jago, L. (1970). *Learning through experience: Children and workers on adventure playgrounds*. London: London Adventure Playground Association.
Jones, S. S. (2009). Imitation and empathy in infancy. *Cognition, Brain, Behavior, XIII*, 391–413.
Kilvington, J. & Wood, A. (2010). *Reflective playwork: For all who work with children*. London: Continuum International Publishing Group Ltd.
Kingston, B. (2008). *Playwork – Mostly harmless? – Ideas Paper 13*. London: Play England.
Kohut, H. (1971). *The analysis of the self: A systematic approach to the psychoanalytic treatment of narcissistic personality disorders*. New York: International Universities Press.
Lambert, J. (1974). *Adventure playgrounds: A personal account of a play-leader's work, as told to Jenny Pearson*. London: Penguin Books.
Lester, S. & Russell, W. (2004). *Training playwork trainers: A resource pack designed for use with playworkers wishing to develop training skills* (Revised 3rd ed.). JNCTP Joint National Committee on Training for Playwork.
Mays, J. B. (1957). *Adventure in play*. Liverpool: Liverpool Council of Social Service.
McKendrick, J. H., Horton, J., Kraftl, P., & Else, P. (2014). Practice: Playwork in times of austerity. *Journal of Playwork Practice, 1*(1), 61–99.
Meynell Games Group. (2016). *14th National Playwork Conference: Conference journey planner*. Eastbourne: Meynell Games Group.
Mygind, A. (1961). *New Town adventure* (pp. 202–203). London: Anarchy Freedom Press.
National Playing Fields Association. (1960). *Adventure playgrounds – A progress report*. London: NPFA National Playing Fields Association.
National Training Organisation for Sport Recreation and Allied Occupations. (2000). *The playwork education and training endorsement handbook*. London: SkillsActive.
Newstead, S. (2007). *Playtime!* Eastleigh: Common Threads Publications Ltd.
Newstead, S. (2011). *The Buskers guide to playwork* (2nd ed.). Eastleigh: Common Threads Publications Ltd.
Newstead, S. (2016). *Deconstructing and reconstructing the unorthodox recipe of playwork*. Unpublished doctoral dissertation, UCL Institute of Education, London.
Nicholson, S. (1971). How not to cheat children – The Theory of Loose Parts. *Landscape Architecture, 62*, 30–35.
Nuttall, E. (2008). *Possible summers*. Retrieved from https://possiblesummers.word press.com/.
Pfeifer, J. H., Iacoboni, M., Mazziotta, J. C., & Dapretto, M. (2008). Mirroring others' emotions relates to empathy and interpersonal competence in children. *NeuroImage, 39*(4), 2076–2085.
Play England. (2008). *Quality in play* (4th ed.). London: Play England.
Playwork Principles Scrutiny Group. (2005). *The playwork principles*. Cardiff: Play Wales. Retrieved from www.playwales.org.uk/login/uploaded/documents/Play work%20Principles/playwork%20principles.pdf.
Rennie, S. (1999). *Play, playwork and the development of personality*. Paper presented at the IPA World Conference, Lisbon, Portugal.
Russell, W. (1994). *JNCTP and ? in the nineties. Welcome speech by Wendy Russell: Chair of JNCTP*. Paper presented at the JNCTP AGM 1994 Coming of Age.

Russell, W. (2006). *Reframing playwork: Reframing challenging behaviour*. Nottingham: Nottingham City Council.
Sandlands, C. (1955). *I visit the Lollard adventure playground*. Illustrated.
Shier, H. (1990). *JNCTP playwork accreditation report* [Report]. London: Joint National Committee on Training for Playwork.
SkillsActive. (2008). *EYFS update – September 2008*. London: SkillsActive.
Sørensen, C. T. (1931). *Parkpolitik i Sogn og Købstad*. (Republished: Copenhagen: Christian Ejlers, 1978. With extra 'author': Ole Thomassen Ed.). København: Kommission hos gyldendalske boghandel nordisk forlag.
Sørensen, C. T. (1968a). [Letter to] Lady Allen of Hurtwood.
Sørensen, C. T. (1968b). Preface. In Lady Allen of Hurtwood (Ed.), *Planning for play* (p. 9). London: Thames and Hudson.
Sturrock, G. (2007). *Towards tenets of playwork practice*. iP-D!P, 1, i–iv.
Sutherland, A. T. & Soames, P. (1984). *Adventure play with handicapped children*. London: Souvenir Press.
Taylor, C. (1985). *Qualification, validation, endorsement and recognition of training for playwork*. Paper presented at the PlayEd 1985 – The Priorities – Issues in Context.
Taylor, C. (2008). *An advocacy for playwork – Ideas Paper 14* [Report]. London: Play England.
Turner, H. S. (1961). *Something extraordinary*. London: Michael Joseph Ltd.
Williams, H. (1986). *Playworks*. Lancaster: PlayEducation.
Wills, R. (1988). *Freedom to play: A history of the child at play*. (n.p.) (n.p.).

3 Nomadic wonderings on playwork research
Putting a dialectical and ethnographic methodology to work again

Wendy Russell

> We need stories (and theories) that are just big enough to gather up the complexities and keep the edges open and greedy for surprising new and old connections.
>
> (Haraway, 2015, p. 160)

> There is no moving beyond, no leaving the 'old' behind.
> There is no absolute boundary between here-now and there-then.
> There is nothing that is new; there is nothing that is not new.
>
> (Barad, 2014, p. 168)

Wo(a)ndering about the ethics and politics of knowledge production through research

The zipline seat had been put out of action and the children were not tall enough to get it. I set it down for Jacee and she had a go, screeching as she hurtled towards the tyre stop at the other end. Yousuf came and was waiting on the platform. Jacee stayed on the zipline seat in the middle of the wire, leaning back and swinging round, refusing to get off. Then Jamal came up and tried to get the zipline seat off Jacee. Jacee, in the face of competition from her older brother, got down, so now I had the situation that Jamal had the seat and I had told Yousuf he was next. Yousuf was complaining that it was his turn. I was standing close to the zipline seat and put out my hand to hold onto the rope. Now both Jamal and I were hanging on to the rope. I got the feeling that if he had really wanted a go, he would and could have forced it away from me. But he didn't. I was kind of smiling, saying, "Come on, Jamal, you can have a go when Yousuf's had a go, it's his turn, he's been waiting, give me the zipline or you take it up to Yousuf," "No." and it turned into yes, no, yes, yes, no, and a game. So: "Give me the zipline." "No." "Yes." "NO"." "Yes." Lots of smiling going on. And so on, then "This is a game isn't it?" "Yes." In the same singsong reply voice. "Are you enjoying this?" "Yes." "Why?" "Because it's fun." More smiling. Eventually, Yousuf says, "Forget it, let him have a go." Yousuf walks off and Jamal relinquishes the zipline – the game is over and he doesn't have a turn anyway.

This is a moment of everyday playworking as recorded in the field notes for my doctoral research. Nothing special, it cannot claim to encapsulate the essence of playworking, nor be presented as an example of 'good practice'. Yet it says much about the messiness and mundanity of movements, desires, materiality, relational power, emergence and the throwntogetherness (Massey, 2005) of playwork spaces. For me, after over 40 years of trying to make sense of both playwork and children's play, it is the vignette's very ordinariness that matters, since it is this that offers rich possibilities for exploring a different take on both (Karen Barad calls this a 'cut'; more on this a little later). As a provocative opening position, I thought I would 'play' with the suggestion that maybe playworkers (myself included) have been putting play too much centre stage and that this is a political and ethical issue for playworkers.

In this chapter, I return to and put to work again selected elements of my doctoral research in order to explore what researching play from a playwork perspective might mean for me. This 'putting to work again' is inspired by the opening quotations from Donna Haraway and Karen Barad. It does not move beyond nor does it leave behind the original research; it does, however, explore the potential of stories – and theories – that can make connections and leave space open for becoming different.

The original research was an ethnographic study of the dialectics of playwork using Cultural History Activity Theory (CHAT) as a framework for analysis. Playwork's fundamental contradictions stem from the tensions between the sector's definition of play as "freely chosen, personally directed and intrinsically motivated" (Playwork Principles Scrutiny Group (PPSG), 2005, Playwork Principle no. 2) and claims made for the instrumental value of playwork in order to access public funding. Both are pertinent to a discussion on researching play from a playwork perspective, since playwork's theories are *situated*: that is, they have developed within a particular context in order to show a particular value for both play and playwork. In addition, they are situated within what many have argued was the 20th century's dominant academic discipline for theorising childhood, that of psychology (Dahlberg, Moss, & Pence, 2013; Moss, 2007; Rose, 2008).

The process of knowledge production is not neutral: researching play from a playwork perspective does not produce universal, fixed, objective truths about play. To trouble this idea further, I draw on the work of theoretical physicist and feminist philosopher Karen Barad. I am no physics expert, but I can understand the difficulties that the physics community had to contend with when it was discovered that light can be both a wave and a particle, two phenomena hitherto understood as mutually exclusive. According to Barad (2010), it was Niels Bohr who suggested that the problem might lie in the nature of concepts (wave, particle) themselves, and that concepts themselves are "specific material arrangements of experimental apparatuses" (Barad, 2010, p. 253). The starting point of the researcher (for example, classic Newtonian physics) and the apparatus used to observe phenomena enact what Barad (2007) calls an 'agential cut', a particular meaning that excludes other meanings. Furthermore, what this also does is dissolve the boundaries between what Newtonian physics saw as distinct entities: researcher and researched, self and other, subject and object become entangled in co-constituting movements and meanings. The apparatuses used for research, including language itself and the power given to particular ways of knowing, delimit the cut of what is produced in terms of knowledge and accompanying practices. Research, therefore, is an ethical and political event: as such, we have a responsibility to imagine how things might be otherwise and to deliberately seek a different cut in order to bring to light what our habitual perspectives exclude. Given this, I also draw on Braidotti's (2012) notion of nomadic ethics to continue my wanderings and wonderings on childhood, play and playwork in an attempt to resist the fixing and codifying of ideas. The analysis offered is not so much *reflective* (an accurate mirror representation) as *diffractive*, spreading in different directions, an interference of things-as-they-are in order to imagine how they might be otherwise.

The chapter opens with a brief summary of major playwork perspectives and then moves on to explore critical ethnography as a research methodology that can open up space for difference in playwork theory and practice through focusing on multiplicities and on everyday messy practice like the opening scenario. My own engagement with playwork and play scholarship is introduced, particularly in terms of my interest in playwork's contradictions. This interest led me to use CHAT – a dialectical method – as the epistemological, methodological and analytical framework for my study, which is described in the following section, together with an exploration of the particular (Lefebvrian) approach to dialectics that I employed. The process of using CHAT to explore ethnographic data led to an immersion in literature not commonly used in playwork theorising, including space (Lefebvre, 1991); the politics of childhood (Katz, 2011); violence (Ray, 2011; Springer, 2011); playwork subjectivities as multivoiced (Engeström, 2001), emotional (Hochschild, 1983) and performative (Butler, 1999; Powell & Carey, 2007); and ethics (Levinas, 1969; Rushing, 2010). In this sense, the original study offers what might be called a 'minoritarian' (Braidotti, 2012) playwork perspective on researching children's play. Space does not permit in-depth discussion of all these aspects here: rather the focus is on providing just enough background to allow an exploration of the interrelations between CHAT and further musings and what this can tell us about researching play from a playwork perspective. In particular, the chapter reconsiders playwork's definition of play and explores what the desire to define play might do, together with an exploration of what a shift from a psychological to a spatial perspective on play can offer.

What is 'a playwork perspective'?

Playwork, as with other communities of practice, is multivoiced, although some voices are louder than others. Playwork has its dominant theorists who have served the sector well and whose work has influenced the development of official articulations of playwork, as seen in the National Occupational Standards (NOS) (SkillsActive, 2016) and in the Playwork Principles (PPSG, 2005). Having been involved in playwork education and training, and for a while playing a role in the development of qualifications and the Playwork Principles, I take some responsibility for the taken-for-granted assumptions underpinning the dominant playwork perspectives on children's play. Over the last 15 years or so, however, I have been seriously questioning these, not in order to expose them as 'wrong', but to pay attention to what they might exclude. Playwork theory has developed over time and those who have contributed to it have served it well: what is offered here is a diffractive analysis that reads new insights through existing ones. As Barad says, "diffractive readings bring inventive provocations; they are good to think with. They are respectful, detailed, ethical engagements" (Dolphijn & van der Tuin, 2012, p. 50).

Mostly, playwork articulations of play are somewhat defensive, making a generalised and principled case for playwork practice not to defer to the hegemonic construct of the child as in need of professional adult protection, correction and socialisation. Playwork's foundational theories can be (all too) briefly summarised thus:

> An evolutionary standpoint (Hughes, 2012) asserts that playing has evolved in order to provide children with the mechanism by which they develop adaptive capabilities, yielding both ontogenetic and phylogenetic benefits. A psychotherapeutic perspective (Sturrock & Else, 1998) claims that playing is healing or that it can prevent the development of neuroses or psychosis originating in childhood. A developmental approach (Brown, 2008) sees a rich environment for play as fundamental to children's development. All three stances aim to illustrate why over-protective and over-directive adult practices ('adulteration') can constrain children's engagement in a wide range of play forms and therefore be detrimental for their health and development.
>
> (Russell, 2013a, p. 4)

What all these strands have in common is that they are grounded in psychology, a discipline which offers a powerful and particular agential cut on childhood and play and understands 'the child' and 'the playworker' as discrete selves in isolation from, but interacting with, other discrete selves and environments. Playwork's ethos, although unique, reflects the dominance of psychology in the 20th century and the increasing reach of its gaze in the lives of children (Rose, 1999). How might a different playwork perspective open up what else can be said about children's play? I explored this through ethnography and an engagement with less commonly employed theory, and have continued to explore it since.

Critical and performative ethnography put to work again

I chose ethnography as the methodology for my fieldwork, because I wanted to write (*-graphy*) the tribe (*ethne*) that is playwork. I wanted to work alongside playworkers in order to *feel* again what playwork was like over a period of time and to document the everyday material discursive practices of playwork, its messiness and its routines, habits and rituals, its affects and emotions, its very ordinariness. Playwork's literature mostly "presents a particular understanding of children's play and consequent justificatory account of the value of playwork together with normative assertions of how playworkers should ply their craft" (Russell, 2013a, p. 97). This can be seen, for example, in Brown (2003), Brown and Taylor (2008), Hughes (2012), Kilvington and Wood (2010), Sturrock and Else (1998). Although there is a move towards a more narrative style (for example, Brown, 2014; Nuttall, 2012, and playwork blogs), there still remains little on what playwork actually looks like.

Yet, I was also worried about bringing the authority of an academic researcher's gaze to those aspects of playwork that do not constitute a part of playwork's public identity. Presenting a different picture of playwork felt risky. As Denzin (2006) points out:

> Ethnography is a not an innocent practice. Our research practices are performative, pedagogical, and political . . . The pedagogical is always moral and political; by enacting a way of seeing and being, it challenges, contests, or endorses the official, hegemonic ways of seeing and representing the other.
>
> (p. 422)

I give one example here of an aspect that is not explored in depth in this chapter but may serve to illustrate the point being made: that of violence. Although I had set out not to pay attention to peak experiences or exceptional events, I ended up devoting a chapter to this topic in my doctoral thesis, because it was so much a part of the everyday playwork I experienced, both in my playworking days and in my fieldwork (including interviews and workshops where I shared my early thinking). Whilst older texts talk about violence (for example, Hughes, 1975; Turner, 1961), I found it to be all but invisible in contemporary playwork literature (which talks a bit about aggression and a lot about behaviour, but little on violence). I offered two responses to this. First, universal psychological statements about children and their play obscure the heterogeneity and the spatiality of children's lives, particularly in terms of class and poverty. My analysis brought these issues to the fore and situated them within theories of the politics of space (Lefebvre, 1991) and a class politics of childhood (Katz, 2011) to explore the entanglements of capitalism, social policy, poverty, violence and play as resistance. Second, "the silence may also have something to do with protection of a romantic construction of play together with an internalisation of (gendered) feelings of shame if violence does erupt" (Russell, 2013a, p. 175). Disturbing this silence felt a little risky, as if I might reveal something that could shatter the promotion of children's play as an unmitigated force for good. And yet, I also felt it was important, that there was another story to tell about children's lives that was being obscured. Playwork has multiple perspectives.

There is a growing body of work in contemporary writing on ethnography which embraces multiplicity, actively seeking to disturb classical ethnography's desire to explain and to represent the group under investigation in terms of universal, fixed and essential stereotypes that elide difference and that reproduce colonialised versions of the same. Post-colonial, more-than-representational, posthuman and post-qualitative approaches seek to disturb the comfortable familiarity and certainty of such knowns and to look instead for multiplicity, difference, movement, affect, assemblages, vitality, performativity and corporeality (for example, Lather, 2015; Martin & Kamberelis, 2013; St. Pierre, 2013; Vannini, 2015). Such approaches can build on what playwork has already said about play and explore what more can be said. Taking such an approach also helps to move beyond static binary distinctions of 'insider' or 'outsider' research that assumes objectivity is both possible and desirable. In classical ethnography, 'going native' was considered bad research practice, as it threatened objectivity. Yet, I was not seeking objectivity: rather, I was looking at what more could be brought to the study of everyday playwork and what this might mean for researching children's play. Just as well since, in classical ethnography terms, I went native over 40 years ago.

I discovered adventure playgrounds in the mid-1970s when I worked on one in East London over the school summer holiday. I was smitten and have worked in the play and playwork sector ever since, first as a playworker (mostly on adventure playgrounds in north London), then moving into development, research, and education and training. It is possibly relevant that my entry into the playwork community of practice was at a time when playwork was much more closely allied to radical community work and youth work rather than early years and education (a shift that emerged following the 1989 Children Act). As Conway (2005) recalls, "most playworkers I knew were a mixture of hippy idealists, anarcho-punks and grass-roots community activists with strong libertarian and left-wing beliefs" (p. 2). Certainly, my memories were of a practice that felt itself to be apart from 'the establishment' and on the side of the children and families with whom we worked. If we read any books about childhood at all, they were more likely to be Colin Ward or John Holt rather than Kathy Sylva or Jerome Bruner. These foundations still influence playwork theorising, and the sense of recalcitrance (Battram & Russell, 2002) and the need to question the powerful voices of authority has remained strong with me. For the last 15 years or so, I have been working as an academic, and this has allowed me the opportunity to read beyond the dominant sources that playworkers have used, opening up new areas for exploration. This shows the unpredictability and idiosyncrasy of the process of knowledge production. That I was in an academic environment with access to a wide range of literature and colleagues was happenstance, leading to a particular entanglement of my own passion for playwork, history, literature, conversation and so on.

The dialectics of playwork

My research explored how playworkers navigate the tensions and contradictions they face in their day-to-day work. There is a fundamental tension between supporting play for its own sake and seeking public funding for work which can address identified problems of social policy. As Cranwell's (2003) historical studies show, public provision for children's play has always been driven by whatever problem of childhood was exercising the government and society at that time, with play being corralled in the name of physical and moral health, school attendance, social education, crime prevention and so on. Today's themes could be addressing obesity and physical inactivity, crime reduction, community cohesion, contact with nature and the development of resilience. The increasing instrumentalisation, commodification and marketisation of public services within a context of austerity that shifts responsibility for health and well-being onto the individual (Hoedemækers, Loacker, & Pedersen, 2012) means that now more than ever playworkers seek ways to articulate value (as a rationale for funding) that move away from appreciating play's intrinsic value (Russell, forthcoming). The way that this particular contradiction was theorised in my doctoral study was through dialectics, using the Marxist concepts of use and exchange value. Exchange value for play*work* as a form of labour lies in its capacity to effectively and economically address social policy concerns, and the urgency of this in the current economic and political climate is reflected in the moves towards research projects aimed at providing evidence of such instrumental and exchange value (see for example, Gill, 2014). Playwork's use value has been articulated in a number of ways, but generally lies in the co-production of spaces that support children's open-ended and autotelic playing. Any attempt to direct playing towards policy outcomes risks commodifying it and turning it into something other than play. These contradictions are not straightforward dualistic opposites, and the study needed an epistemological and methodological approach that could embrace the complexities and entanglements of childhood, play, playwork, common sense understandings and social policy. This is where CHAT came in.

Cultural Historical Activity Theory and dialectics

Dialectics is at the core of CHAT and is understood here as a method. It is a vast and contested terrain, and I have tried to steer a path through it in a way that can accommodate fluidity, movement and difference. Although dialectics is often understood as the analysis of opposites, it offers much for acknowledging and moving beyond static binary oppositions and as such is the basis for perpetual change. I ended up drawing a lot on the work of French philosopher Henri Lefebvre in this research, particularly his work on the production of space (Lefebvre, 1991) and on dialectics (Lefebvre, 2009). Lefebvre was also critical of over-simplistic dualistic opposites: for him, there was always something more, always a third. His approach to dialectics had three influences: Marx, whose dialectical materialism focused on social practice; Hegel, whose dialectics was about thought and language; and Nietzsche, who considered the role of poesy, the irrational and, of course, play (Schmid, 2008). These three 'cuts' of dialectics become entangled, in tension with each other to produce something new, but not in any complete or finished way, as dialectics is a form of ceaseless becoming. It is this non-essentialist, non-dualistic, non-deterministic triad and its possibility for irrational Nietzschean play that makes it such a fitting foundation for a diffractive analysis of play and playwork.

CHAT developed from the work of Vygotsky, whose method sought to move away from the then-dominant behaviourist conception of activity as stimulus and response and towards seeing it as object-oriented and *mediated* through material and symbolic tools, creating a triad of subject, object and mediating artefact. In later developments of the theory, Engeström (1987) broadened the original model out beyond individuals' actions to a *collective* activity *system* (see Figure 3.1), adding the rules that guide the activity, the community of actors and the division of labour. It also encompasses the four processes of labour identified in Marxist theory: production, distribution, exchange and consumption.

It was this model that was used to analyse playwork as a collective activity system networked with other collective activity systems. There is a tension in the model between seeing the collective activity system as a whole and analysing discrete elements of and processes within it (Jones, 2009). Engeström (1987) addresses this through noting that his model allows for "the possibility of analysing a multitude of relations" (p. 94), but that "the essential task is always to grasp the systemic whole, not just separate connections". The relationships within the activity system as a whole can shift and change: objects can become mediating artefacts, as can rules, which can also become objects, and so on. In this way, the points and processes of the triangle do not exist as discrete components, they are constantly being brought into being through 'intra-actions', a term Barad (2007) uses in preference to 'interaction' to emphasise how phenomena (both human and non-human, including material and symbolic objects, affects, knowledges and spaces) do not pre-exist but emerge through entanglements. For Barad, "the so-called subject, the so-called instrument, and the so-called object of research

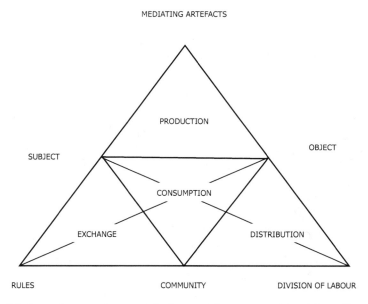

Figure 3.1 Second-generation model of an activity system adapted from Engeström (1987)

are always already entangled" (Dolphijn & van der Tuin, 2012, p. 15). In my analysis, the points and processes of the CHAT model were used as heuristic devices and as a way of structuring the written thesis rather than being seen as independently existing entities, although this will inevitably have affected the analysis itself. A central principle of Vygotsky's method is that phenomena should be studied as processes rather than fixed, static entities: each phenomenon has a history characterised by changes (Cole & Scribner, 1978). Any analysis needs to take histories into account (which is why part of my study considered playwork's history and interviewed pre-1989 playworkers). However, as Vygotsky (1978) noted, development is not a neat, linear progression; it is idiosyncratic, uneven and characterised by ruptures and upheavals. Development occurs through efforts to resolve internal contradictions in the system: it is this that makes it a dialectical and historical model.

The stories that I have created from my research are not presented as a universal assertion concerning the truth of playwork. Nor are they an entirely personal fantasy superimposed onto my research participants via the literature. A conclusion that embraces the dialectics of playwork allows for multiple ways of making sense of play and playwork. The idea of the researcher as bricoleur seems fitting here. Bricolage involves using multiple tools, methods and disciplines: it requires a critical appreciation of competing discourses and paradigms, emphasising the hermeneutic and dialectic nature of interdisciplinary enquiry. It involves moving to and fro between data, literature and different ways of knowing (theory, affect, intuition and my 40 years' immersion in the sector). As Kincheloe (2005, p. 341) states, "bricoleurs are not aware of where the empirical ends and the philosophical begins because such epistemological features are always embedded in one another".

What follows is a brief account of some aspects of playwork as a collective activity system by way of illustrating how this cut can reveal other ways of knowing about play. In particular, the analysis considers two things: first, aspects of the Playwork Principles (PPSG, 2005) as mediating artefacts that affect playwork understandings of play, and second, playwork's object as the production of a space where children can play, which allows a spatial perspective to researching play to add to the dominant psychological one.

Playwork's contradictory understanding of play as a mediating artefact

My research sought to pay attention to how the politically and geographically situated everyday practices of playworkers have developed over time and place and how playworkers navigate the contradictions inherent in their work. These contradictions are not straightforward oppositions, nor is there one single playwork story that can pronounce which practice is right or wrong, although broad principles can, and have, been established. Currently, the sector asserts its professional and ethical framework in the form of a set of Playwork Principles (PPSG, 2005). The Playwork Principles make a bold statement of service ideal "For playworkers, the play process takes precedence and playworkers act as advocates for play when engaging with adult led agendas" (PPSG, 2005, Playwork Principle no. 4).

This makes playwork the only section of the children's workforce that explicitly professes at least a levelling, if not a reversal, of power relations between professional adult and playing child, thereby bringing playwork's fundamental contradictions to the fore. The playwork concept of 'adulteration' (Sturrock & Else, 1998), understood as the pollution of children's ludic habitat with adult desires, rests on the assumption that adult intervention into children's play alters it, compromising the espoused belief that play should be "freely chosen, personally directed and intrinsically motivated" (PPSG, 2005, Playwork Principle no. 2). Such characteristics of play can be found in much of the literature (for example, Burghardt, 2005; Caillois, 2001; Garvey, 1977; Huizinga, 1955) and are useful in curbing the excesses of adult desire to teach or control. Yet, if taken literally, they become nonsensical. This section explores the contradictions such definitions give rise to for playworkers.

Although playworkers' relationships with children aim to be democratic, ultimately playworkers operate in adult-provided and adult-supervised institutions of childhood. In this sense, playwork itself is as an intervention: children's play can be 'freely chosen' only up to the point at which responsible adults deem it to be unacceptable for whatever reason. There is much debate in the sector on the topic of intervention and what such a point of unacceptability might be (see, for example, Hughes, 2012; Kilvington & Wood, 2010; Russell, 2013a; Sturrock & Else, 1998).

Common sense also tells us that children's freedom of choice may equally be restricted by the resources available and by other children. As Sutton-Smith (1997) points out, if children play in groups then there is necessarily the need for compromise and negotiation, as the opening vignette shows. Freedoms are limited – and simultaneously supported – by the resources that can be brought into play.

However, there is a more fundamental critique of the notion of play as freely chosen and personally directed. The language of 'choice' implies a rational weighing up of options, something that does not fit well with play's emergent, spontaneous, opportunistic and self-organising characteristics. Questions about whether children can choose how to play, or whether playworkers might be adulterating play (as in the opening scenario perhaps) share a particular starting point grounded in what Lester (2015) terms "an unquestioned orthodoxy of thought with its accompanying clichés and material effects" (p. 53). This orthodoxy understands humans as isolated, autonomous and rational beings who can choose how to act upon a world that is separate from them. In this worldview, agency – the capacity to act on the world – is seen as something which individuals possess. Yet this basic premise, unquestioningly accepted as common sense, is challenged by scholars across a range of diverse academic disciplines, including theoretical physics (Barad, 2007), science and technology studies (Haraway, 1991, 2015), geography (Whatmore, 2006), political science (Bennett, 2010) and philosophy (Braidotti, 2013), to give but a few examples. It is no longer adequate to envision humans as apart from others both human and nonhuman. Old binary distinctions of self and other (subject and object), human and nonhuman, nature and culture, time and space are melting. This thinking has been applied to research methodologies (for example, Lather, 2013, 2015; MacLure, 2010, 2013), and to other contexts, such as early years education and childhood studies (Lenz-Taguchi, 2014; Taylor & Blaise, 2014), but to date has not been very evident play scholarship or playwork research (see Lester, 2015 as an exception).

Barad's (2007, 2010) ideas of intra-action and entanglements require a different way of understanding concepts such as self and identity, as we have seen. Similarly, agency, the power to act, does not reside in individuals but emerges through intra-actions. This raises a challenge to the idea that play is freely chosen, and that playworkers can choose to intervene in particular ways. Yet, far from absolving people from responsibility in a world understood as intra-active, Barad also suggests that this make ethics even more important. If responsibility does not lie with individuals alone, this means that responsibility is even greater than if it did: "entanglements are . . . irreducible relations of responsibility" (Barad, 2010, p. 265). Ethics itself is entangled with ways of being and with the processes of knowledge production: the particular cut taken excludes some ways of understanding (and therefore being in) the world in favour of others. The ethical responsibility lies in looking for different cuts (Russell, 2015).

In the opening scenario, the playworker is already implicated in the unfolding event, not apart from it. It is not a question of identifying one isolated intervention that can support the freely chosen play of each individual child. The complexities of the entanglement matter in a way that can shift attention (offering a different agential cut) from each child's individual right to freely chosen play towards the ongoing co-production of a space in which play can emerge: a spatial rather than individual cut. This is more than a purely theoretical matter. The idea of an agential cut acknowledges that the way we perceive things affects our actions: it is *performative*. The singular outcome of this event becomes one phenomenon within the ongoing process of the co-production of relational space and so less an issue of who can freely choose what and more a question of how the space works. That the negotiations became a game, or that nobody ended up using the zipline, in and of themselves perhaps matter less than an appreciation of the ongoing entanglements that can help create conditions that support playfulness. In this sense, play is self-organising, where 'self' refers to the play itself rather than each individual child. It emerges from the flows and movements and from the entanglement of bodies, desires, material objects (the zipline, the platform), histories and so on and then moves on in a way that is singular and could not have been predicted in any accurate manner.

This is where the chapter returns to the opening provocation that maybe playwork has been paying too much attention to play as a concept. The provocation is used playfully here, just to see what more it might offer. Having explored playwork's definition of play, attention is now taken to what the practice of defining play might do. Defining is a boundary-making process. In order to define play, there needs to be a boundary between 'play' and 'not-play'. The debates within play scholarship rest on whether definitions of play can be applied always and only to the myriad phenomena that might be called play (for example, Burghardt,

2005; Sutton-Smith, 1997). Categorisations are helpful in helping to make sense of the world, but they are also performative. As Sutton-Smith (1995, p. 283) says, such boundary-making processes turn play into a 'separable text', apart from all other aspects of children's lives. In practice and policy terms, play becomes a time and space bound activity, rationalised into a thing to be provided, with particular forms of play (physical, outdoor, natural, risky, etc.) being accorded greater value.

Let's return again to the opening scenario. Who is playing here, when and how? Where might the boundaries between play and not-play be? What matters in any analysis of this short scene? And finally, what might such questions do to our attempts at meaning making?

Or: what if we think of different questions to ask that can help us move beyond the binaries of "play and not-play, this play and that play, good play and bad play" (Russell, 2015, p. 198), and pay attention instead to the dynamic flows and forces that produce that particular entanglement of zipline, children and playworker? This assemblage is then freed from the fixing of categorisation, becoming one very ordinary fluid mo(ve)ment in the co-production of a space where playfulness can emerge, constantly shifting with the ever-open possibility for becoming different. We can move away from arguments about whose choice mattered and pay attention instead to how the space works: to the flows, affects and assemblages that come together and fall away again in a ceaseless movement that at times might be recognisable as playing. In my research, I did this using Lefebvre's (1991) work on the production of space.

Playwork's object as the production of space where children can play

Given that the Playwork Principles (PPSG, 2005) state "the role of the playworker is to support all children and young people in the creation of a space in which they can play" (Playwork Principle no. 5), this was taken in my analysis as the object of playwork as a collective activity system, recognising what has been said regarding the already-entangled nature of the CHAT activity system. This aspect of the research has been published in detail elsewhere (Russell, 2012, 2013b) and is introduced here briefly in terms of its capacity to offer a different cut on play and playwork, with the potential for different material discursive practices.

In Lefebvre's (1991) analysis, space is more than a neutral container: it is *produced* by interrelationships between physical, social and symbolic elements and the actions of individuals and institutions. These interrelationships are political because they represent power relations. Space is produced through the entanglements of three interdependent moments: the perceived, or experienced space of mundane everyday spatial practices; the conceived space of planners; and the lived space of art, love and play.

> A key feature of lived space is that it defies the representations of conceived space: it cannot be planned, provided, measured or reduced to exchange

> value. It cannot be represented in the modern, rational science of certainty, determinism and absolute truths and thus sits uncomfortably with current evidence-based policy discourse that provides the basis for public funding.
>
> (Russell, 2012, p. 56)

In my original analysis, I suggested that this cut allows playworkers to appreciate the tensions between adult ultimate control of the space and ideas of exchange value (perceived space), planning in terms of designing the space and the naming of zones and resources that assumes particular correct usage and outcomes (conceived space) and the importance of recognising small moments of nonsense and playfulness as a significant aspect of how the culture of the space is co-produced (lived space). These small moments can often get buried under the hegemonic rationality of conceived space and the humdrum of everyday perceived space, yet should be appreciated as fundamental to a space that is *designed* to support children's play, that is, a space where the rationality, boredom and fear of the everyday world can be transformed into any fantastical, scary or ordered world of the players' own desires (Sutton-Smith, 1997). Because of play's very nature, playwork settings will be volatile places: in a sense, that is what they are designed to be. What my fieldwork showed was the complex messiness of small and singular moments, the fuzziness of boundaries between what is and is not playing and the many ways in which situations can escalate or die away as a result of the whole entanglement which produces that space at that time.

Lefebvre's (1991) theorising on the production of space, and particularly his dialectical triad of conceived, perceived and lived space, emerged as a fitting basis for analysing playwork within the CHAT dialectical and historical framework. The dialectic here is that articulations of playwork's value (for example, Gill, 2014; Manwaring & Taylor, 2006) tend to reside in conceived and perceived space, and necessarily so, because lived space defies representation in this way and cannot be planned in any precise or predictable way. Nonetheless, this analysis allows an appreciation of how space is co-produced through entanglements of people, histories, contexts and material and symbolic artefacts and, through this, an appreciation of the contingent and situated nature of each mo(ve)ment and encounter. This helps to move the analysis beyond simple cause-and-effect in terms of planning, intent, intervention and value articulations and beyond individual children. Yet, this is not an either/or binary: conceived space and perceived space are not the opposites of lived space.

Closing wo(a)nderings

> I remember hearing Brian Sutton-Smith speak about his lifetime research into children's play. Having regaled his audience of playworkers with some of the fantastical, rude, sometimes offensive and cruel stories children told and the things they did, and weaving these stories into his theoretical synthesis of play as a parody of emotional vulnerability, the first question from the audience was about how playworkers should respond to some of the more extreme

> forms of bullying that he described. I remember thinking that this was not a question that applied to his research; its great strength was that it did not have to address that issue.
>
> (Russell, 2013a, p. 198)

I opened this chapter with the observation that researching play from a playwork perspective produces knowledge which is *situated*. Playwork's *locus of enunciation* (Mignolo, 2009), its starting point, has a normative purpose: to profess the importance of play and, by extension, of playwork, and to articulate what playwork is and how it should be practised. As Barad (2007) points out, knowledge, being and ethics are inseparable. We can get stuck in habitual ways of advocating for play and playwork, and these habits, as apparatuses, enact an 'agential cut' (Barad, 2007): they perpetuate particular perspectives that exclude others. I have argued here that disturbing these habits of thought and action is an ethical endeavour, and I have offered a diffractive analysis of my ethnographic research in order to see what more might be said about play from a playwork perspective. Using CHAT as a heuristic framework, whilst at the same time persistently resisting categorising and shoe-horning raw data into themes, allowed me to pay attention to playwork's inherent contradictions without being paralysed by them. In particular, bringing a Lefebvrian spatial cut to explore playwork's object allows us to go back into a political analysis and can help us move beyond seeing play as a time- and space-bound activity residing in individual children. The mundane opening scenario becomes one example of how the space is co-produced, how everything is entangled to produce that moment. Attention can be paid to "small moments in lived space, the importance of caring and openness, of being comfortable with uncertainty, alongside (and often in a dialectical relationship with) the bigger instrumental and universal assertions of the value of play and playwork" (Russell, 2013a, p. 234).

References

Barad, K. (2007). *Meeting the universe halfway: Quantum physics and the entanglement of matter and meaning*. London: Duke University Press.

Barad, K. (2010). Quantum entanglements and hauntological relations of inheritance: Dis/continuities, spacetime enfoldings, and justice-to-come. *Derrida Today, 3*(2), 240–268.

Barad, K. (2014). Diffracting diffraction: Cutting together-apart. *Parallax, 20*(3), 168–187.

Battram, A. & Russell, W. (2002). *The edge of recalcitrance: Playwork, order and chaos*. Paper presented at Spirit of Adventure Play Is Alive and Kicking, Play Wales Conference, Cardiff, June.

Bennett, J. (2010). *Vibrant matter: A political ecology of things*. Durham and London: Duke University Press.

Braidotti, R. (2012). Nomadic ethics. In D. W. Smith & H. Somers-Hall (Eds.), *The Cambridge companion to Deleuze* (pp. 170–197). Cambridge, UK: Cambridge University Press.

Braidotti, R. (2013). *The posthuman*. Cambridge: Polity Press.
Brown, F. (Ed.) (2003). *Playwork theory and practice*. Maidenhead: Open University Press.
Brown, F. (2008). Fundamentals of playwork. In F. Brown & C. Taylor (Eds.), *Foundations of playwork* (pp. 7–13). Maidenhead: Open University Press.
Brown, F. (2014). *Play and playwork: 101 stories of children playing*. Maidenhead: Open University Press.
Brown, F. & Taylor, C. (Eds.). (2008). *Foundations of playwork*. Maidenhead: Open University Press.
Burghardt, G. M. (2005). *The genesis of animal play: Testing the limits*. Cambridge, MA: The MIT Press.
Butler, J. (1999). *Subjects of desire*. New York: Columbia University Press.
Caillois, R. (2001). *Man, play and games* (trans. Meyer Barash). Urbana and Chicago: University of Illinois Press.
Cole, M. & Scribner, S. (1978). Introduction to Vygotsky. *Mind in society: The development of higher psychological processes* (pp. 1–14). Cambridge, MA: Harvard University Press.
Conway, M. (2005). *From guerrilla playwork to the centre of government policy on play?* PlayEd 2005: What Is the Future for Playwork? The 17th Play and Human Development Meeting. Ely, Cambs, 1st and 2nd March. PlayEducation.
Cranwell, K. (2003). Towards playwork: An historical introduction to children's out-of-school play organisations in London (1860–1940). In F. Brown (Ed.), *Playwork theory and practice* (pp. 32–47). Buckingham: Open University Press.
Dahlberg, G., Moss, P., & Pence, A. (2013). *Beyond quality in early childhood education and care: Languages of evaluation*. Abingdon, Oxon: Routledge.
Denzin, N. K. (2006). Analytic autoethnography, or déjà vu all over again. *Journal of Contemporary Ethnography*, 35(4), 419–428.
Dolphijn, R. & van der Tuin, I. (2012). Interview with Karen Barad. In *New Materialism: Interviews and Cartographies* (pp. 48–70). Ann Arbor, MI: Open Humanities Press.
Engeström, Y. (1987). *Learning by expanding: An activity-theoretical approach to developmental research*. Helsinki: Orienta-Konsultit. Retrieved from http://lchc.ucsd.edu/mca/Paper/Engestrom/Learning-by-Expanding.pdf.
Engeström, Y. (2001). Expansive learning at work: Toward an activity theoretical reconceptualization. *Journal of Education and Work*, 14(1), 133–156.
Garvey, C. (1977). *Play*. London: Fontana.
Gill, T. (2014). *The play return: A review of the wider impact of play initiatives*. London: Children's Play Policy Forum. Retrieved from www.playwales.org.uk/login/uploaded/documents/Play%20Policy/The%20Play%20Return.pdf.
Haraway, D. J. (1991). *Simians, cyborgs and women: The reinvention of nature*. Abingdon, Oxon: Routledge.
Haraway, D. J. (2015). Anthropocene, capitalocene, plantationocene, chthulucene: Making kin. *Environmental Humanities*, 6, 159–165.
Hochschild, A. R. (1983). *The managed heart: Commercialization of human feeling*. Berkeley: University of California Press.
Hoedemækers, C., Loacker, B., & Pedersen, M. (2012). The commons and their im/possibilities. *Ephemera*, 12(4), 378–385.
Hughes, B. (1975). *Notes for adventure playground workers*. London: Children and Youth Action Group.

Hughes, B. (2012). *Evolutionary playwork and reflective analytic practice* (2nd ed.). London: Routledge.
Huizinga, J. (1955). *Homo ludens: A study of the play element in culture*. Boston: Beacon Press.
Jones, P. E. (2009). Breaking away from *Capital*? Theorising activity in the shadow of Marx. *Outlines, 1*, 45–58.
Katz, C. (2011). Accumulation, excess, childhood: Toward a countertopography of risk and waste. *Documents d'Anàlisis Geogràfica, 57*(1), 47–60.
Kilvington, J. & Wood, A. (2010). *Reflective playwork: For all who work with children*. London: Continuum.
Kincheloe, J. L. (2005). On to the next level: Continuing the conceptualization of the bricolage. *Qualitative Inquiry, 11*(3), 323–350.
Lather, P. (2013). Methodology-21: What do we do in the afterward? *International Journal of Qualitative Studies in Education, 26*(6), 634–645.
Lather, P. (2015). The work of thought and the politics of research: (post) qualitative research. In N. K. Denzin & M. D. Giardina (Eds.), *Qualitative inquiry and the politics of research* (pp. 97–117). Walnut Creek, CA: Left Coast Press.
Lefebvre, H. (1991). *The production of space* (trans. D. Nicholson-Smith). London: Blackwell.
Lefebvre, H. (2009). *Dialectical materialism*. Minneapolis: University of Minnesota Press.
Lenz-Taguchi, H. (2014). New materialisms and play. In L. Brooker, M. Blaise, & S. Blaise (Eds.), *The Sage handbook of play and learning in early childhood* (pp. 79–90). London: Sage.
Lester, S. (2015). Posthuman nature: Life beyond the natural playground. In M. MacLean, W. Russell, & E. Ryall (Eds.), *Philosophical perspectives on play* (pp. 53–67). London: Routledge.
Levinas, E. (1969). *Totality and infinity: An essay on exteriority* (trans. A. Lingis). Pittsburgh: Duquesne University Press.
MacLure, M. (2010). The offence of theory. *Journal of Education Policy, 25*(2), 275–283.
MacLure, M. (2013). The wonder of data. *Cultural Studies, Critical Methodologies, 13*(4), 228–232.
Manwaring, B. & Taylor, C. (2006). *The benefits of play and playwork: Recent evidence-based research (2001–2006) demonstrating the impact and benefits of play and playwork*. London: CYWU and SkillsActive.
Martin, A. D. & Kamberelis, G. (2013). Mapping not tracing: Qualitative educational research with political teeth. *International Journal of Qualitative Studies in Education, 26*(6), 668–679.
Massey, D. (2005). *For space*. London: Sage.
Mignolo, W. D. (2009). Epistemic disobedience, independent thought and de-colonial freedom. *Theory, Culture and Society, 26*(7–8), 1–23.
Moss, P. (2007). Meetings across the paradigmatic divide. *Educational Philosophy and Theory, 39*(3), 229–245.
Nuttall, E. (2012). *Possible summers*. Retrieved from https://possiblesummers.word press.com/.
Playwork Principles Scrutiny Group (PPSG). (2005). *Playwork principles*. Cardiff: Play Wales. Retrieved from www.playwales.org.uk/login/uploaded/documents/Playwork%20Principles/playwork%20principles.pdf.
Powell, J. L. & Carey, M. (2007). Social theory, performativity and professional power: A critical analysis of helping professions in England. *Human Affairs, 17*, 78–94.

Ray, L. (2011). *Violence and society*. London: Sage.
Rose, N. (1999). *Governing the soul: The shaping of the private self* (2nd ed.). London: Routledge.
Rose, N. (2008). Psychology as a social science. *Subjectivity, 25*, 446–462.
Rushing, S. (2010). Preparing for politics: Judith Butler's ethical dispositions. *Contemporary Political Theory, 9*(3), 284–303.
Russell, W. (2012). 'I get such a feeling out of . . . those moments': Playwork, passion, politics and space. *International Journal of Play, 1*(1), 51–63.
Russell, W. (2013a). *The dialectics of playwork: A conceptual and ethnographic study of playwork using cultural historical activity theory*. Unpublished doctoral dissertation, University of Gloucestershire, Gloucester.
Russell, W. (2013b). Towards a spatial theory of playwork: What can Lefebvre offer as a response to playwork's inherent contradictions? In E. Ryall, W. Russell, & M. MacLean (Eds.), *The philosophy of play* (pp. 164–174). London: Routledge.
Russell, W. (2015). Entangled in the midst of it: A diffractive expression of an ethics for playwork. In M. MacLean, W. Russell, & E. Ryall (Eds.), *Philosophical perspectives on play* (pp. 191–204). London: Routledge.
Russell, W. (forthcoming). Nonsense, caring and everyday hope: Rethinking the value of playwork. In B. Hughes & F. Brown (Eds.), *Aspects of playwork, Play and Culture Studies* (Vol. 14). MD: University Press of America.
Schmid, C. (2008). Henri Lefebvre's theory of the production of space: Towards a three-dimensional dialectic. In K. Goonewardena, S. Kipfer, R. Milgrom, & C. Schmid (Eds.), *Space, difference and everyday life: Reading Henri Lefebvre* (pp. 27–45). Abingdon, Oxon: Routledge.
SkillsActive. (2016). *Playwork national occupational standards*. London: UK Commission for Emploment and Skills.
Springer, S. (2011). Violence sits in places? Cultural practice, neoliberal rationalism, and virulent imaginative geographies. *Political Geography, 30*, 90–98.
St. Pierre, E. A. (2013). The posts continue: Becoming. *International Journal of Qualitative Studies in Education, 26*(6), 646–657.
Sturrock, G. & Else, P. (1998). 'The Colorado Paper' – The playground as therapeutic space: Playwork as healing. In G. Sturrock & P. Else (Eds.) (2007), *Therapeutic playwork reader one 1995–2000* (pp. 73–104). Eastleigh, Hampshire: Common Threads.
Sutton-Smith, B. (1995). The persuasive rhetorics of play. In A. D. Pellegrini (Ed.), *The future of play theory: A multi-disciplinary enquiry into the contributions of Brian Sutton-Smith* (pp. 275–295). New York: State University of New York Press.
Sutton-Smith, B. (1997). *The ambiguity of play*. Cambridge, MA: Harvard University Press.
Taylor, A. & Blaise, M. (2014). Queer worlding childhood. Discourse. *Studies in the Cultural Politics of Education, 35*(3), 377–392.
Turner, H. S. (1961). *Something extraordinary*. London: Michael Joseph.
Vannini, P. (2015). Non-representational ethnography: New ways of animating lifeworlds. *Cultural Geographies, 22*(2), 317–327.
Vygotsky, L. S. (1978). *Mind and society: The development of higher psychological processes*. Cambridge, MA: Harvard University Press.
Whatmore, S. J. (2006). Materialist returns: Practising cultural geographies in and for a more-than-human world. *Cultural Geographies, 13*(4), 600–610.

4 Researching children's play as a playworker-ethnographer

Hannah Smith Brennan[1]

Introduction

I was a playworker in London, United Kingdom, for five years and saw hundreds of children enjoy and grow in multiple ways. I also heard parents express profound appreciation for how our work helped their children – to process their emotions, to gain confidence, to develop friendships, to succeed in school, the list went on. These experiences convinced me of playwork's positive impact on children and families. I considered being a playworker in these local government-run afterschool clubs as both practical and political. I was supporting working parents by looking after their children; protecting children's rights to, and through, play; and providing spaces where underprivileged children grew and flourished. I saw this work as fundamentally about social justice in contemporary contexts where children were simultaneously gaining and losing rights (Beck, 2006; Cockburn, 2005; James, Jenks, & Prout, 1998; Moss & Petrie, 2002).

My professional experiences spurred me to explore the importance of play and the ramifications of its curtailment in urban settings, like the one where I grew up and now lived and worked. As it turned out, these were also key concerns in the playwork literature at the time (Brown & Taylor, 2008; Gill, 2007; Hughes, 2003). I wanted to understand how my convictions dovetailed or converged with local government policy requirements to support children's informal learning and 'empowerment' (see Jeffs & Smith, 2005). This involved looking more closely at important questions which had emerged from my professional practice: what playworkers do; how we see our work; the relationships between policies, procedures and playwork perspectives; and the contributions we make.

I created a doctoral research project, the very process of which aimed to protect and promote children's play. I wanted my research methods to not interrupt, but instead to blend with what playworkers were doing to support children's play, and at the same time produce evidence of the impact of playwork. I used critical ethnography as a framework to examine play and playwork in these clubs. Within this framework I conducted ethnographic fieldwork in two local authority-run, closed-access afterschool provisions for primary school children for nine months. My two key methods – participant observation and semi-structured interviewing – allowed me to listen to the views and experiences of participating playworkers, children and parents and also to observe and participate in the afterschool sessions daily.

I soon discovered that practitioner research was more complicated than I had anticipated. As a result of completing this research, I improved as a practitioner and researcher and gained insights useful to qualitative research into this kind of play. To my surprise, through the process, I distinguished my own playwork perspective. I came to see how strongly this perspective had influenced the research design and that my interest in specific issues was a product of the contexts in which I had trained and worked. As critical awareness of my own playwork perspective grew, so my understandings of the research itself evolved. I came to see that the playworker, like the ethnographer, tries to be there without being there. The playworker, like the ethnographer, also seeks to give weight to the voices of those who are less powerful. While achieving these goals in any given moment is often messy and complex, the use and interaction of these two approaches proved fruitful, and I came to see critical ethnography as particularly well suited to researching play from a playwork perspective.

This chapter draws from my practitioner research to examine similarities between critical ethnography and playwork practice. I explore the opportunities this approach gave me to value 'insider' knowledge, to use my skills as a playworker in the research and to engage playwork practitioners. I briefly define what playwork is, my playwork background and the evolution of my playwork perspective. I then discuss ethnographic perspectives, the critical ethnographic framework I used and the common goals and methods critical ethnography and playwork practice share. The discussion here raises questions about what critical ethnography in practitioner research can contribute to the field, and what this may mean for the study of play from a playwork perspective and the development of a body of playwork research. The use of critical ethnography in playwork research has the power to reveal playworker/'child at play' relationships in new and important ways, to contextualise these meaningfully and to inform playwork practice.

Playwork perspectives – evolution of my own playwork perspective

From 2000 to 2005, I worked in state-provided afterschool care for primary school children in the mixed socio-economic area of west London that I grew up in. These local government-run clubs provided safe, affordable childcare for low-income, working parents and aimed to counteract social exclusion and support poorer children's social development and school achievements (Bennett, 2003; Office for Standards in Education (Ofsted), 2001). At this time, all clubs providing childcare for children under eight years old had to be registered with Ofsted. To obtain and maintain this registration, clubs had to meet Ofsted's standards. These included all clubs being fully health and safety risk-assessed and following specific policies, such as "plan and provide activities and play opportunities to develop children's emotional, physical, social and intellectual capabilities"

(Ofsted, 2001). In contrast to the 'formal' learning of school, part of our job description was therefore to support this kind of 'informal' learning and development (Jeffs & Smith, 2005). This provided a template for programmed activities, and this idea of informal learning intrigued me. As a playworker, I fully embraced the goal of working from a child-centred approach – to nurture growth and exploration, and to support children's exposure to new experiences and pursuit of their interests and talents.

The wealth of children's play literature also influenced and shaped my professional perspective. Beyond the extensive work across the neuro and human sciences (Axline, 1964; Burghardt, 2005; Freud, 1922; Hughes, 2003; Huizinga, 1955; Pellegrini, Blatchford, Kato, & Baines, 2004; Piaget, 1951; Spencer, 1873), sociological arguments were particularly resonant for me. These promoted the value of play as beneficial for the individual, their communities and the larger society. This understanding of the value of play was also reflected in the playwork literature of the time. For example, the influential report 'Best Play: What Play Provision Should do for Children' (Children's Play Council (CPC), National Playing Fields Association (NPFA), and Playlink 2000) argues that play provides opportunities for development of empathy, self-identity, self-esteem, happiness and fulfilment, all of which benefit communities and society as a whole. I had seen children change through their play and agreed with this perspective. I saw play as valuable on multiple levels: to the individual, for positive developmental experiences which support children's adjustment to school and social life in general; to parents, as their children enjoy opportunities for fun, activity, creativity and learning; and to communities, the economy and society, as it supports individuals to grow into autonomous, well-rounded, effective adults.

In addition, my playwork colleagues and I shared widespread public concern about social and economic factors negatively affecting childhood in late 20th and early 21st century Britain (see Ball, Gill, & Spiegal, 2008; Bascombe, 2008; Freeman, 1997; Hendrick, 1997; James et al., 1998). We worried about poverty, health, youth crime, play deprivation, increased traffic and numbers of cars, computer, mobile phone and television use, safety, family stressors and employment patterns. We believed that increases in supervised play and care provision were in part due to drastic reductions in children being allowed to use outside environments for unsupervised play, activities and travel (Gill, 2007). With some children spending increased amounts of time in afterschool clubs, these had become important childhood contexts. Sometimes, these were the main locations outside of school where children played and socialised (Barker & Smith, 2000). We shared concerns for the concentric effects of these changes – on children's freedom to play, and on families and communities. These concerns further fuelled our passionate advocacy for playwork ideals and practices. We saw ourselves, in tiny ways, as helping to alleviate these concerning factors (Brown & Taylor, 2008).

I learned that a key part of my job was to empower children, to confer "power to an individual through an enabling or facilitating process" (Bonel & Lindon, 2000, p. 280). 'Empowerment' was about engaging children in processes that would build their confidence and self-esteem, taking child-centred approaches to learning and participation, and enabling and facilitating children's decision-making and self-direction (Brown, 2003, Brown & Taylor, 2008). The term was used broadly in playwork contexts to mean children reclaiming personal power in their play, having or being afforded the power to make choices and to affect their surroundings. This strong, definitive and good-sounding word invigorated and encouraged me. I also learned that playwork was about *not* intervening, play *not* having specific outcomes and children choosing and directing their *own* play. My work with children supported them to experience, enjoy, learn and develop during and through their play in irreducible and irreplaceable ways (Brown & Taylor, 2008; Hughes, 2001; Sturrock & Else, 1998). That there is vital learning inherent to children's free choice and exploration made complete sense to me (Ailwood, 2003; Lester & Russell, 2008). I saw this as messy, multilayered and valuable to the whole child's development – expanding their physical, social and emotional skills and equilibrium, their creative and cultural explorations and their intellectual capabilities (Brown, 2003). I sought to educate parents on our playwork approach, to encourage them to see play's value and to defend play spaces in which children could just 'be'. I felt I was carefully buffering children at play, protecting them against powerful adult expectations and pressures (Playwork Principles Scrutiny Group (PPSG), 2005, Playwork Principle no. 4). In the clubs I worked in, play and learning were co-existing requirements.

Designing my doctoral research, I questioned none of this. Influential ideas filtered through the literature and the media into the workplace and ignited me. I chose a research methodology to help me advocate for children's play, to fight inequality, to make society better. In the study's early stages I used my playwork background to understand what participants were saying and doing in relation to play. I looked, for example, at whether the children's experiences were at the centre of decision-making processes (Brown, 2003; Brown & Taylor, 2008) and whether playworkers ensured the play process took precedence and acted as 'advocates for play when engaging with adult led agendas (PPSG, 2005, Playwork Principle no. 4). In my new playworker-ethnographer role I could look in-depth at relationships between playwork theory and practice, and at what playwork practitioners and children were saying and doing. At first this seemed straightforward. It meant valuing the play environment (Brown, 2003) and investigating whether children were getting to play as playwork prescribed (PPSG, 2005). I was yet to discover the complex, sometimes adversarial relationship between ideas about play and learning, and their implications for both children and playworkers.

Conducting the research provided opportunities to articulate these influences and to hear my colleagues formulate their playwork perspectives. I realised that while our job titles said 'playworker', playwork was only part of our job description. I began to see and understand the incongruities between the Playwork Principles (PPSG, 2005) and strategic, outcome-oriented approaches to play and learning in these Ofsted-regulated contexts. I began to see play and playwork in these clubs as tense convergence points between government efforts to ensure children's prosocial behaviour and learning while playing, and playwork priorities which were about preserving children's play free from adult agendas. I discovered widespread concern for disadvantaged children's cognitive and social development impacting playwork practice in the clubs I trained, worked and researched in. These dominant concerns and contemporary discourses contributed to instrumental ideas about learning through play. They were key to policy and research debates, influenced playwork training, and trickled down into playwork practice (Lester & Russell, 2008).

I emerged from this background to do practitioner-research in these same local government-run clubs. I set out to better understand relationships between playworkers and children, what helped and hindered children's play, empowerment and informal learning, what these concepts meant and what differences they made. As my critical awareness grew through the research, my playwork perspective evolved. These concerns, priorities and conflicting messages had shaped my choice to do this research in these particular settings and how I did it, and the experiences of the playworkers and children involved. In search of answers to these questions, I discovered much about *why* I was asking them. I came to see how strongly my playwork perspective influenced the research design and that my interest in specific issues was a product of the contexts in which I had trained and worked. During the process I observed playwork practitioners steer children's play in an expression of broader societal concerns to ensure they developed in desirable ways. As a playworker I had done this myself. I learned that empowerment is a "complex and somewhat fragile concept whose role is neither straightforward nor static" (Stein, 1997, p. 13). I discovered that being an ethnographer and a playworker was also neither straightforward nor static. Understanding the larger context around play and playwork in these settings explained a lot about the divergent requirements on playwork practitioners to both control and facilitate children's play. In ethnography, and critical ethnography specifically, I found ways to explore these interlocking layers.

What is playwork?

Playwork is a theoretically grounded professional framework for creating and maintaining spaces for children to play. Playwork settings include: afterschool clubs, holiday play schemes, adventure playgrounds, parks, play buses and breakfast clubs. The nationally recognised Playwork Principles currently establish playwork's professional and ethical framework and aim to provide the playwork perspective on play for working with children and young people (PPSG, 2005). Playworkers support children's "freely chosen, personally directed, intrinsically motivated" play outside of the educational curriculum (PPSG, 2005). Playworkers see play as "a generic term applied to a wide range of activities and behaviours [that] children and young people do when not being told what to do by adults" (Play England, 2009, p. 6). Playworkers seek to ensure that children access the broadest range of play types (Hughes, 2002, 2006) because "children and young people's capacity for positive development will be enhanced if given access to the broadest range of environments and play opportunities" (PPSG, 2005, para. 1). The Playwork Principles define playworkers as advocates for children's play, whether defending it from adult-led agendas or supporting children to create their play space, and that the essence of playwork is to support and facilitate the play process. This goal should inform the development of play policy, strategy, training and education. In addition, up-to-date knowledge of play and reflective practice should inform playwork so that practitioners can recognise both their impact on the play space and the impact of children's play on them. Finally, playworkers are to use a low-intervention style that enables children to develop their play, with playworkers weighing the developmental benefits of exposure to risk with ensuring each child's safety and well-being. I explore this understanding of playwork in the light of critical ethnography later in this chapter.

ETHNOGRAPHIC PERSPECTIVES

Ethnography

Ethnography is a generic term for a collection of related methods and techniques well suited to research into children's lives (Back, 1996, 2004; Connolly, 1998; Corsaro, 2005; Hey, 1997; James, 2001). These include participant observation, semi-structured interviewing and reflexive practice. Doing ethnography requires active engagement in the lives of the host community, periods of immersion, being both participant and observer and being in close contact with research participants. This embedded approach seeks first hand understanding by embracing complexity and diversity to penetrate different worldviews through the eyes of 'insiders'. This collection of methods and techniques shares the basic premise that knowledge is culturally defined, and that immersion is necessary to understanding life as lived. It intends to facilitate the sharing of cultural knowledge through accessible methods and to amplify the voices of the marginalised – often called 'insider advocacy' (Hammersley & Atkinson, 1995, p. 124).

Immersion enables the researcher to observe patterns of behaviour, to determine values and perspectives, similarities and differences (Woods, 1996). The ethnographer seeks to soften the effect of their presence by learning appropriate social behaviours, and through the long duration of fieldwork. Thus, over time, research participants "forget their 'company' behaviour and fall back into familiar patterns" (Fetterman, 1998, p. 36). Lengthy immersion and semi-structured interviewing afford the researcher opportunities to refine questions, to check ideas, to challenge concepts formed prior to fieldwork and to search for ever-deeper social, cultural and personal understanding. Rather than measuring particular predetermined concepts about play and playwork, immersion in the afterschool clubs allowed me to listen to participants' ideas, values and experiences and to participate in and observe their actions over time.

Ethnography frequently seeks to level power relations between researcher and researched (Brettel, 1993; Hammersley & Atkinson, 1995). Reflexivity – a multifaceted critical analytical process and mode of awareness to recognise the researcher's own cultural and political positions, attitudes and behaviours – is a key tool in this. For ethnographers, the deconstruction of notions of objectivity and challenges to traditional power and representation require a re-evaluation of the traditional position of the researcher, seeking to identify and locate ourselves as part of the ethnographic data we generate. From the position that all knowledge is personal and cultural in some sense, producing ethnographic data necessarily implicates the researcher's views and agendas. Therefore, the ethnographer is a 'human instrument' (Fetterman, 1998, p. 31), and who and where we are shapes the knowledge we produce (Ribbens & Edwards, 2000). This 'observation of participation' (Tedlock, 1991, p. 69) marks a shift in what researchers endeavour to achieve (Barker & Smith, 2001; Connolly, 1998).

Ethnography values participants' 'insider' (Blaikie, 2000) knowledge as an expression of personal, social, cultural and historical truths (Silverman, 2001). While highly contextual and often contradictory and messy, 'insider' knowledge constitutes the currency of the social world (Clifford & Marcus, 1986). This approach sees subjective perceptions of reality as significant in shaping social beliefs and behaviour, a mundane web of meaning that deserves investigation and 'thick' description (Geertz, 1973). To value 'insider' knowledge is to validate what people say and do as reflecting meanings produced in particular sociocultural contexts (Bourdieu, 1992; Foucault, 1980). Whilst our contexts shape how we experience and respond to the world, culture exists in the meanings people produce and reproduce daily (Geertz, 1973; Marcus & Fischer, 1986). People are creative beings, social actors constrained but not determined by social structures (Carspecken, 1996), and the social world is created through dynamic interaction between culturally and historically produced human responses and discourses (Foucault, 1980). Ethnographic practitioner research conducted from an 'insider' viewpoint can generate different relations between the researcher and the researched, enabling unique opportunities for understanding (Brettell, 1993). It can be quicker, for example, to reach a point where language and practices under study are familiar. These 'insider' accounts can inform us about the people and contexts that produce them, and 'insider advocacy' can be a means of advocating for insiders' experiences and agendas.

Ethnography uses these methods and techniques to represent and thereby amplify the voices of those silenced by unequal power relations commonly replicated in other forms of research (Hammersley & Atkinson, 1995). The example of children as a socially silenced group is relevant here. Seen as not quite complete beings until adulthood, in the past, research into children's lives was often conducted *on* rather than *with* them (James & Prout, 1997). Ethnography has proven effective for actively involving children as research participants (Alldred, 2000; Corsaro, 2005; James, 2001). These values make it well suited to the kind of playwork and research I was interested in – that which seeks to challenge the traditional marginalisation of children in research and society, to enable a voice for children and playworkers, to validate their lives and to use research findings to advocate on their behalf.

Critical ethnography in playwork practitioner research

Critical ethnography is inherently both political and pedagogical. Emerging from the critical theory school, this approach seeks to challenge social, political and economic inequalities and for research findings to contribute to positive social change (Carspecken, 1996; Denzin & Lincoln, 2003). Proponents of critical ethnography are explicit about these particular social values: that social power relations are unequal and the lives of those negatively affected by such inequalities can be improved. Whereas conventional ethnography provides thick description of how things are (Geertz, 1973), critical ethnography critiques power, structure and agency within larger economic, political and historical contexts. In this way, it seeks to highlight and disrupt power relations and social inequalities in order to advocate for a more just society. These goals have produced significant growth in the body of knowledge about children (Robinson, 1994; Corsaro & Molinaro, 2000) and proved useful to my aspirations.

I used critical ethnography as a framework to understand social inequality and attitudes imbedded in policies, institutions, practices and structures that marginalise particular social groups, in this case, children. In this research, the 'insiders' I particularly focused on were the playwork practitioners and the children. Critical ethnography became an influential lens through which I saw the research and interacted with the participants. I wanted to avoid excessive ethnographic description, instead to strike a balance between descriptive and historically located accounts. I chose critical ethnography because of its social justice focus and goal of democratising the research process to support participants in representing their own voices, values and agendas (Carspecken, 1996; Petrie, 1994). This approach helped me understand and construct my playwork perspective and build the critical awareness and skills to navigate this ambiguous yet rich dual practitioner-researcher role. It also enabled me to see and understand important conflicts. For example, while as playworkers, we intend to prioritise and facilitate play, institutional and social expectations mean we often allow activities geared toward particular socialisation outcomes to take precedence (Ansell & Smith, 2008).

I used Carspecken's (1996) five-stage approach to produce an analysis of immediate experience and broader social forces impacting children and playworkers. This approach meshed well with my concerns as a playworker to value participants' processes, to advocate for children's rights, to empower the voices of those who are often silenced and to be present yet inconspicuous (Brown, 2003; Brown & Taylor, 2008). I wanted the experience of participating in this research to be valuable to the playworkers in a number of ways: to provide chances to explore ideas, to engage in the self-reflection outlined in the Playwork Principles (PPSG, 2005, Playwork Principle no. 6), to put a critical lens on whether they were supporting play as they intended and to potentially see ways to alter their practice. Critical ethnography allowed me to incorporate these goals into the research design and ultimately provided deep reflection for myself also. As a playwork practitioner-turned-researcher, I was also partly an 'insider'. The 'insider advocacy' approach helped me understand personal, social, cultural and historical truths – theirs and mine.

By using a critical ethnographic approach, I was able to do a number of key things. I drew on field notes, transcribed semi-structured interviews and policy documents to link 'thick' description with playwork theories and practices, and with local and national policies. I pulled out themes for exploration in greater depth in relation to empowerment, play and informal learning. I also explored relationships between organisational structures and expectations, playwork approaches, everyday service delivery and experiences in these settings. This approach helped me to understand my own and my colleagues' playwork perspectives, different perceptions of children and childhood, their impacts on the resources and opportunities provided for children and how they shaped playworkers' experiences. In the process, I also discovered that critical ethnography and playwork practice share important commonalities. The next section looks at how these proved relevant and valuable to this research and the insights it produced.

Critical ethnography and playwork practice

Critical ethnography and playwork practice both deal with questions of power and representation. Any "issues of power and inequality necessarily permeate social research of any type"; the researcher must strive to "spot and analyse power relations" (Carspecken, 1996, p. 40). Children represent a socially "muted, disempowered group" (Hardman, 1973, p. 85), subject to adult control over whether they receive their rights, from survival to development, protection to participation (Freeman, 1997; United Nations International Children's Emergency Fund (UNICEF), 1991). This power permeates everything from large-scale decision-making in the form of governance, policy-making and environmental design, to everyday interactions in schools and afterschool settings. Indeed, "children remain the sector of society whose rights are most systematically ignored – especially the right to play" (Brown, 2014, p. 2). Playwork advocacy on children's behalf seeks to contest adult agendas and to prioritise the child over the adult when it comes to play (PPSG, 2005). Advocacy on behalf of 'muted' groups means protecting and representing the agendas of those for whom decisions are usually made. Both critical ethnography and playwork practice seek to empower the disempowered, to represent their voices and to advocate for their rights. To achieve these goals, both critical ethnography and playwork use the methods of low intervention, reflective practice, and open-ended questioning.

Ethnographers and playworkers seek to be supportive yet unobtrusive (Webb & Brown, 2003), showing "low intervention/high responsiveness" (Hughes, 1996, p. 51). This means generally not intervening in what is happening, but being available and responsive in ways that enable those we work with to extend rather than limit what they are doing. This involves adopting a reactive strategy (Corsaro, 2003). As Brown and Webb point out, this makes playworkers particularly well suited to undertaking ethnographic research with children (Brown & Webb, 2003). My playwork colleagues tried to understand play, to be available and to support children, yet also to minimise the effects of their presence. They would often occupy themselves with other tasks, being present if needed but neither obtrusive nor obviously watching the children. They were playful if called upon, taking direction from the children and responsive to play cues through which children invited them or other children into their play (Sturrock & Else, 1998). If children asked for help with a dispute, staff would respond with open questions to help the children use their own authority to resolve matters. I did all these things in my previous role as a playworker and also during my research as a participant observer. Whether the actions of a playworker or participant observer, these practices sought to show children that this was their space, that they deserved to control their play and that adults were there for support if needed.

As a playworker, I was already familiar with asking open questions, probing gently, stepping back, observing naturally occurring processes and reflecting on the impact of my behaviour. These skills helped me navigate being a critical ethnographer. My use of participant observation and semi-structured interviews allowed me to hear peoples' views, experiences and values and to observe and be involved in collective processes daily. Like playwork practice, participant observation involves striking a balance between creating good relationships and understanding participants' perspectives and experiences while maintaining enough distance to allow in-depth observation. Developing trust takes time and careful negotiation. As Corsaro and Molinaro (2000) argue, the process of being accepted by children in a way that enables them to relate to the researcher is a slow and delicate one. Semi-structured interviews are essentially intentional conversations designed to elicit information on particular topics. This involves posing open-ended questions, valuing respondents' viewpoints and adapting the conversation in response to what they say. This is similar to how a playworker might question a child (Hughes, 2002). When doing ethnography, similar to the practice of playwork, semi-structured enquiry and participant observation are frequently combined. For ethnographers and playworkers alike, this combination enhances the quality of information gleaned and understandings reached because what people say and do often differ (Hammersley & Atkinson, 1995).

However, the two approaches of playwork practice and ethnography also had tensions in common. While trying to be unobtrusive, concerns to appear professional, committed, in control and industrious also characterised both roles. Throughout the research, my playwork colleagues enthusiastically articulated their identities as carers and guides, dedicated to the children. They expressed commitment to children's rights to be valued and to control their own play, to socialise with other children and to grow in their confidence and independence. Some went as far as to connect the importance of these with children acquiring skills for life in a world where the odds may be against them. I felt these commitments also, as a playworker and a critical ethnographer. Playworkers also described expectations that being professional involved appearing in control and industrious, busily protecting and caring for the children. This contrasted with being supportive yet unobtrusive, leaving children to control their play. As a critical ethnographer, I also felt this and sought to find a balance.

Reflective practice is central to both ethnography (Corsaro & Molinaro, 2000) and playwork (Kilvington & Wood, 2010). It is an invaluable set of written and verbal techniques for ongoing assessment and adjustment of what we do. For ethnographers, as a 'human instrument', who and where we are shapes our conduct and the knowledge we produce. For practitioners, up-to-date knowledge of play and reflective practice informs our responses to children playing (PPSG, 2005, Playwork Principle no. 6). As ethnographers and practitioners, reflecting on our biases and behaviours may help us to recognise and temper our impacts on those we work with. For myself as an ethnographer and for the playworkers, verbal and written critical self-reflection were essential to quality in our work. Talking with my supervisors and writing my daily research journal provided valuable space to reflect on the research process, on my different roles and relationships with participants and on my own playwork knowledge and perspective. This practice gave me the space to assess my responses and rejuvenate adequate distanciation (Jackson, 1987). This means maintaining a degree of distance, to be able to observe and understand. Throughout the fieldwork, my position required a balance between nurturing relationships with participants, while retaining enough distance to allow for observation and data recording. Ultimately, being in this dual role proved invaluable. The combination of my 'insider' insight and my 'outsider' analytical position as a researcher meant that my views became an amalgamation of these two perspectives. Furthermore, as playwork professionals, reflecting on our practice individually and with our colleagues allows us to develop our practice to more closely resemble our ideals and the Playwork Principles (PPSG, 2005).

In these highly regulated afterschool contexts, in my dual position as a playworker-ethnographer (both 'insider' and 'outsider'), it meant that I was there to understand, rather than to assess. As a playwork 'insider' I knew the contexts and could appreciate and navigate what was going on. Staff knew, for example, that I supported playwork and understood the opportunities and challenges it could bring, including fatigue, confusion over the different directives received from administration and trainings and having various roles that required distinct ways of interacting with children. These shared experiences aided our meaningful conversations and also meant that staff called on my playwork support from time to time during the research. As a researcher 'outsider', I observed, enquired and made discrete notes in private (something other staff expressed they wished they could do in order to develop their own practice).

To support reflection throughout the research, conversations and semi-structured interviews provided space for participants to formulate their perspectives (Flick, 2002; Mason, 2002). My deference to their 'insider' knowledge surprised some and changed the predicted power dynamics of our relationships. I frequently asked what perhaps appeared to be naïve open-ended questions, not assuming I knew the answers, using what Hastrup (1993) terms 'defamiliarisation' (p. 148). I also sometimes returned to points for further clarification to encourage greater explanatory depth (Kvale, 1996; Wolcott, 1994). Some of the playworkers found this odd. Based on our former professional relationships, they thought I knew the answers to some of my questions. Some of the children also found the experience of having an adult defer to their knowledge odd. After clarifying that I wanted to know *their* thoughts, they generally responded by continuing in greater depth.

Producing research of use to playworkers, in which their experiences and perceptions drove my narrative, proved complex. The need for the analytic distanciation as an 'outsider' and my new role as participant observer put me in a position unfamiliar to us all. I was there to observe and absorb, to collaborate and support, to understand the nuances and context-specific constraints. But I was also doing a PhD. Fundamentally geared toward meeting doctoral requirements, I had to draw conclusions and critiques, ultimately focussing on analyses other than the narratives of the playworkers. Amidst mixed feelings about this role and my evolving interpretations, I wanted to be useful but also to remain in the background, to support but also to solidify my new ideas. This conflict was partly inherent to navigating participant observation, and partly about a growing critical reflection not only on the settings but on my own theory, practice and purpose. I realised the challenge of going into research to support and advocate for colleagues because my perspectives changed as a result of getting involved in academic research. As valuable as these insights are, it is important to remember that academic perspectives hope to compliment, not trump, the more complex realities of work on the ground.

We are ourselves embedded in the power relations that we have to understand and navigate. Both playwork practice and bringing a playwork perspective to research into play face the challenges and constraints of operating within traditional power structures that playwork and ethnography both seek to counteract. Practitioner research provides space to reflect and discuss gaps between intentions and outcomes with someone who understands the profession but is one step removed. Incorporating reflective practice as integral to playwork and ethnographic research works well to develop applicable insights. Adding a critical perspective further strengthens this potential.

Conclusion

This chapter has drawn from my practitioner research to examine similarities between critical ethnography and playwork practice. I have explored the opportunities this approach gave me to value 'insider' knowledge, to use my skills as a playworker in the research and to engage playwork practitioners. Practitioners in these seemingly disparate roles share mutual concern for social justice. They critique established power relations, advocate for marginalised people and use low-intervention, reflective methods. Incorporating these sensibilities and techniques met my research goals in three key ways. I gave precedence to children's and playworkers' voices, prompted playworkers' critical reflections and made sense of the complexities of playwork practice and ethnographic research. This approach helped me understand the impacts of diverse perceptions of children and childhood on the playworkers and the play spaces they provided for the children.

A key objective of my practitioner research was to gain greater understanding of my work and to use this insight to better achieve my professional goals. In the context of this research, examining play from a playwork perspective meant looking at play and playwork as political – as intimately embedded in questions of power, social justice and representation of those who are often marginalised – and adjusting my practice to meet my goals. Critical ethnography gave me a number of things. It provided a framework compatible with the Playwork Principles (PPSG, 2005) through which I developed a socially and politically contextualised view of myself and what I observed and came to understand the significant influence of non-play-related policies on my early playwork identity. Practitioner research methodologies that produce such distinctions of our own professional perspectives are valuable. They allow us to understand how changing political agendas affect us, to find ways to navigate these and to advocate for our professions within the context of contemporary concerns. As a result of this approach, I grew greatly in my critical awareness of my own standpoint, improved as a practitioner and as a researcher and gained insights useful to the burgeoning field of playwork research.

These insights are important in their specificities and beyond, as they highlight and raise questions about contemporary relations between society, governments and children (Smith, 2010). Children are a powerful symbol of the future in contemporary UK society, and debates about instrumental, outcome-orientated valorisation of children's play stem from this (Lester & Russell, 2008). Observing playwork practice and triangulating field data with documentary analysis became an effort to understand "cultural norms and anxieties about play" (McKendrick, Horton, Kraftl, & Else, 2014, p. 66). I came to see how particular ideas about play and childhood had shaped my own and my colleagues' views and produced mixed messages and requirements in the workplace. Recognising this helped me understand what playworkers said and did within the policy and practice guidelines of the clubs. Critical ethnography gave me a framework to value their 'insider' knowledge, to use my playwork skills and to engage them in critical reflection. In my own and my colleagues' work, I realised that without critical reflection on our practice, our goals and behaviours can diverge, instead reproducing relationships we intend to challenge.

The commonalities between ethnography and playwork make valuable contributions to this study of play from a playwork perspective and to the development of a body of playwork research more broadly. This approach contributes to the body of knowledge in which children's agendas and experiences of play and play environments are central to research concerns. It can be used to advocate for the profession's impact on children's play. It engages in research, the very process of which can improve practice for practitioners and practitioner-researchers. Ethnography is particularly compatible for qualitative research into the broad domain of children's play. Furthermore, critical ethnography may be uniquely well suited for qualitative research into play in playwork environments and beyond. As we look to important questions of what playwork practitioners and policy-makers need to know about play and playwork in the future (McKendrick et al., 2014), the combination of critical ethnography and playwork practice has the potential to impact playwork and practitioner research, evidence-based playwork practice and our deeper understanding of the role of children within our society.

Note

1 Also known as Dr Hannah Henry Smith.

References

Ailwood, J. (2003). Governing early childhood education through play. *Contemporary Issues in Early Childhood*, 4(3), 286–298.
Alldred, P. (2000). Dilemmas in representing the voices of children. In J. Ribbens & R. Edwards (Eds.), *Feminist dilemmas in qualitative research* (pp. 147–170). London: Sage.
Ansell, N. & Smith, F. (2008). Young people, care and social well-being. In S. J. Smith, S. J. Marston, R. Pain, & J. P. Jones (Eds.), *Handbook of social geography* (pp. 351–367). London: Sage.
Axline, V. (1964). *Play therapy*. Boston: Houghton Mifflin.
Back, L. (1996). *New ethnicities: Racism and multiculture in young lives*. London: UCL Press.
Back, L. (2004). Inscriptions of love. In H. Thomas & J. Ahmed (Eds.), *Cultural bodies: Ethnography and theory* (pp. 27–54). Oxford: Blackwell.
Ball, D., Gill, T., & Spiegal, B. (2008). *Managing risk in play provision: Implementation guide*. Nottingham: DCSF.
Barker, J. & Smith, F. (2000). *Children's experiences of afterschool clubs*. www.hull.ac.uk/children5to16programme/conference/barker.pdf.
Barker, J. & Smith, F. (2001). Power, positionality and practicality: Carrying out fieldwork with children. *Ethics, Place and Environment*, 4(2), 142–147.
Bascombe, D. (2008). Children's rights: UN committee points to UK failures. *ChildRight*, 25(November), 11–14.
Beck, U. (2006). Living in the world risk society. *Economy and Society*, 35(3), 329–345.
Bennett, J. (2003). Starting strong: The persistent division between care and education. *Journal of Early Childhood Research*, 1(1), 21–48.
Blaikie, N. (2000). *Designing social research*. Cambridge: Polity.
Bonel, P. & Lindon, J. (2000). *Playwork: A guide to good practice*. Cheltenham: Stanley Thornes.
Bourdieu, P. (1992). Thinking about limits. In M. Featherstone (Ed.), *Cultural theory and cultural change* (pp. 37–49). London: Sage.
Brettell, C. B. (1993). Introduction: Fieldwork, text, and audience. In C. B. Brettell (Ed.), *When they read what we write: The politics of ethnography* (pp. 1–24). London: Bergin and Garvey.
Brown, F. (2003). *Playwork: Theory and practice*. Buckingham: Open University.
Brown, F. (2014). *Play and playwork: 101 stories of children playing*. Buckingham: Open University.
Brown, F. & Taylor, C. (2008). *Foundations of playwork*. Berkshire: Open University.
Brown, F. & Webb, S. (2002). Playwork: An attempt at definition. *Play Action*, 11–18.
Burghardt, G. M. (2005). *The genesis of animal play: Testing the limits*. Cambridge, MA: MIT Press.
Carspecken, P. F. (1996). *Critical ethnography in educational research: A theoretical and practical guide*. New York and London: Routledge.
Children's Play Council, National Playing Fields Association & PlayLink. (2000). *Best play what play provision should do for children*. London: National Playing Fields Association.

Clifford, J. & Marcus, G. (1986). *Writing culture*. Berkeley: University of California Press.

Cockburn, T. (2005). Children's participation in Social policy: Inclusion, chimera or authenticity? *Journal of Social Policy and Society*, 4(2), 109–119.

Connolly, P. (1998). *Racism, gender identities and young children*. London: Routledge.

Corsaro, W. A. (2003). *We're friends, right? Inside kids' culture*. Washington, DC: Joseph Henry Press.

Corsaro, W. A. (2005). *The sociology of childhood*. Thousand Oaks, CA and London: Pine Forge.

Corsaro, W. A. & Molinaro, L. (2000). Entering and observing in children's worlds: A reflection on a longitudinal ethnography of early education in Italy. In P. Christensen & A. James (Eds.), *Research with children: Perspectives and practices* (pp. 179–200). New York, NY: Falmer Press.

Denzin, N. K. & Lincoln, Y. S. (2003). *Strategies of qualitative inquiry*. London: Sage.

Fetterman, D. M. (1998). *Ethnography second edition: Step by step*. London: Sage.

Flick, U. (2002). *An introduction to qualitative research*. London: Sage.

Foucault, M. (1980). *Power/knowledge*. New York: Pantheon Books.

Freeman, M. (1997). *The moral status of children: Essays on the rights of the child*. Netherlands: Kluwer Law International.

Freud, S. (1922). *The standard edition of the complete psychological works of Sigmund Freud*. London: Hogarth.

Geertz, C. (1973). *The interpretation of cultures*. London: Fontana.

Gill, T. (2007). *No fear: Growing up in a risk averse society*. London: Calouste Gulbenkian Foundation.

Hammersley, M. & Atkinson, P. (1995). *Ethnography: Principles in practice*. London and New York: Routledge.

Hardman, C. (1973). Can there be an anthropology of children? *Journal of the Anthropological Society of Oxford*, 4(2), 85–99.

Hastrup, K. (1993). Native anthropology: A contradiction in terms? *Folk*, 35, 147–161.

Hendrick, H. (1997). Constructions and reconstructions of British childhood: An Interpretive Survey, 1800 To The Present. In A. James & A. Prout (Eds.), *Constructing and reconstructing childhood* (pp. 34–62). Oxon: Routledge Falmer.

Hey, V. (1997). *The company she keeps: An ethnography of girls' friendship*. Buckingham: Open University Press.

Hughes, B. (1996). *Play Environments: A question of quality*. London: Playlink.

Hughes, B. (2001). *Evolutionary playwork and reflective practice*. London and New York: Routledge.

Hughes, B. (2002). *A playworker's taxonomy of play types* (2nd ed.). London: Play Education.

Hughes, B. (2003). Play deprivation, play bias and playwork practice. In F. Brown (Ed.), *Playwork theory and practice* (pp. 66–80). Buckingham: Open University Press.

Hughes, B. (2006). Play types: Speculations and possibilities. London: London Centre for Playwork Education and Training.

Huizinga, J. (1955). *Homo ludens: A study of the play element in culture*. Boston: Beacon Press.

Jackson, A. (1987). *Anthropology at home: ASA monographs*. London and New York: Tavistock Publications.

James, A. (2001). Ethnography in the study of children and childhood. In P. Atkinson, A. Coffey, S. Delamont, J. Lofland, & L. Lofland (Eds.), *Handbook of ethnography* (pp. 246–257). London: Sage.
James, A., Jenks, C., & Prout, A. (1998). *Theorizing childhood*. Cambridge: Polity Press.
James, A. & Prout, A. (1997). *Constructing and reconstructing childhood*. London and New York: Routledge Falmer.
Jeffs, T. & Smith, M. (2005). *Informal education: Conversation, democracy and learning*. Nottingham: Educational Heretics Press.
Kilvington, J., & Wood, A. (2010). *Reflective playwork: For all who work with children*. London: Continuum.
Kvale, S. (1996). *Interviews: An Introduction to qualitative research interviewing*. Los Angeles, London and New Delhi: Sage.
Lester, S. & Russell, W. (2008). *Play for a change: Play, policy and practice, a review of contemporary perspectives*. London: Gloucester University.
Marcus, G. E. & Fischer, M. J. (1986). Two contemporary techniques in cultural critique in anthropology. In G. E. Marcus & M. J. Fischer (Eds.), *Anthropology as cultural critique: An Experimental moment in the human sciences* (pp. 137–164). Chicago: University of Chicago Press.
Mason, J. (2002). *Qualitative researching*. London: Sage.
McKendrick, J. H., Horton, J., Kraftl, P., & Else, P. (2014). Bursting the bubble of opening to door? Appraising the impact of austerity on playwork and playwork practitioners in the UK. *Journal of Playwork Practice*, 1(1), 61–69.
Moss, P. & Petrie, P. (2002). *From children's services to children's spaces: Public policy, children and childhood*. Oxon: Routledge Falmer.
Office for Standards in Education (Ofsted). (2001). *Out of school care: Guidance to the national standards*. Nottingham: DfES.
Pellegrini, A. D., Blatchford, P., Kato, K., & Baines, E. (2004). A short-term longitudinal study of children's playground games in primary school: Implications for adjustment to school and social adjustment in the USA and the UK. *Journal of Social Development*, 13(1), 107–123.
Petrie, P. (1994). *Play and care out of school*. London: HMSO.
Piaget, J. (1951). *Play, dreams and imitation in childhood*. London: Routledge and Keegan Paul.
Play England. (2009). *Making it Happen: Implementing the Charter for Children's Play*. London, Play England.
Playwork Principles Scrutiny Group. (2005). *Playwork principles*. Playwork. Retrieved from www.playwales.org.uk/login/uploaded/documents/Playwork%20Principles/playwork%20principles.pdf.
Ribbens, J. & Edwards, R. (Eds.) (2000). *Feminist dilemmas in qualitative research*. London: Sage.
Robinson, H. A. (1994). *The ethnography of empowerment: The transformative power of classroom interaction*. London: Falmer.
Silverman, D. (2001). *Interpreting qualitative data*. London: Sage.
Smith, H. H. (2010). *Children's empowerment, play and informal learning in two after school provisions*. Unpublished doctoral dissertation, Middlesex University, Middlesex.
Spencer, H. (1873). *The principles of psychology*. NewYork: D. Appleton and Co.
Stein, J. (1997). *Empowerment and women's health: Theory, methods and practice*. London: Zed Books.

Sturrock, G. & Else, P. (1998). 'The Colorado Paper' – The playground as therapeutic space: Playwork as healing. In G. Sturrock & P. Else (Eds.) (2007), *Therapeutic playwork reader one 1995–2000* (pp. 73–104). Eastleigh, Hampshire: Common Threads Publications Ltd.

Tedlock, B. (1991). From participant observation to the observation of participation: The emergence of narrative ethnography. *Journal of Anthropological Research*, 47(1), 69–94.

United Nations International Children's Emergency Fund. (1991). *United Nations Convention on the Rights of the Child*. Svenska: UNICEF Kommitten.

Webb, S. & Brown, F. (2003). Playwork in adversity: Working with abandoned children in Romania. In F. Brown (Ed.), *Playwork theory and practice* (pp. 158–175). Buckingham: Open University Press.

Wolcott, H. F. (1994). *Transforming qualitative data*. Los Angeles and London: Sage.

Woods, P. (1996). *Researching the art of teaching: Ethnography for educational use*. New York: Routledge.

5 Playing at research
Playfulness as a form of knowing and being in research with children

Philip Waters

Introduction

Picture this: I'm in a wooded copse within the grounds of a small Cornish school watching and being with children as they freely play. My attire is unusual. My head is adorned with an Australian-style outback hat that is strategically tilted forward to partially disguise my face, the purpose being to give an illusion of mystery as to my identity. A long, oil-skinned riding coat flaps behind me like a superhero's cape that shelters my shin-high leather boots. Across my chest is a rustic leather satchel, behind which hides a chain that hosts a fob-watch that I occasionally flip open to reveal the time. Suddenly, and without suggestion, I drop to the floor and place my ear to the ground.

> A child leans over me. "What you doing?" she asks.
> "Listening for them," I say.
> "Who?"
> "The little people."
> "Little people?"
> "Yes. Piskies. They've escaped."

Other children gather around us. I shift position and place my ear to another spot. One child places an ear to the ground next to me. "I don't hear them!" he exclaims loudly.

"They're over here," another child says, ear pressed to the trunk of a tree.

"Ah, the little blighters," I begin, standing up. "They're fast and sneaky," I say, walking to the tree and placing my ear against it.

We are joined by other children; some watching, some squeezing between us to listen to the tree, others hesitant to join in but curious nevertheless . . .

It would take quite a leap of faith, I think, for some researchers to consider that the above situation might be a method of research, or that I, dressed as an intrepid explorer, might be a serious researcher in the midst of a study. Both are, of course, true. In this chapter, I present a case for playfulness being a legitimate form of praxis in work with children and as an approach to conducting research. I critically examine the concept of 'playfulness' as applied to practice-led research evolved within the development of a pedagogic method called Narrative Journey (Waters, 2014a, 2014b). In presenting a case for playfulness as research, I draw on a range of texts that examine the playfulness of both children and adults and relate these to my own research and critical reflections. Themes discussed will include the role of playfulness in adult and children's lives; the functional and beneficial merits for being playful, including its relational prospects; perspectives on inter-subjectivity and embodied ways of knowing; and reflections on playwork praxis that position children and adults together as co-players. In this treatment of playfulness, I wish to challenge dominant ways of conducting research that situate children as either objects, subjects or participants – all of which 'other' children in research activities (Lahman, 2008) – whilst equally challenging praxis, politics and philosophies that exclude adults as players within children's activities – all of which *other* adults. It is worth noting that *praxis* is defined here as *informed action* (Freire, 1970) – an embodied and dialogic means of working with both theory and practice. Or, put another way, research activity is considered here as playful informed action.

The role of playfulness

Although there are qualitatively few differences between studies of adult and child playfulness (Tegano & Moran, 2007), there are quite distinct differences in research exploring *play as behaviour* as opposed to playfulness as an internal state. Indeed, behaviours are observable and measurable while internal states are less so (Barnett, 1998). It is not surprising, then, that many of the studies conducted on playfulness are about its functional qualities, about what it provides for the individual or social group and how these functional qualities manifest. In the context of my research, I use playfulness as an engagement device for interacting with children, a method or approach to adult/child correspondence that is employed as a functional device for research purposes. But equally, it is also a mood state, a form of activity that can be devoid of intentionality, purposefulness or application and instead operates as a means for *being* with children that is natural and child-centred.

While not exhaustive, studies of playfulness have been broad and encompassing, including its contribution to social capital (Barnett, 2007); its capacity for leisure and entertainment purposes – of self and others (Qian & Yarnal, 2011) and for humour (McGhee, 2010); its role in the psychological benefits that help develop resilience and/or coping mechanisms (Santer, Griffiths, & Goodall, 2007); its therapeutic contribution to mental health (Proyer, 2014a, 2014b); and its pedagogic contribution to formal and informal learning (Frimberger, 2013).

There is also a body of literature which explores playfulness from the perspective of the player, particularly where it is seen as a means for expressing desires, dreams, fantasies, wishes, traumas, conflicts and emotions (Barnett, 1998); for thinking flexibly and taking risks with ideas (Youell, 2008); as a form of release for tensions in the workplace (Qian & Yarnal, 2011); as a style for approaching problems (Skard & Bundy, 2008); as a process of adaptation (Ryan-Bloomer &

Candler, 2013); and as a quality of life (Proyer, 2014b). Taking a different stance, Reddy (1991) asserts that playfulness is an "interpersonal phenomenon that is always taking place in a relational dimension" (cited in Rosa, 2011, p. 205). In this sense, it is a dyadic process that comes to form only in the presence of another (Youell, 2008). However, relational aspects of playfulness, especially in contexts of child and adult interactions, have been little researched. Moreover, in this chapter, playfulness is interrogated within a broader treatment that accepts the relational over the solitary and the ecological over the social. That is, playfulness is not merely the subjective state of an individual; it is the relational subjectivity of co-players exposed to an environment as they engage with each other and the physical landscape. And so, while playfulness might be relational, it is also embodied (Rautio, 2013).

Else (2009) proposes that playfulness, like play, ought to be considered as an integral feature that spans the entirety of the life course, its expressions of which can be seen in every facet of human endeavour:

> Play is not just a phenomenon for children; it is present throughout life and is there in the creativity and energy of many different kinds of people. In looking to the greatest minds, it is possible to find many examples of playfulness and playful approaches from every discipline of human activity.
> (Else, 2009, p. 131)

While it is clear that play and playfulness are inextricably linked and that one has bearing on the other, it is equally clear that a distinction should be drawn between them. Such a distinction is offered by Lieberman (1977), Proyer (2012) and Bateson and Nettle (2014), who suggest that play and playfulness are separate facets of a much broader treatment of play. O'Brien and Duren (2011) are more specific about this, suggesting that it is a distinction between play as a self-initiated and intrinsic form of activity and playfulness as the disposition towards that activity. Youell (2008) takes a more subjective viewpoint when she describes playfulness as the very essence of play, proposing it is a much deeper part of the human condition than biological expressions of play normally allow. A similar view is supported by Lester and Russell (2010), who advise that play and playfulness, despite having different meanings, are interlinked aspects of our being. This is not unlike the position of Alcock (2013) and Moran (2000), who, drawing on the work of Heidegger (1962) and Merleau-Ponty (2004), advocate that playfulness should be understood in terms of the way it is *experienced* rather than how it is *expressed* as a component or causal part of another structure. Of course, the distinction might also be a semantic one, summarised here by Howard, Bellin, and Rees (2002), as a difference between external and internal aspects of play:

> Whilst certain activities may appear more play-like, we can never be sure whether the individual is feeling playful. Playfulness would appear to be an internalised construct that develops over time as a result of experience and interaction . . . Play is an act defined by observable characteristics. The

construct of playfulness comprises the internal qualities brought to the activity by the players themselves. Namely, how the player feels about the activity. So, whilst it may be possible to define or label certain activities as play in respect of the characteristics they display, the development that occurs during the activity is dependent on the perceptions of the player.

(p. 4)

Furthermore, I am inclined to agree with Newstead's (2010) observation when she says, "Playworkers are not interested in play as an event or an action, they are interested in playfulness as a characteristic and an ability" (p. 13).

In this chapter, I adopt the distinction that play is a form of behaviour (expression) and that playfulness is one's disposition towards that behaviour (experience). This understanding of playfulness is the focus in my research and to which I now turn in the context of playwork praxis.

Playwork and playfulness

Within the playwork sector, the distinction between expression and experience is a notable one. For the most part, play is considered the child's manifestation of internal intent, which is formed, on the one hand, as patterns of behaviours which are defined as *play types* (Hughes, 2002a, 2006), or more generally, as *play cues* and *returns* (Sturrock & Else, 1998). Both these forms describe play behaviour in the way it is manifested and observed and thus relies on an observer's perspective. Less attention has been given to understanding how children might experience play themselves from their own perspectives, and further, how adults might experience play with children as co-players, or equally, as players in their own right. It is worth noting here that a shift from play to playfulness is also a shift from observation to experience. We cannot, of course, observe dispositions in the same manner we might observe behaviours; they are internal facets of the human condition. But we can come to understand dispositions through direct experience, through playful play (Bateson & Martin, 2013).

There are, of course, a number of sub-texts that underscore the way adults work in environments where children play. The playwork profession, for example, is governed by an ethical framework called the Playwork Principles (Playwork Principles Scrutiny Group (PPSG), 2005) – for a useful critique, see Brown (2008). The Playwork Principles were devised to ensure that playworkers operate within a set of standards that are formed both by praxis and underpinning theories of play from a playwork perspective. For instance, Principle no. 2 states: "Play is a process that is freely chosen, personally directed and intrinsically motivated. That is, children and young people determine and control the content and intent of their play, by following their own instincts, ideas and interests, in their own way for their own reasons" (PPSG, 2005). Whilst there is little scope to explore this in depth here, it is worth noting that in the many environments where children play, *free choice* is not always as easily attainable (King & Howard, 2014). Likewise, the praxis of adults within these environments cannot always support the following of one's own instincts, especially if those instincts position the child in friction with behavioural, social, cultural or environmental boundaries.

In my opinion, the Playwork Principles do more than set the benchmarks and protocols for the playwork sector. They deeply embed a cultural praxis phenomenon that requests of adults to curtail their own play and be wary of adulterating children's play, or as Hughes (2001) puts it: "the hijacking of the child's play agenda by adults with the intention of substituting it with their own" (p. 163). Sturrock and Else (1998) take this further and suggest that the adulteration of children's play might be due to the adult's unplayed out material:

> The attraction to many of the work [playwork] may be that they have, themselves, unworked out play material that they feel impelled to express . . . There is a danger of a multifold contamination in this situation. On adventure playgrounds we see it in the grandiose structures built by some workers that become 'too good to play on', their pristine preservation overriding the deconstructive aspects of the play cycle. Or, more abstractly, where the play themes or narratives are presented solely by the workers. A further adulteration is evident in the form of 'infantile toxicity'. Here the playworker becomes drawn into the child's play frame and becomes over-involved in the play.
>
> (p. 20)

While unplayed-out material and hijacking children's play are useful concepts that might govern the way playworkers engage children, playfulness suggests a more nuanced, collaborative relationship with children. Yet still, its lack of place in the playwork profession is a curious matter and in part might be due to viewing children's play through a particularly skewed lens. First, there is the historical model of children's play happening in semi-derelict sites called junk playgrounds (adventure playgrounds), and as such, today's playwork profession is based on an adventure playground movement (Chilton, 2013). The problem here is that much of what playworkers do in praxis is devised on a spatial understanding of children's play (Newstead, 2015), where the culture and praxis of the adventure playground don't fit as well into other environmental contexts, such as the school or home environment. Furthermore, such a position disables the profession from developing a unified praxis like, for example, play therapy, which is not defined by place but by application.

Secondly, much of the current literature supporting playwork praxis is based on a model of human evolution that positions the child within a narrative of isolated development, as an individual venturing into the world alone, or as Hughes (2001) suggests, as a 'lone organism' (p. 254). Bio-evolutionary perspectives of play, while of course important, have tended to neglect the social and cultural relativity in children's everyday activities, which might, and often do, involve adults, and even adults that play (Lindqvist, 2001a).

It is worth noting that much of the theory underpinning playwork praxis, including the Playwork Principles, was created as a need for the profession to justify a theoretical basis for the way they work that is different from other professions working with children, commonly known as the playwork perspective (PPSG, 2005). More importantly, and this is where I have empathy, it was also to create a workforce that recognises the diminishing need for children to have space and time to play freely away and separate from dominant adult contexts. However, whilst I see the benefit and well-intentioned merits for such a philosophical approach to praxis, my critique is that it locates play within the domain of childhood and positions adults on the outside with few liberties to play or be playful, a position that counters quite a lot of the research on the benefits of playfulness for the human condition across the life course.

My approach to playwork practice, and to some extent, to the way I conduct research with children, is grounded in a Foucauldian view of power (Foucault, 1980; Gadda, 2008), meaning that power is distributed, shared, used and abused within relational contexts. Underpinning my arguments in this chapter, then, is a notion of how power presents itself in playful contexts. Being an adult is not the issue: rather, it is how players (young or old) use and abuse power. For example, children abuse other children's opportunities to play freely in all sorts of ways; for example, large children physically dominate small children, skilled children oppress less skilled children and so on. This is not to deny, of course, that being an adult player among children is not still a sensitive position and one that should not be taken lightly by the playworker. In this context, I agree with Wilson (2009), who reminds us that playwork practitioners ought to be aware of their broader life experiences and remain mindful of the needs, desires and intent of younger co-players, which are the merits of professional playwork praxis in my opinion. But playing and being playful (not in a fabricated or false way, because children see right through the pretence) has to be genuine and meaningful, and in the context I am proposing here, praxis should be one of ". . . openness, playfulness, humility, restraint and patience" (Russell, 2013, p. 17).

Taking this all into consideration, I adopt the view that playfulness is a mood state which has an infectious appeal that can induce states of playfulness in others and so embrace playfulness as both a disposition and a relational activity, a duality that is partially described by Jerome Bruner when he says that "play is an approach to action and not a form of activity" (Moyles, 1989, p. 11). Here, of course, playfulness is substituted for play: the implications being that playful approaches for engaging children and in conducting research might provide something different than other types of approaches and/or methodologies. Indeed, I believe "playful thought can generate radically new approaches to challenges set by the physical and social environment" (Bateson & Martin, 2013, p. 1). Moreover, and this is where Bruner and I part company on the matter, I believe that playfulness can be both an approach to action – as in how one might go about conducting research – as well as the activity itself – the method(s) employed within research activity. Before unpacking these concepts further, I will now establish the background context to my own research which was conducted in a small school in Cornwall, with the aim of evolving a form of pedagogic praxis called Narrative Journey.

Narrative Journey

Narrative Journey is a method that uses narrative cues and story framing to incite children's interest in the natural world (Frampton, Jenkin, & Waters, 2015; Waters, 2011, 2014a, 2014b, 2014c). Developed in my work with the Eden project,[1] Narrative Journey evolved as an experiential and place-based learning tool for situating learning within the playful interactions and constructions that learners have with each other and with their immediate environment. In its simplest form the practitioner offers into the play environment a narrative cue – a short, simple, verbal, or bodily-expressed *call to action* – from which the emerging *adventure* (should there be one) is left to the children as an open-ended experience. Offered for the playful possibilities they might induce, narrative cues come with no boundaries or restrictions on how they might be used. In many respects, they are similar to *play cues* introduced to the playwork sector by Sturrock and Else (1998), the only difference being that narrative cues are located within a story perspective as opposed to just a play one.

In more complex iterations of the Narrative Journey method, a series of cues might be presented that, when strung together in a meaningful way, creates the narrative conditions for an unfolding saga. Unlike isolated narrative cues, *story framing* provides the basis for a narrated world in which children and practitioners co-construct characters, plots and themes in moment-by-moment, playful collaborations. Story framing is not the same as *play frames*, which are imagined boundaries that harness play activity, or what Sturrock and Else (1998) otherwise refer to as "projected or thrown fantasy" (p. 13). Instead, story framing is the narrative device a practitioner applies to create the conditions for an unfolding story. It often has all the ingredients you would expect to see in traditional storymaking activities, such as genre, plot, characterisation, tension, calls to action etc. (Waters, 2016; Yorke, 2013), but with scope for playful deviations by any one or combination of players. In the context of my research, Narrative Journey is being explored as a method for physically engaging children in the natural environment as a process of supporting health and well-being outcomes. Narrative framing thus provides the theme and context for actions to emerge, whereas narrative cues are the motivational devices for encouraging certain types of actions over others. Although Narrative Journey has play and playfulness at its core, it remains a pedagogic rather than ludigogic (Sturrock, Russell, & Else, 2004) method.

Narrative Journey partly evolved as a praxis response to an historical and ongoing conflict within the UK's early childhood sector about the purpose of play. On the one hand, play is defined as intrinsic, which in praxis terms equates to play inherently belonging to children with the ambition that it should not be shaped, manipulated or structured by adults (Elkind, 2007; Hughes, 1990, 2001; Lester & Russell, 2008, 2010; PPSG, 2005; Thomson, 2014; Wragg, 2013). On the other hand, play is considered important for its *instrumental* qualities, for its capacity as a vehicle for therapy, formal learning and for socially engineering aspects of children's lives (Bairaktarova, Evangelou, Bagiati, & Brophy, 2011; Brooker, Blaise, & Edwards, 2014; Fleer, 2015). As such, Narrative Journey draws its practices from across allied fields like playwork, place-based education and performative storytelling and situates itself as a method that can be used both instrumentally and in support of more intrinsic forms of play.

By reframing practice as playful, practitioners are positioned as players within, rather than as observers or adjudicators on the outside of, children's experiences. Although this is a privileged position that demands a great deal of sensitivity towards children's play needs, it requests of the practitioner to follow the lead of children wherever and whenever possible, while at the same time not shying away from contributing play content as long as it does not dominate or forcefully dictate children's actions, intentions or intrinsic motivations. Playfulness in this context, within Narrative Journey pedagogy, is a means by which adults can legitimately be in playful situations with children. Furthermore, as a form of playful pedagogy, it sits midway between two fairly embedded forms of playwork praxis. On the one hand, there is the low-intervention strategies proposed by Hughes (2001; 2002b), which some authors propose are a 'non-interventionist' approach (Kilvington & Wood, 2010, p. 89). On the other hand, there are the complex intervention strategies advocated by Sturrock and Else (1998), and later, Sturrock et al. (2004), where clearly, the agendas of children and adults overlap. Narrative Journey tends to move between the two intervention approaches, aligning to one or the other depending on the context and pedagogical requirements.

Playfulness as research

Given the amount of research conducted on the subject of play, it is interesting that very few researchers have considered its merits as a mode for performing scholarly inquiry. Conversely, where playfulness has been used as a research instrument, it is rarely taken seriously. Frimberger (2013), for example, who used playful methods within intercultural research with fellow PhD students, suggests that adults find it challenging to adopt a playful persona as opposed to a normative professional persona, and would struggle in accepting that playfulness ". . . did not just serve our own entertainment but was part of a properly scientific research endeavour" (p. 82).

That researchers struggle to take playfulness seriously as a research activity is not surprising when one takes into consideration the plethora of research that epitomises childhood and play as a bounded sanctity. Frimberger (2013), for example, suggests that participants in her research ". . . were transported into a more playful childhood habitus" (p. 156), a notion that further subjects playfulness to a childhood domain and in the process decomposes its use as a *serious* method in research. Alcock, on the other hand, while recognising its lowly academic status, views playfulness as a qualitative process that naturally lends itself to an interpretive paradigm. Her treatment of playfulness, while not as a method, recognises its contribution as a safeguarding and backgrounding context for research activity:

> The process of gaining access to staff, parents, and finally children was uncomplicated, mainly because the research focus on playfulness and humour was

perceived as positive and nonthreatening for children by both teachers and parents.

(Alcock, 2013, p. 181)

Another factor that positions playfulness as a neglected research method is the bias of employing observational techniques over other methods in the study of children's play. Woodhead and Faulkner (2000) suggest that such a bias has meant we have spent more time *watching* and less time *being* with children:

> Whilst observational techniques provide much information into the nature of children's play, and allow us to make inferences about development and involvement in activities, they do not tell us about children's perceptions and do not therefore allow us to make judgements about individual definitions of playfulness. This is particularly relevant where the distinction between the observable act of play is distinguished from playful intention.
>
> (p. 5)

My research, while it also falls under the banner of the interpretive paradigm (Angen, 2000), incorporates an ecological stance (Neisser, 1993) that embraces the actions and interactions of players within a play environment, where playfulness is both a method of *playwork* praxis and an approach to conducting research and where all factors contribute to multiple constructions and deconstructions of knowledge. Moreover, as a relational activity, playfulness does more than afford children the capacity to discover what is known out there in the world. It also asks what is *unknown*, what is undiscovered, the very idea of which bestows upon children control over their own learning (Bruner, 1990; Mello, 2001). In Narrative Journey praxis, playfulness is the means for potential forms of knowing and potential ways of experiencing and is only partially orientated towards knowledge that can be *foraged* or *excavated*. It favours more a knowledge construction thesis, a *knowing* in action, or embodied, ecological and tacit forms of experiential learning (Castillo, 2002; Siemens, 2006; Snowden, 2002).

In championing the legitimacy of playfulness as a method in scholarly inquiry, I primarily draw on the work of Aitken (2001), Alcock (2013) and (Edmiston, 2008) and use their work to frame an ethical argument for my own playful interventions in research with children. I begin with Aitken, who proposes that researchers ". . . need to be in the field in a different kind of way, a less structured way, a more serendipitous way, a less contrived way, a more playful way" (Aitken, 2001, p. 502) if we wish to genuinely understand the reality of children's every day lived experiences. He argues convincingly that knowledge is often situated – specific to a situation, context or knowledge maker – and that academic field workers have traditionally held privileged positions over sites of inquiry (Aitken, 2001). This problem is further complicated by research governing bodies – especially ethics committees – that struggle to understand the necessity of research praxis that situates the immediacy of children's experience as legitimate research data, or actions and interactions as knowledge under construction (Waters & Waite, 2016). Of particular relevance to my own research is Aitken's playful methodology, an example of which is given here when he describes playing a cave man for a museum exhibit where a visiting group of young children adopt him into their play world:

> I am not sure what I became in that simulated cave in my simulated animal skins – a pet, a plaything, a confidant, an ally against adults – but for the next half hour I felt as though I were a trusted part of those children's world.
> (Aitken, 2001, p. 496)

Important here is Aitken's sense of attunement with children. In becoming a trusted part of their world, he was positioned to experience the children's perspective as close as one ever could in research activities with children. They were open to him without condition or restraint, to which all he had to do was accept the immediacy of their play, to be guided by them and to be situated by their actions and intentions. Indeed, it could be argued that a research position like this is rarely afforded when children are approached via traditional methodologies – see Punch (2002) for an overview – but is readily offered when adults display the sorts of qualities that children recognise and appreciate, the qualities in this case being play and playfulness.

Of course, this doesn't mean that children will not have certain expectations about researchers. For example, Alcock (2013), despite her playful ethnographic approach to being in the field with children, noticed that children would still treat her as another adult, a cross between teacher and parent, of which a passive responsive role was all she could do to minimise the effect of her presence. Adopting the reactive approach developed by Corsaro and Molinari (2000), Alcock worked hard to succumb to an identity assigned by children, which in many respects is a position that playworkers adopt when they relinquish power (Santer et al., 2007). This stance is also supported by McIntosh (2006), who says: "Here, children should react to the presence of the researcher rather than the researcher taking an active role in establishing relationships and defining boundaries for the research" (p. 5). A similar consideration is also given by Graue and Walsh who suggest the reactive approach is ". . . not one of acting like a child but rather of not acting like an adult" (Graue & Walsh, 1998, p. 107).

While there is merit in these stances, my interpretation of the *reactive approach* is one of adult disempowerment. It is about recognising the relational context of children and researchers and finding ways to balance power more fairly and equitably, which might include embracing forms of "playful resistance" (Russell, 2013, p. 47). Being playful, as long as it is genuine, is an appropriate and reactive way to be in research activities with children. Playfulness is not acting like a child; it is a mood state that can be employed in the service of research activity. In this context, being playful and playing with children, while proposed here as both an approach to research and a research methodology, suggests that the researcher can take an active role in establishing a research relationship. Using Aitken's *cave man* as an example, he was both playfully active and reactive in his relationship with the visiting children. Likewise, in my own research praxis, as well as in my Narrative Journey and playwork praxis, being playful can be both the *reaction* to children's intentions as well as an *active* means of engaging them.

Edmiston (2008), like others (Burghardt, 2005; Fromberg, 1992; Lester & Russell, 2010), positions playfulness as a stance or attitude towards life. Indeed, Lindqvist suggests it "permeates all spheres of life . . . and appear[s] wherever agency and intentionality open space" (Lindqvist, 2001b, p. 21). In this *space*, playfulness becomes a site of possibility; an 'as if' or 'what if' non-literal dimension (Bruner, Jolly, & Sylva, 1976; Lester & Russell, 2008), a dimension where, Turner (1992) suggests, "People play in the subjunctive mood" (p. 133). Interestingly, this opposes the earlier argument about playwork practice evolving within a spatially informed perspective (the adventure playground movement), where geographical, social, cultural and material applications shape the nature and intent of those spaces. Spatiality, in the context of playfulness, is more a non-literal, imagined and co-authored dimension of human interaction Of course, that's not to say that while in this non-literal dimension, the social, physical and cultural properties of everyday life disappear. They do not. Instead, they remain as backdrops that frame or give context to experience, play or otherwise, that eventually give way to a more imagined, *parallel world* where there are countless other ways of being and doing:

> When people play together, pretending that they are elsewhere, everyday life dims in the light of an imagined world that seems to materialize and take on a brighter reality . . . Play worlds are created and entered in imagination. A play world begins to take form when people pretend that they are actually there. The external actions in pretend play are the external objectifications of a world conceived in minds, language, and interacting bodies.
> (Edmiston, 2008, pp. 9–10)

Key to both Narrative Journey and playwork praxis, and to some extent my research practices, too, are the contexts established for entering or co-authoring imagined realities. Playfulness, as has already been suggested (Reddy, 1991 cited in Rosa, 2011; Youell, 2008), is not just the realm of the individual. It is a relational context for many players, a platform, or site (Nicolini, 2010), where two (or more) separate subjectivities come together to form a third, or hybrid, subjectivity. In playwork terms, this is what Sturrock and Else (1998), and later Sturrock (2003), call the *ludic third*, while in a literacy and language framework, it is what Roskos and Christie (2011) call the *play-literacy nexus*, a space where play, language and literacy behaviours converge and interact. It is not a physical space, per se, but rather a context in which literacy-rich pretence might be expressed. However, I choose to think of this context as an active state rather than a passive site and so use the term *narrative thirding* (Waters, 2014c). Narrative thirding, then, while it is created by the subjectivities of individual players (the playfulness they bring to the situation), is also the site (the space for playful engagement) that contains the subjectivities of players. It is both created in the moment and ceases to end when players stop narratively playing.

Narrative thirding in practice, like the complex intervention proposed by Sturrock and Else (1998), has some resemblance with the inter-subjective approach that Tegano and Moran(2007) use in classroom activities. They suggest that:

> An inter-subjective adult, who has developed shared understandings with children about their play, is more likely to be aware of the complexity of children's play. To be inter-subjective means to be involved in play, immersed in play, aware of play at an intimate level.
>
> (p. 177)

In this context, playfulness is not only a disposition or means of engagement; it is also a way of seeing or for observing through the eyes of children, which is a particularly useful method when conducting research with children. However, Edmiston (2008) offers a slight proviso here, and suggests that: "Unlike children, who are often very physically and socially active as they play . . . adults rarely use imagination socially to embody other worlds" (p. 10). In Narrative Journey praxis, the opposite is usually true. Adults are expected, through their practice and reactive responses, to actively contribute narrative content. They are expected to be playful. Thus, concepts like narrative thirding help to support practitioners and researchers to maintain a position as player within children's activities where knowledge is co-constructed. The researcher might later reconstruct meaning in a theoretical way so as to frame it for certain audiences. But the construction of the knowledge is a collaborative one, because it is devised by playful means within playful contexts between playful beings.

Conclusion

As a playwork practitioner, I have extended the periphery of my praxis by exploring how my own sense of playfulness can be used in both praxis and research with children. As a researcher, I am aware that playwork informs the way I think about researching children's experiences, about the impact my presence has on children and their everyday worlds and how research intrusions, as in any ethnographic field study, is likely to have an effect. Narrative Journey praxis is used to expose children to possible ways of being that are primarily delivered through a mechanism of playful pretence. In this chapter, I have proposed that 'narrative thirding' is the site of that playful pretence; it neither belongs to me nor the children and is as much informed by the environmental context in which it is situated at any given time or place. All of these factors (and more) come together to construct knowledge not as concrete or objective facts, but as ways of being and knowing. Playful research methods hide the *serious* side of being adult and at the very least present a relationship that is dressed in a narrative pretence where players collectively engineer their actions, not as *fake* ways of engaging with each other, but as genuine imagined ways of being and knowing.

Acknowledgement

This work was funded by the European Regional Development Fund Program 2007–13 and the European Social Fund Convergence Program for Cornwall and the Isles of Scilly, UK.

Note

1 Eden is an educational garden and environmental charity created in an exhausted quarry in the china clay mining area of Cornwall, UK.

References

Aitken, S. C. (2001). Playing with children: Immediacy was their cry. *The Geographical Review*, *91*(1–2), 496–508.

Alcock, S. (2013). Toddler's complex communication: Playfulness from a secure base. *Contemporary Issues in Early Childhood*, *14*(2), 179–191.

Angen, M. J. (2000). Evaluating interpretive inquiry: Reviewing the validity debate and opening dialogue. *Qualitative Health Research*, *10*(3), 378–395.

Bairaktarova, D., Evangelou, D., Bagiati, A., & Brophy, S. (2011). Early engineering in young children's exploratory play with tangible materials. *Children, Youth and Environments*, *21*(2), 212–235.

Barnett, L. A. (1998). The adaptive powers of being playful. In M. C. Duncan, G. Chick, & A. Aycock (Eds.), *Diversions and divergences in fields of play* (pp. 97–120). Greenwich, CT: Ablex Publishing.

Barnett, L. A. (2007). The nature of playfulness in young adults. *Personality and Individual Difference*, *43*(4), 949–958.

Bateson, P. & Martin, P. (2013). *Play, playfulness, creativity and Innovation*. Cambridge: Cambridge University Press.

Bateson, P. & Nettle, D. (2014). Playfulness, ideas, and creativity: A survey. *Creativity Research Journal*, *26*(2), 219–222.

Brooker, L., Blaise, M., & Edwards, S. (2014). Contexts for play and learning. In L. Brooker, M. Blaise, & S. Edwards (Eds.), *The SAGE handbook of play and learning in early childhood* (pp. 1–4). London: SAGE.

Brown, F. (2008). The playwork principles: A critique. In F. Brown & C. Taylor (Eds.), *Foundations of playwork* (pp. 123–127). Berkshire: McGraw-Hill & Open University Press.

Bruner, J. (1990). *Acts of meaning*. Cambridge, MA: Harvard University Press.

Bruner, J. S., Jolly, A., & Sylva, K. (1976). *Play: Its role in development and evolution*. London: Penguin.

Burghardt, G. M. (2005). *The genesis of animal play: Testing the limits*. Cambridge, MA: MIT Press.

Castillo, J. (2002). A note on the concept of tacit knowledge. *Journal of Management Inquiry*, *11*(1), 46–57.

Chilton, T. (2013). *Adventure playgrounds – A brief history*. [Pamphlet]. Bognor Regis: Fair Play for Children.

Corsaro, W. A. & Molinari, L. (2000). Entering and observing in children's worlds: A reflection on a longitudal ethnography of early education in Italy. In P. H.

Christensen & A. James (Eds.), *Research with children: Perspectives and practices* (pp. 239–259). London: Falmer Press.

Edmiston, B. (2008). *Forming ethical identities in early childhood play*. London and New York: Routledge.

Elkind, D. (2007). *The power of play: How spontaneous, imaginative activities lead to happier, healthier children*. Cambridge, MA: Da Capo Press.

Else, P. (2009). *The value of play*. London: Continuum.

Fleer, M. (2015). Pedagogical positioning in play – Teachers being inside and outside of children's imaginary play. *Early Child Development and Care, 185*(11–12), 1801–1814.

Foucault, M. (1980). *Power/knowledge: Selected interviews and other writings, 1972–77* (trans. C. Gordon, L. Marshall, J. Mepham, & K. Soper). New York: Pantheon Books.

Frampton, I. J., Jenkin, R., & Waters, P. (2015). Researching the benefits of the outdoor environment for children. In S. Hay (Ed.), *Early years education and care: New issues for practice from research* (pp. 125–140). London: Routledge.

Freire, P. (1970). *Pedagogy of the oppressed*. London: Penguin.

Frimberger, K. (2013). *Towards a Brechtian research pedagogy for intercultural education: Cultivating intercultural spaces of experiment through drama*. Unpublished doctoral thesis, Glasgow: University of Glasgow

Fromberg, D. (1992). A review of research on play. In C. Seefeldt (Ed.), *The early childhood curriculum: A view of current research* (pp. 42–84). New York: Teachers College Press.

Gadda, A. (2008). *Rights, Foucault and power: A critical analysis of the United Nation Convention on the Rights of the Child*. University of Edinburgh: Edinburgh Working Papers in Sociology.

Graue, M. E. & Walsh, D. J. (1998). *Studying children in context: Theories, methods, and Ethics*. Thousand Oaks, CA and London: SAGE.

Heidegger, M. (1962). *Being and time* (trans. J. Macquarrie & E. Robinson). New York: Harper and Row.

Howard, J., Bellin, W., & Rees, V. (2002). *Eliciting children's perceptions of play and exploiting playfulness to maximise learning in the early years classroom*. Paper presented at the BERA Annual Conference, Exeter.

Hughes, B. (1990). Children's play – A forgotten right. *Environment and Urbanization, 2*(2), 58–64.

Hughes, B. (2001). *Evolutionary playwork and reflective analytic practice*. London: Routledge.

Hughes, B. (2002a). *A playworker's taxonomy of play types* (2nd ed.). London: Play Education.

Hughes, B. (2002b). *The first claim – Desirable processes: A framework for advanced playwork quality assessment*. Cardiff: PlayWales.

Hughes, B. (2006). *Playtypes: Speculations and possibilities*. London: London Centre for Playwork Education and Training.

Kilvington, J. & Wood, A. (2010). *Reflective playwork: For all who work with children*. London: Continuum.

King, P. & Howard, J. (2014). Factors influencing children's perceptions of choice within their free play activity: The impact of functional, structural and social affordances. *Journal of Playwork Practice, 1*(2), 173–185.

Lahman, M. (2008). Always othered: Ethical research with children. *Journal of Early Childhood Research*, 6(3), 281–300.
Lester, S. & Russell, W. (2008). *Play for a change: Play, policy and practice: A review of contemporary perspectives – Summary report*. London: Play England.
Lester, S. & Russell, W. (2010). *Children's right to play: An examination of the importance of play in the lives of children worldwide*. Working Paper No. 57. The Hague, Netherlands: Bernard van Leer Foundation.
Lieberman, J. N. (1977). *Playfulness: Its relationship to imagination and creativity*. New York: Academic Press.
Lindqvist, G. (2001a). When small children play: How adults dramatise and children create meaning. *Early Years*, 21(1), 7–14.
Lindqvist, G. (2001b). Elusive play and its relation to power. *Focaal – European Journal of Anthropology*, 37, 13–23.
McGhee, P. E. (2010). *Humor: The lighter path to resilience and health*. Bloomington, IN: AuthorHouse.
McIntosh, J. (2006). How dancing, singing and playing shape the ethnographer: Research with children in a Balinese dance studio. *Anthropology Matters Journal*, 8(2), 1–17.
Mello, R. (2001). The power of storytelling: How oral narrative influences children's relationships in classrooms. *International Journal of Education and the Arts*, 2(1). Retrieved from www.ijea.org/v2n1/.
Merleau-Ponty, M. (2004). *The phenomenology of perception* (trans. C. Smith). London: Routledge.
Moran, D. (2000). *An introduction to phenomenology*. London: Routledge.
Moyles, J. R. (1989). *Just playing? The role and status of play in early childhood education*. Buckingham: Open University Press.
Neisser, U. (1993). Introduction. In U. Neisser (Ed.), *The perceived self: Ecological and interpersonal sources of self-knowledge* (pp. 3–21). New York: Cambridge University Press.
Newstead, S. (2010). A new definition of playwork? *Playwords*, 41, 12–13.
Newstead, S. (2015). Editorial. *Journal of Playwork Practice*, 2(2), 113–114.
Nicolini, D. (2010). Practice as the site of knowing: Insights from the field of telemedicine. *Articles in Advance Organization Science*, 22(3), 602–620.
O'Brien, J. C. & Duren, G. J. (2011). Play and playfulness. In J. W. Solomon & J. C. O'Brien (Eds.), *Pediatric skills for occupational therapy assistants* (3rd ed., pp. 390–413). Atlanta, GA: Elsevier Inc.
Playwork Principles Scrutiny Group. (2005). *Playwork principles*. Retrieved from www.playwales.org.uk/login/uploaded/documents/Playwork%20Principles/playwork%20principles.pdf.
Proyer, R. T. (2012). Examining playfulness in adults: Testing its correlates with personality, positive psychological functioning, goal aspirations, and multi-methodically assessed ingenuity. *Psychological Test and Assessment Modeling*, 54(2), 24.
Proyer, R. T. (2014a). Perceived functions of playfulness in adults: Does it mobilize you at work, rest, and when being with others? *European Review of Applied Psychology*, 64(5), 241–250.
Proyer, R. T. (2014b). A psycho-linguistic approach for studying adult playfulness: A replication and extension toward relations with humour. *The Journal of Psychology*, 148(6), 717–735.

Punch, S. (2002). Research with children: The same or different from research with adults? *Childhood*, 9(3), 321–341.

Qian, X. L. & Yarnal, C. (2011). The role of playfulness in the leisure stress-coping process among emerging adults: An SEM analysis. *Leisure/Loisir*, 35(2), 191–209.

Rautio, P. (2013). Mingling and imitating in producing spaces for knowing and being: Insights from a Finnish study of child-matter intra-action. *Childhood*, 21(4), 461–474.

Reddy, V. (1991). *Playing with others expectations: Teaching and mucking about in the first year*. Oxford: Blackwell.

Rosa, E. D. (2011). The creative role of playfulness in development. *Infant Observation*, 14(2), 203–217.

Roskos, K. & Christie, J. (2011). The play-literacy nexus and the importance of evidenced-based techniques in the classroom. *American Journal of Play*, 4(2), 204–224.

Russell, W. K. (2013). *The dialectics of playwork: A conceptual and ethnographic study of playwork using cultural historical activity theory*. Unpublished doctoral dissertation,Gloucestershire: University of Gloucestershire

Ryan-Bloomer, K. & Candler, C. (2013). Playfulness of children at home and in the hospital. *International Journal of Play*, 2(3), 237–253.

Santer, J., Griffiths, C., & Goodall, D. (2007). *Free play in early childhood: A literature review*. London: Play England.

Siemens, G. (2006). *Knowing knowledge*. Retrieved 23 January, 2014, from www.elearnspace.org/knowingknowledge_LowRes.pdf.

Skard, G. & Bundy, A. C. (2008). Test of playfulness. In L. D. Parham & L. S. Fazio (Eds.), *Play in occupational therapy for children* (2nd ed., pp. 71–93). St Louis, MO: Mosby Elsevier.

Snowden, D. (2002). Complex acts of knowing: Paradox and descriptive self-awareness. *Journal of Knowledge Management*, 6(2), 100–111.

Sturrock, G. (2003). *The Ludic third*. London: Ludemos Press.

Sturrock, G. & Else, P. (1998). 'The Colorado Paper' – The playground as therapeutic space: Playwork as healing. In G. Sturrock & P. Else (Eds.) (2007), *Therapeutic playwork reader one* 1995–2000 (pp. 73–104). Eastleigh, Hampshire: Common Threads.

Sturrock, G., Russell, W., & Else, P. (2004). *Towards Ludogogy, Parts l, ll and lll: The art of being and becoming through play*. Leigh-on-Sea: Ludemos.

Tegano, D. W. & Moran, J. D. (2007). Play and creativity: The role of the intersubjective adult. In D. J. Sluss & O. S. Jarrett (Eds.), *Investigating play in the 21st century: Play and cultural studies* (Vol. 7, pp. 175–187). Lanham, MA: University Press of America, INC.

Thomson, S. (2014). 'Adulterated play': An empirical discussion surrounding adults' involvement with children's play in the primary school playground. *Journal of Playwork Practice*, 1(1), 5–21.

Turner, V. (1992). *Blazing the trail: Way marks in the exploration of symbols*. Tucson & London: The University of Arizona Press.

Waters, P. (2011). Trees talk: Are you listening? nature, narrative and children's anthropocentric place-based play. *Children, Youth and Environments*, 21(1), 243–52.

Waters, P. (2014a). Into the woods: Stories and nature in playwork training. *Children, Youth and Environments*, 24(3), 221–235.

Waters, P. (2014b). Narrative journey: Storying landscapes for children's adventurous outdoor play and experiential learning. *Horizons*, *67*, 32–36.

Waters, P. (2014c). Tracking trolls and chasing pixies: Stories, creativity and children's outdoor experiential learning. *Departures in Critical Qualitative Research*, *3*(3), 236–260.

Waters, P. (2016). Stories in action at the zombie apocalypse training camp. *Permaculture*, (88), 8–12.

Waters, P. & Waite, S. J. (2016). Towards an ecological approach to ethics in visual research methods with children. In D. Warr, M. Guillemin, S. Cox, & J. Waycott (Eds.), *Ethics and visual research methods: Theory, methodology and practice*. London: Palgrave Macmillan.

Wilson, P. (2009). *The playwork primer*. College Park, MD: Alliance for Childhood.

Woodhead, M. & Faulkner, D. (2000). Subjects, objects or participants: Dilemas of psychological research with children. In P. H. Christensen & A. James (Eds.), *Research with children* (pp. 9–35). London: Falmer Press.

Wragg, M. (2013). Towards an inversion of the deficit model of intervention in children's play. *European Early Childhood Education Research Journal*, *21*(2), 283–291.

Yorke, J. (2013). *Into the woods: How stories work and why we tell them*. London: Penguin Books.

Youell, B. (2008). The importance of play and playfulness. *European Journal of Psychotherapy and Counselling*, *10*(2), 121–129.

6 Process, participation and reflection

How playwork practice influenced a mixed-methods approach to researching children's perception of choice in their play

Pete King

Introduction

In this chapter, I will argue that from a playwork perspective in researching play, there is a recognition of children's rights within the research, children having an active participation in some form and the need for adult reflection throughout the research process. I have been involved in children's play and playwork for 20 years as a practitioner, development officer, trainer and lecturer. Most of my professional work has been with children aged between five and 11 years. Throughout this time, professional playwork education, policy and practice has been underpinned by play being described as freely chosen, personally directed for no external goal (Joint National Committee on Training for Playwork (JNCTP), 1985). The description of play as freely chosen has been area of interest since my early days as a practitioner and as a student studying both play and playwork. It has also remained with me throughout my academic research. The notion of freely chosen play lacked any research evidence from a child's perspective. This lack of children's perception is not unique, as evident in educational policy development and policy implementation (Devine, 2000; Wood, 2004). This notion of freely chosen play from a child's perspective became the focus of my doctoral research.

Although children's behaviour has been studied and interpreted by adults and within early years, the research undertaken has often focused on easily observable aspects of play, for example, social play (Broadhead, 2006). As well as social play, this can also include pretend play, where the benefits of play meet other agendas, such as problem solving in education, the importance of physical play in children's health and the use of play in children's emotional well-being (play therapy) (Santer, Griffiths, & Goodall, 2007). However, as Smith, Takhvar, Gore, and Vollstedt (1986) point out "how we observe play may affect the kinds of play we record" (p. 40) and often, the research may not consider children's views. I was interested in children being actively involved as research participants in my doctoral research so that they were able to express their views.

Smith (1986) stated that the study of children's play focused on cognitive growth and creativity as important outcomes, particularly in areas of education.

During this period in the 1970s and 1980s, the growth of a new 'profession' in the United Kingdom arose in playwork (see the Introduction of this monograph). Playwork is about supporting children's play in non-educational environments (adventure playground, open access play and closed access, out of school clubs) with the emphasis that play should be freely chosen and not being focused on the educational benefits of play (Hughes, 2001). The focus of my research was children's perception of choice in their play with children aged between 6 to 12 years, an age group that has been termed middle childhood, which has been defined as "the period sandwiched between 'early years' and 'youth' that is generally associated with the primary school years" (Kellett & Ding, 2004, p. 161).

Researching children's perception of choice in their play meant involving children in the research as much as possible, not as passive objects, but as active participants. Involving children had been a key aspect of my playwork practice, where children were encouraged to participate and be involved in consultation about all aspects of their playwork provision. One common tool for which I adopted was Hart's (1992) Ladder of Participation.

The problem of devising innovative research using child participants, particularly in the very subjective area of children's play, poses problems, particularly in relation to the reliability and validity of the research process and subsequent results. Alderson and Morrow (2004) identify three aspects that the researcher needs to focus on when designing research that involves children. These are the research relationships (for example, listening skills), power (for example, respecting children's rights and interests) and emotions (for example, being aware of your own feelings). In addition, research can be influenced by the researcher's own personal experience of childhood and their personal and professional experience as an adult (Greig & Taylor, 1999). This points to the need for the researcher to adopt a reflective stance throughout the research process, just as the playwork practitioner should be doing throughout their professional practice (Kilvington & Wood, 2010).

This chapter has provided a rare but thoughtful opportunity to consider the relationship between my playwork practice and undertaking doctoral research. It identifies three aspects which link my professional practice as a playworker and my academic research into children's play. These three aspects are:

1   Process: the play process and the research process;
2   Participation: children's participation in practice and in research;
3   Reflection: play process reflection and research process reflexion.

This chapter discusses these three aspects: firstly, from the perspective of how they shaped and developed my playwork practice and how this informed and influenced my research.

Major influences on my playwork practice

As a playwork practitioner, three distinct factors have had a huge influence upon my professional practice. The first was the playwork focus on the process of play, rather than play as an outcome (Howard & King, 2015; Neumann, 1971). The second factor has been regarding participation and consultation with children, accessing children's views and opinions regarding their right to play, as identified within Article 31 of the United National Convention on the Rights of the Child (UNCRC) (United Nations International Children's Emergency Fund (UNICEF), 2009). The third element has been how the adult (playworker) reflects and interprets their position in the child's play cycle when involved in a child's play (Sturrock, 2003; Sturrock, 1999; Sturrock & Else, 1998). These three influences on my playwork practice are discussed in more detail below.

The process of play

The process of play is complex and includes both observable actions and private thoughts (Sturrock, 2003; 1999). Within playwork, the process of play has been conceptualised in the form of a play cycle (Sturrock & Else, 1998). The play cycle involves a signal, or play cue to emerge from the child which can be 'picked up' by another person (child or adult), where the response to the play cue (or play return) is returned back to where the play cue was initiated. The play cue and play return are only two components of the play cycle and other aspects including time, the frame (the specific space) and the loop and flow. For the playworker, the important aspect is how the play cycle, the process of play, is supported (Playwork Principles Scrutiny Group (PPSG), 2005).

The focus on the process of play is conceptualised in the definition of play in policy and strategy developed within each country of the United Kingdom and Republic of Ireland (except England, which has no play policy or strategy) and in the Playwork Principles (PPSG, 2005). These policies and strategies, alongside the Playwork Principles, are based on a definition of play being freely-chosen by the child (Garvey, 1977; Hughes, 2001). This is an adult-generated definition of play (King & Howard, 2014a), which is based on rhetoric (what has been written so it must be true), with little research from a child's perspective as to whether being freely chosen is a defining characteristic which children consider in their play. This was the aspect of my professional practice which first came to light when delivering playwork training, in considering whether freely chosen play is possible for children, when often their 'free play' is situated within a specific slot in a time-table. It is common for pre-school and primary schools in the UK to allocate a time-slot for free play, and it is not uncommon for this to also occur in playwork environments, which appears both controlling and contradictory to play being freely chosen.

Participation

In 1989, the United Nations (UN) passed the United Nations Convention on the Rights of the Child (UNCRC). This is an agreement stating the civil, political, economic, social and cultural rights of every child, regardless of their race, religion or abilities (Jones, 2011). The UK Government ratified the UNCRC in

1992, and it therefore fell onto those working with children and young people in the 1990s in specific areas to implement the relevant 54 rights in their practice. Three articles in particular had a major impact on playwork practice: Article 31 the right to play, Article 12 (freedom of having views) and Article 13 (freedom of expression). With respect to playworkers being an advocate of children's play on adult-led agendas (PPSG, 2005, Playwork Principle no. 4), advocacy involves both consultation and participation to obtain children's views of play. Support for how to consult and involve children in participating in their playwork environments was provided by Hart's (1992) Ladder of Participation in the PlayTrain publication 'Article 31 Action Pack' (Shier, 1995), and by a re-working of this the Ladder of Participation in the Save the Children publication 'Empowering Children and Young People' (Treseder, 1997).

These two aspects of consultation and participation were important when being an advocate for children and young people's play. Hart's (1992) Ladder of Participation placed the level of participation with children on a continuum from non-participation (manipulation, decoration and tokenism), passive participation (adult-initiated, shared decisions with children) to full active participants (child-initiated, shared decision with adults). These three aspects of the right to play, the right to having views and opinions and a right to share them in addition to Hart's (1992) Ladder of Participation strongly influenced my professional practice. For example, whilst managing the play service in Cheltenham, I organised a children's rights conference in Cheltenham (King, 2002), where four groups of children and young people carried out play research in their local communities, supported by an adult keyworker, and shared their views to an audience of adults. The structure of how each adult keyworker supported the play research was based on Hart's (1997) book *Child Participation*. The level of participation involved the adult initiating and supporting each group of children, although the children were active participants in the collection of data and analysis as well as with the design and delivery of their conference presentation. The conference showed that children, when supported, can research and present their views of play to adults and that children's voices are important to help develop professional playwork practice.

Since the 1989 UNCRC, children have been involved in consultation and participation of their playwork space, and as the importance of Article 31 has been further highlighted with the UN General Comment (UN, 2013). This type of consultation and participation of children in their playwork environments has been challenged by Hughes (2001), who believes that in practice, participation and consultation is not necessarily to meet the needs of children and young people, but to meet an adult agenda of adhering to work-enforced policies and procedures. According to Hughes (2001), this appeared to overshadow the primary role of the playworker in supporting the play process where "more than democracy, more than participation, more than equal opportunities, the playworker's first motive has to be to ensure children in play can engage in a developing world that is controlled by them" (p. 166–167). Within the social construction of childhood, where play is integral to childhood (Mayall, 2002) and children are co-constructors of their lives (James & Prout, 1997), the adult view of play made me question if, as adults, we were representing children and young people's views of freely-chosen play correctly. This could only be explored by consultation with children.

Being reflective in the play process

Reflective practice is the process for the practitioner to link theory and practice to aid their learning (Kolb, 1984) where reflection in playwork practice is essential (Hughes, 2001; Kilvington & Wood, 2010). One aspect of reflection that was particularly of interest in my practice was how the adult continually reflected upon their position when supporting children's play. This continual reflection relates to the concept of proposed by Schön (1991) as reflection in action. This self-awareness of practice has been described as the 'witness position' or 'watcher self' (Sturrock, 2003; 1999; Sturrock & Else, 1998), which involves playworkers continually self-evaluating their professional practice, reflecting both the objectivity of their professional work, whilst also considering their own subjectivity. If play is a key aspect of childhood (Mayall, 2002), then everybody has a childhood with their own subjective and personal play experiences. It is commonly believed in playwork that childhood experiences influence playwork practice (Cole, Maegusuku-Hewett, Trew, & Cole, 2006). Therefore, if a person's own childhood play experience may influence practice, then it may be possible a playworker's work experience could influence how they research.

This section has explained how the processes of play, participation and reflection have shaped and influenced my professional practice as a playworker. These three aspects are now discussed in relation to the research process, research design and reflexivity and to my doctoral research.

The research process

The topic of choice in and play can be considered in both objective and subjective terms, for both the researcher and the participants. For the researcher, their ontological perspective (how they view reality) will influence how they undertake the research process with regards to taking an 'outsider' objective approach or an 'insider' subjective approach (Kerstetter, 2012). Whether taking an objective or subjective stance, any research involving children has to ensure that an ethical approach underpins the whole research process (Alderson & Morrow, 2004). This would include the researcher having an understanding of childhood (Alderson, 2005; Farell, 2005) and how they react to childhood (David, Tonkin, Powell, & Anderson, 2005). As play is integral to childhood (Mayall, 2002), then the researcher's understanding of play is another consideration that needs to be taken into account. My perspective of play has been influenced by my playwork practice.

The study of children's perception of choice in their play had to involve research methods that did not rely on observational judgements by adults, as this will often be based on inferential perspectives of play (Smith & Vollstedt, 1985), which involves making claims based on what the adult observes. To avoid making any claims and assumptions about children's perceived choice in their play, it was important to obtain the views of children themselves. James (2007) states that during the 1980s and 1990s, where childhood was considered more as a social construction (James & Prout, 1997), children emerged as social actors and were encouraged to speak out. However, James (2007) questions the authenticity of using children's voices in research with respect to how children's perspectives are presented and particularly how childhood is understood. The epistemological approach in my PhD research required careful consideration into which method was appropriate, particularly as different research paradigms exist. Thomas Kuhn (1970) defined paradigms as "some accepted examples of actual scientific practice-examples which include law, theory, application, and instrumentation together-provided models from which spring particular coherent traditions of scientific research" (p. 10).

Paradigm models are copied within any given field and compete with each other (Tashakkori & Teddlie, 1998). Historically, this has been the case in relation to the paradigms of quantitative and qualitative research where the former is objective with knowledge based on generalised observable facts, whilst the latter is subjective and based on individual experience and perception (Bryman, 2004). Researching children's perception of choice in their play had to consider these two different paradigms, particularly whether children are being used as objects or subjects of research (Woodhead & Faulkner, 2000). In addition, the social construction of childhood has seen a move from children being viewed more as participants in research, rather than as subjects or objects (Kellet & Ding, 2004). This aspect of considering children to be research participants has a clear resonance with my understanding of playwork practice in line with Hart's (1992) Ladder of Participation, where playworkers obtained children's views to influence their playwork practice. As with playwork practice, children can also have a participatory role within the research process. This was considered within my doctoral study.

Both quantitative and qualitative approaches to research have their individual strengths and weaknesses. In recent years, a combined quantitative and qualitative approach to research has evolved (Armitage, 2007; Burke Johnson, & Onwuegbuzie, 2004). This has been termed as mixed-methods research or the third paradigm (Burke Johnson, & Onwuegbuzie, 2004). Mixed-methods research is being increasingly used to gain children's views (Mason & Hood, 2010) and is an approach that stands midway between objectivity and subjectivity or intersubjectivity (Torstenson-Ed, 2007).

In my doctoral study, a mixed-methods approach was used and involved a quantitative exploratory study where children were active participants in collecting their own data in the first part of the research. The second part of the research developed from these initial results and involved both a quantitative quasi-experiment and the undertaking of qualitative interviews. Here, children were more passive participants in the research. The mixed-methods approach reflected different aspects of Hart's (1992) Ladder of Participation. For the exploratory study, children were active participants in collecting their own data for my research reflecting Hart's (1992) assigned but informed. The quasi-experiment and interviews saw children as passive participants, using a Play Choice Scale and answering questions to provide their views and opinions. Although passively participating, the use of interviews to obtain the views of children reflected Articles 12 and 13 of the UNCRC.

The involvement of children in the research process often focuses on data collection. However, the analysis is undertaken by the researcher, and as Woodhead and Faulkner (2000) point out, transcribing and analysing children's data tend to reflect the adult research questions rather than the child's experience. This important point is now discussed in relation to critical realism and critical theory.

Critical realism and critical theory

Combining a quantitative and qualitative paradigm using a mixed-methods approach to research involved both critical realism (Bhaskar, 1975) and critical theory (Cohen, Manion, & Morrison, 2003). Originally developed by Roy Bhaskar (1975), "critical realism adopts a stratified ontology across three domains: the real, the actual and the empirical" (Downward, 2006, pp. 508–509) and considers the internal and external relations between objects and events (Yeung, 1997). Critical theory is concerned with oppressions and inequality in society and seeks to "emancipate the disempowered, to redress inequality and to promote individual freedoms within a democratic society" (Cohen et al., 2003, p. 28). Grover (2004) states the importance of giving voice to the vulnerable, rather than meeting the political and social agendas of others. The approach of critical theory had clear resonance with the aspect of consultation, participation and advocacy as a playwork practitioner, particularly as inequality exists in children's role in society (Mayall, 2002). As a play advocate, this often involved interpreting children's views when undertaking consultation and evaluating children's play experiences. This is an important consideration within critical theory, as Bryman (1992) states that any understanding of reality is likely to be provisional. Whilst critical theory provides the opportunity for participants to voice their views, as James (2007) points out, children's views may be translated by adults in what they feel is normal for childhood. Critical realism and critical theory enable consideration of both the subjective nature of researching play and the objectivity of research.

Taking into account the subjective nature of researching children's play, a critical realism epistemology and critical theory were important when considering the aspects of data collection, analysis and interpretation. Within the mixed-methods approach used, children were involved in data collection. This involved children collecting their own data as well as being interviewed; however, both the analysis and interpretation of all the data were undertaken by an adult (the researcher).

The subjective nature of both the researcher and the research participants in relation to the objectivity of the research can also be considered with regards to playwork practice. Sturrock (2003) and Sturrock and Else (1998) have considered the adult's position within the play cycle of the child, where the adult's subjective knowledge and experience of play needs to be considered with respect to the objectivity of their work. In the research process, the researcher needs to consider their position with regards to both data collection and data analysis. Taking this point in relation to researching children's play, the subjectivity and objectivity within research has a major influence on the ontological (reality), epistemological (knowledge), methodological (design) and methods (research tools) used in conducting research and the subsequent analysis and interpretation, or in other words, on the research design.

Research design

As Kellett and Ding (2004) state, the challenge with regards to research design when conducting research with children is to "find appropriate techniques that neither exclude nor patronise children" (p. 165). According to Punch (2002), the challenge is to strike a balance between not patronising children and recognising their competencies while maintaining their enjoyment of being involved with the research and facilitating their ability to communicate their view of the world. This can be achieved by using innovative methods as:

> Innovative methods can be more interesting and fun (for the children and the researcher). However, they should be referred to as 'research-friendly' or 'person-friendly' techniques, rather than the patronizing term 'child-friendly'.
> (Punch, 2002, p. 337)

These challenges reflect those posed in the playworker's role when consulting children for their views and how they express them (Articles 12 and 13 of the UNCRC). This is reflected in the initial two Playwork Assumptions and the 12 Playwork Values (Bonel & Lindon, 1996). The two Playwork Assumptions focused on play being freely chosen and the adult role in supporting this. The 12 Values included aspects such as empowering children and children being at the centre of the process and consider the legal framework of equal opportunities and health and safety. In 2005, the two Playwork Assumptions and 12 Playwork Values were then superseded by the eight Playwork Principles (PPSG, 2005) (see Introduction in this monograph).

The research design encompassed Bronfenbrenner's Ecological Systems (1986) concept, which has been considered within playwork practice (see Lester & Russell, 2004) and Bronfenbrenner's bio-ecological model for research (1995, 1999). This study focused on the central element of Bronfenbrenner's ecological system (1986), the microsystem. The microsystem is the complex interrelations within the immediate setting and is "a pattern of activities, roles, and interpersonal relations experienced by the developing person in a given setting with particular physical and material characteristics" (Bronfenbrenner, 1986, p. 7).

Bronfenbrenner's (1995, 1999) bio-ecological model for research involves two propositions. The first is the complex interaction between persons, object and symbols in its immediate external environment, referred to as proximal processes, and the second, the form, power, content and direction of these proximal processes. Bronfenbrenner stated that when both aspects are investigated in research design it is referred to as a "process-person-context-time model (PPCT)" (Bronfenbrenner, 1995, p. 621). The process-person-context-time concept allowed factors both within and outside the child's play environment to be taken into account and provided the 'lens' with which to construct the research design within the research process, fitting in with a critical realism and critical theory approach. Bronfenbrenner (1995) explained the complexity of the process-person-context-time process in relation to human development:

> Human development takes place through processes of progressively more complex reciprocal interaction between an active, evolving biopsychological human organism and the persons, objects, and symbols in its immediate external environment. To be effective, the interaction must occur on a fairly regular basis over extended periods of time. Such enduring forms of interaction in the immediate environment are referred to as proximal processes.
> (Bronfenbrenner, 1995, p. 620)

This research placed play and the play activity as the process, children as the person and the three play environments of home, school playground and out of school club as the cross-sectional time the data was collected. The research design incorporated the main themes from the dynamic play model (Miller & Kuhaneck, 2008), the impact of playground design (Barbour, 1999) and a classification of choice (Deci & Ryan, 1985). This provided the framework for the research design which was a two phase mixed-methods sequential study. The first study was an exploratory quantitative questionnaire, the Play Detective Diary, and the results were used to develop the second study. The research tool that was developed for the quantitative exploratory study took into consideration how the data was to be collected and the relationship between the child participants and the researcher. Punch (2002) stated:

> Children tend to lack experience of communicating directly with unfamiliar adults in a one-to-one situation, a more innovative approach such as using task-based methods can enable children to feel more comfortable with an adult researcher.
> (p. 330)

A playful approach in research has been used within children's learning (Howard, 2002), in architectural schools (Rice, 2009) and considered to be an important characteristic in early years teaching practice (Howard & King, 2015). A playful approach to data collection was used which reflected playwork practice. Wilson (2009) makes reference to the "quirky playfulness of the playworkers themselves" (p. 2), which is an important factor in their professional practice (Howard & McInnes, 2013). Playfulness within playwork practice was reflected in the research process of both study one and study two. This was achieved using the Play Detective Diary, the Play Choice Scale within the Manipulation of Affordance Scenario Task (MAST) quasi-experiment and a playful approach which has been used in other areas of children's play (McInnes, Howard, Miles, & Crowley, 2009).

Both studies one and two were developed in relation to the contextual characteristics (the three play environments where each study was carried out of home, school playground and out of school club), child characteristics (social aspect of the child whether playing alone or with other people), strategies (perceived levels of choice), interviewing conditions (Play Detective Diary and the MAST experiments and interviews) and the consequences (data collection and analysis). The research map is shown in Figure 6.1.

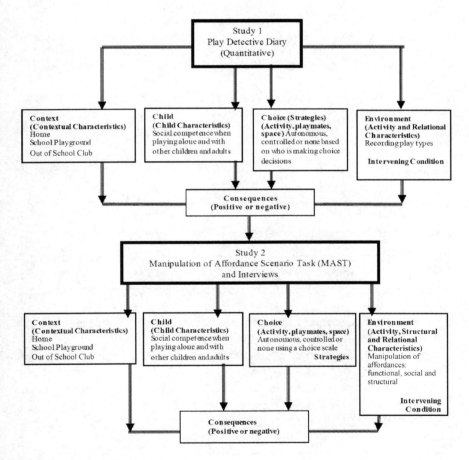

Figure 6.1 Research design map
Based on Barbour (1999), Deci and Ryan (1985) and Miller and Kuhaneck (2008)

The Play Detective Diary and MAST experiments developed for studies one and two, respectively, enabled both quantitative and qualitative data collection and analysis, where children were active participants in the former.

Play Detective Diary

The Play Detective Diary provided a playful approach to collect the data and analysis, as children were asked to be Play Detectives. The Play Detective Diary arose for the need to produce a research tool that was quick, easy and fun to use, in essence to be playful. The Play Detective Diary provided an innovative way of collecting quantitative data from children, in a playful but meaningful way where being a 'Play Detective' provided an approach that had some element of role-play. The collecting of data by the children themselves meant they had ownership of the diary.

Whilst not co-constructors of the research process, children did contribute to the development of the Play Detective Diary and were actively involved in the collection of data by completing their own Play Detective Diary. This relates to Hart's (1992) aspect of assigned but informed, as the design and instructions were by the adult, although data collection would be undertaken by the children themselves. An example of a diary sheet can be found in Figure 6.2.

A more detailed account of participants, results and analysis of the Play Detective Diary can be found in King and Howard (2014a).

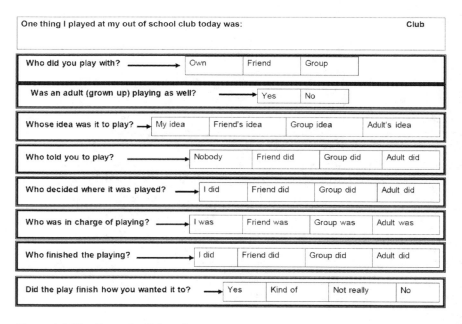

Figure 6.2 Play Detective Diary sheet

Manipulation of Affordance Scenario Task

The results from the quantitative exploratory study were used to develop the quasi-experiment, MAST and interviews. The MAST experiment was based on the concept of affordances (Gibson, 1986), which is about the interaction between the environment and the organisms where an affordance:

> Cuts across the dichotomy of subjective-objective and helps us to understand its inadequacy . . . it is both physical and psychical, yet neither. An affordance points both ways, to the environment and to the observer.
>
> (Gibson, 1986, p. 129)

The use of affordances has been studied in children's mobility in their local environments (Kyttä, 2002) and pre-school environments in the Scandinavian countries (Hyvönen & Juujärvi, 2005). An extensive review of outdoor play also considered the role of affordances and implications for playwork practice (Lester & Maudsley, 2006). For MAST, three types of affordances were manipulated: structural (environment), functional (activities within the environment) and social (people in the environment). The MAST quasi-experiment involved children being passive participants. Children provided a score value of choice in their favourite play activity at home, in the school playground and the out of school club which provided a baseline score for each play environment. For each play environment, the play was subjected to a series of manipulations and upon each manipulation the level of choice was re-scored by the child participant.

The MAST quasi-experiment required the use of photographs to stimulate responses, which can be a powerful tool to use in experimental research (Howard, 2002). The photographs chosen for MAST were used in conjunction with a Play Choice Scale which children could manipulate to provide a numerical value on their perceived level of choice. The Play Choice Scale was made of cardboard and the numbers coloured in using colouring pencils with a value of 0 (no choice) up to 10 (all the choice). The reason for this was to make the Play Choice Scale look less like a 'formal mathematical tool', such as a slide rule, but try and keep in with the experiment as a playful activity which children could explore and investigate (see Figure 6.3). It was interesting to note that when children entered

Figure 6.3 The Play Choice Scale

the room to begin the MAST quasi-experiment, the first thing they noticed was this scale which they picked up and explored.

Children were shown a set of stock photographs which represented typical environments to play at home, on the school playground and in the out of school club. For each photograph, children were asked to state their favourite play activity and where they would play and, using the Play Choice Scale, provide a numerical value between 0 and 10 on how much choice they perceived to have. This provided a baseline value of choice for each environment. Using each photograph and their favourite play activity identified with each one, children were then asked a series of set questions that would cause a potential change in their play. Two questions related to the manipulation of the play space to represent structural affordances. Two questions related to the manipulation of the play activity which reflected functional affordances (types of play) and six questions manipulated social affordances by introducing other people into the activity. After each manipulation, children were asked to use the Play Choice Scale to score for their level of choice. The purpose of manipulating the structural, functional and social affordances was to see if their level of perceived choice changed from their baseline score. Reasons for children's baseline and any change in choice were gained through conducting and recording interviews simultaneously when undertaking the MAST quasi-experiment. Further details of the MAST quasi-experiment and interviews can be found in King and Howard (2014b).

Being reflective in the research process: reflexivity

Reflexivity should be a central part of the research process where researchers critically reflect not only on their role and their assumptions (Davies, 2008), but also on the choice of methods and their application (Punch, 2002) and the relationship with the participants (Alderson & Morrow, 2004). As highlighted earlier, research often reflects the adult research question, not necessarily the child's experience (Woodhead & Faulkner, 2000). This dualism between child data and adult understanding contributes to the need for a reflective approach by the researcher. Reflexivity was an important consideration in all aspects of my research process. Reflexivity allows the researcher to consider the narrative of research and how their personal life interacts with scholarship. It enables the researcher to reflect on their own subjectivities and professional practice (Davies, 2008). Sutton-Smith (1994) makes clear reference to the interaction of somebody's personal and academic life:

> I have reached that point in life when the scholarly pretence of impersonality is no longer a convincing disguise for myself. It is my belief, furthermore, that a central issue in social science at this time is to understand the way in which the narrative of the investigator's personal life interacts with his or her scholarship.
>
> (p. 3)

Sutton-Smith is making reference here to the subjective–objective nature of research. If how we played can have an influence on our practice as suggested (Cole et al., 2006), it is then not unconceivable that our professional practice could influence our research. For the researcher, this is important as their own subjectivity could influence the research process. This process of self-reference in research is termed reflexivity (Davies, 2008). Babcock (1980) stated reflexivity involves a number of dichotomies: private/public, individual/collective, implicit/explicit, and partial/total. These dualisms need to be considered in relation to professional practice and undertaking research.

The reflexive nature of research, for both the quantitative and qualitative research design and implementation, meant being aware of my position in the whole research process. The aspect of reflexivity mirrored the concept of the 'witness position' (Sturrock, 2003; Sturrock & Else, 1998). The witness position is where during playwork practice, the playworker is continuously reflecting on their own thoughts, feelings and reverie when in a play cycle with children, being aware of their own subjectivity, but working objectively. This clearly also applies to researching children's play where, as discussed earlier, the subjective–objective aspect play can make it a difficult topic to study where the researchers experience of play as a child may influence the research. For the researcher who was previously a playworker, this could also be a subjective influence on the research. This clearly relates to the comment by Sutton-Smith on the recognition of the interaction of his personal and academic life.

Conclusion

This chapter focused on three aspects that have informed my playwork practice, and in turn, shaped my doctoral research. The three aspects are:

1   Process: the play process and the research process;
2   Participation: children's participation in practice and in research;
3   Reflection: play process reflection and research process reflexion.

Although it can be argued that these three aspects apply to all aspects of research, from a playwork perspective, it is worthy of consideration on how they interact with each other, and to what degree. Reflecting through my PhD and my professional practice, I have traced this back to being an advocate in supporting children's right to play (Article 31) and for children to have a voice and express their voice (Article 12 and Article 13) in supporting their play in a playwork environment. For me, this is the playwork perspective in researching play: recognising children's rights within the research process which includes children's active participation in some form, and the adults reflecting on their research throughout the research process. This last part on reflection is about recognising that research, as with policies and procedures, is adult-generated, and care is required in the interpretation of children and young people's views. This was considered in relation to critical realism and critical theory epistemology of using a mixed-methods approach based on Bronfenbrenner's process-person-context-time concept.

Within the research literature, the growing trend that emerged out of the social construction of childhood in the 1990s (James & Prout, 1997) saw the growth of children being more actively engaged as participants in research. For me, researching play from a playwork perspective was a natural progression from being a practitioner to a researcher. Hart's (1992) Ladder of Participation is still a useful reference point to use within research design and data collection, even if it is nearly 25 years old. The arguments against children being involved in consultation and participation are sound, particularly as Hughes (2001) makes reference to adults can be "potential bullies" (p. 166) when involving children in consultation. Rather than it being voluntary, children may feel obliged to participate. However, research is about informed consent, non-cohesion and the right to withdraw, and the ethics of research have to ensure any participant involved in research are aware of these aspects. This applies to both professional practice as well as academic research and is particularly relevant for a subjective–objective topic subject as children's play.

References

Alderson, P. (2005). Designing ethical research with children. In A. Farell (Ed.), *Ethical research with children* (pp. 27–36). Maidenhead: Open University Press.

Alderson, P. & Morrow, V. (2004). *Ethics, social research and consulting with children and young people*. Essex: Barnardos.

Armitage, A. (2007). *Mutual research designs: Redefining mixed methods research design*. Paper presented at the British Educational Research Association Annual Conference. Retrieved from www.ethiopia-ed.net/images/1687236896.doc.

Babcock, B. A. (1980). Reflexivity: Definitions and discriminations. *Semiotica, 30*(1–2), 1–14.

Barbour, A. C. (1999). The impact of playground design on the play behaviours of children with differing levels of physical competence. *Early Childhood Research Quarterly, 14*(1), 75–98.

Bhaskar, R. (1975). *A realist theory of science*. Leeds: Leeds Books.

Bonel, P. & Lindon, J. (1996). *Good practice in playwork*. Cheltenham: Nelson Thornes Ltd.

Broadhead, P. (2006). Developing an understanding of young children's learning through play: The place of observation, interaction and reflection. *British Educational Research Journal, 32*(2), 191–207.

Bronfenbrenner, U. (1986). Ecology of the family as a context for human development: Research perspectives. *Developmental Psychology, 22*(6), 723–742.

Bronfenbrenner, U. (1995). Developmental ecology through space and time: A future perspective. In P. Moen, G. H. Elder Jr, & K. Luscher (Eds.), *Examining lives in context: Perspectives on the ecology of human development* (pp. 619–647). Washington, DC: American Psychological Association.

Bronfenbrenner, U. (1999). Environments in developmental perspective: Theoretical and operational models. In S. L. Friedman & T. D. Wachs (Eds.), *Measuring environment across the life span: Emerging methods and concepts* (pp. 3–28). Washington, DC: American Psychological Association Press.

Bryman, A. (1992). Quantitative and qualitative research: Further reflections on their integration. In J. Brannen (Ed.), *Mixing methods: Qualitative and quantitative research* (pp. 57–78). Aldershot: Avebury.

Bryman, A. (2004). *Social research methods* (2nd ed.). Oxford: Oxford University Press.

Burke Johnson, R. & Onwuegbuzie, A. J. (2004). Mixed methods research: A research paradigm whose time has come. *Educational Researcher, 33*(7), 14–26.

Cohen, L., Manion, L., & Morrison, K. (2003). *Research methods in education* (5th ed.). London: RoutledgeFalmer.

Cole, B. Maegusuku-Hewett, T. Trew, R., & Cole, D. (2006). *Do playworkers' childhood play experiences affect their playwork practice?: An exploratory study.* Cardiff: Cardiff Council.

David, T., Tonkin, J., Powell, S., & Anderson, C. (2005). Ethical aspects of power in research with children. In A. Farell (Ed.), *Ethical research with children* (pp. 124–137). Maidenhead; Open University Press.

Davies, C. A. (2008). *Relfexive ethnography: A guide to researching selves and others.* London: Routledge.

Deci, E. L. & Ryan, R. M. (1985). The general causality orientations scale: Self-determination in personality. *Journal of Research in Personality, 19,* 109–134.

Devine, D. (2000). Constructions of childhood in school: Power, policy and practice in Irish education. *International Studies in Sociology of Education, 10*(1), 23–41.

Downward, P. D. (2006). Transforming economics through critical realism: Themes and issues. The *Journal of Critical Realism, 5*(1), 139–182.

Farell, A. (2005). Ethics and research with children. In A. Farell (Ed.), *Ethical research with children* (pp. 1–14). Maidenhead: Open University Press.

Garvey, C. (1977). *Play* (Enlarged ed.). Cambridge, MA: Harvard University Press.

Gibson, J. J. (1986). *The ecological approach to perception.* London: Lawrence Erlbaum Associates.

Greig, A. & Taylor, J. (1999). *Doing research with children.* London: SAGE Publications.

Grover, S. (2004). Why won't they listen to us?: Giving power and voice to children on participating in social research. *Childhood, 11*(1), 81–93.

Hart, R. (1992). *Children's participation: From tokenism to citizenship.* Issue 4 of Innocenti Essays, UNICEF International Child Development Centre.

Hart, R. (1997). *Children's participation: The theory and practice of involving young citizens in community development and environmental care.* London: Routledge.

Howard, J. (2002). Eliciting children's perceptions of play using the activity apperception story procedure. *Early Child Development and Care, 172*(5), 489–502.

Howard, J. & King, P. (2015). Re-establishing early years practitioners as play professionals. In J. Moyles (Ed.), *The excellence of play* (4th ed., pp. 125–137). Maidenhead: Open University Press.

Howard, J. & McInnes, K. (2013). *The essence of play: A practice companion for professionals working with children and young people.* London: Routledge.

Hughes, B. (2001). *Evolutionary playwork and reflective analytic practice.* London: Routledge.

Hyvönen, P. & Juujärvi, M. (2005). Affordances of playful environment: A view of Finnish girls and boys. In P. Kommers & G. Richards (Eds.), *Proceedings of world conference on educational multimedia, hypermedia and telecommunications* (pp. 1563–1572). Chesapeake, VA: AACE. Retrieved from www.editlib.org/p/20301.

James, A. (2007). Giving voice to children's voices. *American Anthropologist, 109*(2), 263–272.

James, A. & Prout, A. (1997). A new paradigm for the sociology of childhood? Provenance, promise and problems. In A. James & A. Prout (Eds.), *Constructing and reconstructing childhood* (2nd ed., pp. 7–33). London: RoutledgeFalmer.

Joint National Committee on Training for Playwork. (1985). *Recommendations on training for playwork* (The Salmon Book). London: The Joint National Committee on Training for Playwork.

Jones, P. (2011). What are children's rights? Cotemporary developments and debates. In P. Jones & G. Walker (Ed.), *Children's rights in practice* (pp. 3–16). London: SAGE.

Kellett, M. & Ding, S. (2004). Middle childhood. In S. Fraser, V. Lewis, S. Ding, M. Kellett, & C. Robinson (Eds.), *Doing research with children and young people* (pp. 161–174). London; Sage.

Kerstetter, K. (2012). Insider, outsider or somewhere inbetween: The impact on researchers' identities on the community-based research process. *Journal of Rural Social Science, 27*(2), 99–117.

Kilvington, J. & Wood, A. (2010). *Reflective playwork: For all who work with children*. London: Continuum.

King, P. (2002). How to . . . put on a children's rights conference. *Playwords, 17*, 45–47.

King, P. & Howard, J. (2014a). Children's perceptions of choice in relation to their play at home, in the school playground and at the out-of-school club. *Children and Society, 28*(2), 116–127.

King, P. & Howard, J. (2014b). Factors influencing children's perceptions of choice within their free play activity: The impact of functional, structural and social affordances. *Journal of Playwork Practice, 1*(2), 173–190.

Kolb, D. A. (1984). *Experiential learning: Experience as the source of learning and development*. Englewood Cliffs, NJ: Prentice Hall.

Kuhn, T. S. (1970). *The structure of scientific revolutions*. Chicago: University of Chicago Press.

Kyttä, M. (2002). Affordances of children's environments in te context of cities, small towns, suburbs and rural villages in Finland and Belarus. *Journal of Environmental Psychology, 22,* 109–123.

Lester, S. & Maudsley, M. (2006). *Play, naturally: A review of children's natural play*. London: Children's Play Council.

Lester, S. & Russell, W. (2004). *Towards a curriculum for advanced playwork practice*. Joint National Committee on Training for Playwork Study Day (JNCTP).

Mason, J. & Hood, S. (2010). Exploring issues of children as actors in social research. *Children and Youth Services Review, 33*(4), 490–495.

Mayall, B. (2002). *Towards a sociology for childhood: Thinking from children's lives*. Buckingham: Open University Press.

McInnes, K., Howard, J., Miles, G., & Crowley, K. (2009). Behavioural differences exhibited by children when practicing a task under formal and playful conditions. *Educational and Child Psychology, 26*(2), 31–39.

Miller, E. & Kuhaneck, H. (2008). Children's perceptions of play experiences and the development of play preferences: A qualitative study. *American Journal of Occupational Therapy, 62*(4), 407–15.

Neumann, E. A. (1971). *The elements of play*. New York: MSS Information Corporation.
Playwork Principles Scrutiny Group. (2005). *Playwork principles*. Retrieved from www.playwales.org.uk/login/uploaded/documents/Playwork%20Principles/playwork%20principles.pdf.
Punch, S. (2002). Research with children: The same or different from research with adults? *Childhood*, *9*, 321–341.
Rice, L. (2009). Playful learning. *Journal for Education in the Built Environment*, *4*(2), 94–108.
Santer, J., Griffiths, C., & Goodall, D. (2007). *Free play in early childhood: A literature Review*. London: Play England/National Children's Bureau.
Schön, D. (1991). *The reflective practitioner*. Aldershot: Ashgate Publishing Ltd.
Shier, H. (Ed.). (1995). *Article 31 Action Pack: Children's rights and children's play*. Birmingham: Play-Train.
Smith, P. K. (1986). Play research and its applications: A current perspective. In P. K. Smith (Ed.), *Special aspects of education: 6 children's play: Research and practical applications* (pp. 1–16). London: Gordon and Breach.
Smith, P. K., Takhvar, M., Gore, N., & Volstedt, R. (1986). Play in young children: Problems of definition, categorisation and measurements. In P. K. Smith (Ed.), *Special aspects of education: 6 Children's play: Research and practical applications* (pp. 39–56). London: Gordon and Breach.
Smith, P. K. & Vollstedt, R. (1985). On defining play: An empirical study of the relationship between play and various play criteria. *Child Development*, *54*(4), 1042–1050.
Sturrock, G. (1999). The impossible science of the unique being. In P. Else & G. Sturrock (Ed.) (2005), *Therapeutic playwork reader one 1995–2000* (pp. 122–130). Eastleigh: Common threads Publications Ltd.
Sturrock, G. (2003). Towards a psycholudic definition of playwork. In F. Brown (Ed.), *Playwork: Theory and practice* (pp. 81–97). Buckingham: Open University Press.
Sturrock, G. & Else, P. (1998). 'The Colorado Paper' – The playground as therapeutic space: Playwork as healing. In P. Else & G. Sturrock (Ed.) (2005), *Therapeutic playwork reader one 1995–2000* (pp. 73–104). Eastleigh: Common threads Publications Ltd.
Sutton-Smith, B. (1994). Paradigms of intervention. In J. Hellendoorn, R. van der Kooij, & B. Sutton-Smith (Eds.), *Play and intervention* (pp. 3–22). New York: State University of New York Press.
Tashakkori, A. & Teddlie, C. (1998). *Mixed methodology combining qualitative and quantitative approaches*. London: Sage.
Torstenson-Ed, T. (2007). Children's life paths through preschool and school: Letting youths talk about their own childhood – Theoretical and methodological conclusions. *Childhood*, *14*(47), 47–66.
Treseder, P. (1997). *Empowering children and young people – Training manual: Promoting involvement in decision-making*. London: Save the Children.
United Nation Convention on the Rights of the Child. (2013). *General comment No. 17 (2013) on the right of the child to rest, leisure, play, recreational activities, cultural life and the arts (art. 31)*. Retrieved from http://tbinternet.ohchr.org/_layouts/treatybodyexternal/Download.aspx?symbolno=CRC%2fC%2fGC%2f17&Lang=e.
United Nations International Children's Emergency Fund. (2009). *A summary of the United Nations Convention on the Rights of the Child*. Retrieved from www.unicef.org.uk/tz/rights/convention.asp.

Wilson, P. (2010). *The playwork primer.* College Park, MD: Alliance for Childhood.

Wood, E. (2004). A new paradigm war: The impact of national curriculum policies on early childhood teachers' thinking and classroom practice. *Teaching and Teacher Education, 20,* 361–374.

Woodhead, M. & Faulkner, D. (2000). Subjects, objects or participants? Dilemmas of psychological research with children. In P. Christiansen & A. James (Eds.), *Research with children: Perspectives and practices* (pp. 10–39). London: Falmer Press/ Routledge.

Yeung, H. W. (1997). Critical realism and realist research in human geography: A method or a philosophy in search of a method? *Progress in Human Geography, 21*(1), 51–74.

7 Using action research to explore play facilitation in school-based school-age childcare settings

Eva Kane

Introduction

Playwork, it could be argued, is driven by a children's perspective on play, as described in the second Playwork Principle:

> Play is a process that is freely chosen, personally directed and intrinsically motivated. That is, children and young people determine and control the content and intent of their play, by following their own instincts, ideas and interests, in their own way for their own reasons.
>
> (Playwork Principles Scrutiny Group (PPSG), Playwork Principle no. 2)

This understanding of play as controlled by the players allows an instrumental view of play to be challenged. Play, when seen as being useful for something else than itself and having deferred benefits (instrumental), can be challenged by the idea that it is intrinsically motivated. It opens up opportunities for taking both the child's and the adult's views of play into account, where the child plays for fun and the adult also recognises the benefits of play. This opening up of play as 'more than' has influenced the way I designed the research described in this chapter. I wanted to work together with childcare staff to challenge our view of play and taken-for-granted practices. In this chapter, I will explain why I undertook action research to explore play in school-age childcare staff's practice and in what way this may be considered research from a playwork perspective.

School-age childcare is an unprecise term which I decided to use as a generic word when talking about what otherwise might be called leisure-time centres in Sweden and out of school clubs with a playwork ethos in England. This chapter is based on my doctoral thesis, 'Playing practices in school-age childcare: an action research project in Sweden and England' (Kane, 2015).

My journey from playwork to research

My research about play and playwork started with an attempt to understand what these concepts could mean. Since research involves avoiding assumptions, clarifying concepts and specifying the contexts in focus, I was quickly challenged to go beyond my preconceived understandings. I had spent very little time as an actual playworker, yet I had worked to support children's afterschool clubs in Belfast. Taking part in courses delivered by Bob Hughes at PlayBoard Northern Ireland gave me a first introduction to the theory of evolutionary playwork that he has developed (Hughes, 2001). I understood this theory as exploring the drive to play seemingly inherent in human life, as well as asking questions about how we can safeguard time and space for play in children's lives and what may happen if we don't. At the same time, PlayBoard, as an organisation promoting playwork practice in Northern Ireland and the UK (King, 2015), was driven by a view of play as a child's right in line with Article 31 of the United Nations Convention on the Rights of the Child (UNCRC) (United Nations (UN), 1989).

When I later started working for PlayBoard Northern Ireland, I became involved in training for staff that focused on play and specifically, outdoor play. I had previously been involved with adult learning in a non-formal context where it had been important to provide an environment based on experiential learning ideas (Kolb & Fry, 1975). I now found that this approach suited playwork training very well and that many other trainers and educators in the field seemed to employ similar theories to their work. I had also become involved with the introduction of a formal qualification, National Vocational Qualification (NVQ) in Playwork, in Northern Ireland (Kane, 2003). My previous experiences had led me to understand knowledge as something that develops in a specific context with specific people and that there were different and equally valuable forms of knowledge (see, for example, Wenger, 1998). The NVQ's used terms such as skills, knowledge and attitudes, and I had previously used terms such as practical, theoretical and tacit knowledge (Polanyi, 1958/1974). How playworkers developed all these types of knowledge as part of their practice, especially in relation to facilitating play, became a growing interest of mine.

As the PlayBoard project grew, there was also a need to evaluate it, or in other words, to assess the impact of the intervention. My team had developed a quality mark for afterschool/out of school settings that promoted outdoor and physically active play and healthy snacks. This quality mark included three training courses. We wanted to know if the quality mark had made any difference to the children and to the types of play opportunities staff provided. As I started to look around for ways of exploring this, I got in contact not only with experienced evaluators of community projects, but also with researchers. I realised that it would also be interesting to explore what happens when this kind of an initiative is introduced in a setting, not only to see if the original goals for the project were achieved, but to go beyond that and learn about how change in school-age childcare practice can be initiated and what actually changes. I started talking to people at the Queen's University in Belfast about putting together a research proposal and realised that the type of research conducted in the field where I could find financial support was often quantitative, but I was not interested in this type of research, as I wanted to explore together with staff how it may be possible to facilitate and enable children's play in a school-based setting. It was what staff did, their professional practice and how it could be developed that interested me.

After my return to Sweden after 20 years in Northern Ireland and then working in school-age childcare in a school in Stockholm, I successfully applied for a PhD position at Stockholm University to undertake a research project steeped in play and playwork. Play, as I understood it from my playwork experience, was a process initiated and controlled by the players, so I aimed to find settings and staff who wanted to be part of a PhD research project about play as well as being prepared to be active participants in initiating and controlling change in their setting. Playwork was also an inspiration for my PhD since it attempts to advocate on behalf of children:

> The thing that sets playwork apart from all other professions is the methods employed. One of the unique things about playwork is that it is the only profession which seeks to work predominately to the child's agenda.
> (Brown, 2009, p. 6)

This approach of working to the child's agenda could also be considered foundational in Swedish school-age childcare. The governing documents state that staff should "make an inventory of needs and interests of the pupils in their group to be able to offer a meaningful and varied service" (Swedish National Agency for Education, 2014, p. 32). The intention when developing my research was to work together with staff to explore how it may be possible to work to the child's play agenda. This suggested a type of research called action research.

Action research as a tool to explore play facilitation

There are a number of different ways of conducting action research; it can be considered more of an umbrella term and a family of methods (Greenwood & Levin, 1998; Reason & Bradbury, 2001). Action research can be applied both in a range of work places as well as in academic institutions across a variety of scientific disciplines (Dick, 2006). The person most commonly referred to as the father of action research is the social psychologist Kurt Lewin (1890–1947). Lewin's research focused on solving social problems and his interest was primarily in group dynamics. He was influenced by John Dewey (1859–1952), psychologist, philosopher and educationalist. Dewey believed in learning from, and thereby expanding, experience. He was passionate about democracy and extensively explored environments conducive for learning (Dewey, 1916, 1938). He believed, together with other pragmatists (Elkjaer, 2009), that the value of knowledge lies in its practical consequences and that there is no distinct division between theoretical and practical judgements. This is also recognisable in Lewin's work and later in the work of the social psychologist David Kolb, who developed the experiential learning cycle (Beard & Wilson, 2002, p. 194). Lewin's cyclical action research steps are usually described as:

- Identify an idea or a problem
- Fact finding

- Plan
- Take action
- Evaluate
- Amend plan
- Take action

(based on Smith, 2001; 2010)

This may look easy, but as always, the job of a model is to describe in a more linear and simplified fashion something that may not be as easy when put into practice. It may be relatively easy to identify something that we want to find out more about or that we might want to change. However, the next thing we are asked to do is to fact find: that is, to explore if what we believe to be happening is really happening and if it is happening the way we assume. This step may already present a challenge, since we often believe that we know what is happening and therefore do not spend sufficient time on this stage.

Greenwood and Levin (1998, p. 7) suggest that to call anything action research, it needs to contain a balance between research, participation and action. Reason and Bradbury (2001) argues that all action research has five dimensions that need to be accounted for. It should have practical outcomes, be participatory in nature, allow for human flourishing, recognise many ways of knowing and allow for emergence (here understood as the unfolding or evolving nature of the project). Some of these dimensions have strong links to the way playwork is described in the Playwork Principles, for example: "[t]he role of the playworker is to support all children and young people in the creation of a space in which they can play" (PPSG, 2005, Playwork Principle no. 5). This support by playworkers will have practical outcomes, suggests a high level of participation and will evolve over time. Similarly, action research is conducted together *with* people in contrast to other research that may be conducted *on* people (Heron & Reason, 2007) or *for* people (Levin & Greenwood, 2011). Playwork is also in many cases a force for change in the community (see, for example, Chan, 2008; Cranwell, 2007), and this is another similarity. Change and its practical outcomes may be considered an ultimate aim of action research, often driven by values of equity and justice. The underpinning fundamental idea of this type of research is that "the social world can only be understood by trying to change it" (Brydon-Miller, Greenwood, & Maguire, 2003, p. 15). I believe action research also shares another fundamental approach with playwork: they are both experimental. As a playworker, you experiment with resources and modify the environment (Hughes, 2001) to see what can happen, and similarly, in action research there is a process of trial and error, even if it is informed differently (Dick, 2015).

Kemmis and McTaggart (2005) present the following list of action research, informed by different theories, in this family of methods: participatory research, critical action research, classroom action research, action learning, action science, soft systems approaches and industrial action research. To this list of action research methods, I would also add action research inspired by appreciative inquiry, which is based on the positive aspects of what is already working well and appreciating "the best of what is" (Cooperrider & Srivastva, 1987, p. 24). The steps in the cycle are "discovery (appreciate the best of what is), dream (imagine/ envision what could be), design (innovate/co-constructing what should be) and destiny (deliver/sustaining what will be)" (Ludema, Cooperrider, & Barrett, 2001, p. 192).

When reflecting on the action, it may be possible to generalise from our experiences, and when this is done, it is possible to test the principle in new situations and engage in new action. In this way, there is no longer a circle, but a spiral, and you never come back to the same place! When you engage in action-based research based on previous experience, new questions will emerge during reflection, and so this expansive spiral will become a way of working. This type of action research can be considered "first person action research" (Reason & McArdle, 2004, p. 1). This is when a person, or in this case a playwork team, engages in researching their own practice.

As a formal researcher reporting on a PhD research project, it is seldom possible to have an eternal project that continuously throws up new questions, and therefore, you will have to choose what to write about. Alternatively, a different method may be required. "Second person action research" (Reason & McArdle, 2004, p. 1) is when an outsider explores an issue together with a team in a setting and is often called participatory action research. This may allow for a team to develop a way of working while the involvement of the researcher is time-limited. "Third person action research" (Reason & McArdle, 2004, p. 1) is more common within larger organisations and companies and usually involves inviting a researcher to be part of a change process led by the organisation themselves. The research that I developed was "second person action research", where I attempted to develop a relationship with the staff that would allow us to work as co-researchers in a project that explored how it may be possible to facilitate children's play in a school-based school-aged childcare setting.

Playing, according to research, seems to happen within a particular play frame (Bateson, 1976; Jensen, 2013). A play frame, according to Else (2008), is "the environment in which the play takes place" (p. 80). A play frame contains "playactions, each child's micro contributions to influence or move play on" (Jensen, 2013, p. 18). Guilbaud (2003, p. 10) adds to this understanding by arguing that a play frame constitutes an alternative reality created by the players. I understand a play frame to be both the physical environment as well as the narrative of the playing, a particular approach and understanding of what is going on in a particular place (time-space) that frames the play. In the same way, I also needed to frame my research by choosing a particular perspective and/or theory from which to understand what was happening. I had to choose not only a particular type of action research, but also a particular theory to help me make sense of what happened in that action research, and I wanted the theory to reflect and work together with a playwork perspective. Greenwood and Levin (1998) suggest that action research can be based on, for example, Marxist theory, pragmatism, systems theory and social psychology.

Kemmis (2009), a researcher known for critical participatory action research (informed by critical theory and drawing primarily on Habermas) calls action research a practice-changing practice. Kemmis (2009, p. 464–470) argues that there are three types of action research: (i) technical, where change in practice is measured against pre-set standards, for example, standards identified in the Common Inspections Framework (Office for Standards in Education (Ofsted), 2015); (ii) practical, where what changes in the practice and how to achieve it is based on the decision of an individual researcher; and (iii) critical, where what practice changes and how to achieve this change is a collective decision with the aim of sustainable transformation. The third type of action research is informed by critical theory (Kemmis, 2013) and therefore asks questions that go beyond prevailing knowledge, challenges assumptions and makes inquiries about power and social position. In my case, it was important to ask whose knowledge about play facilitation had value, whose voice I wanted to listen to and attempt to put forward.

My role as a second person action researcher (Reason & McArdle, 2004) was as a process leader and a participant in the discussions about what was happening, how it was talked about, what should be changed and how. The fifth Playwork Principle states that "the role of the playworker is to support the children to create a space for play" (PPSG, 2005, Playwork Principle no. 5). The second person action research I developed had a similar intention. I wanted to support the staff to create a space in which they could play with their practice as well as support the children attending their setting to create their own space for play. In action research, the role of the researcher is somewhat different to that of more mainstream research.

One possible and still used approach is informed by positivist ideas about "value-free scientific knowledge" (St. Pierre, 2013, p. 648), where it is assumed that the researcher is an objective observer of processes or conducting experiments (for example, randomised control trials) to test theories. The researcher then perceives there to be a division between theory and practice. Action researchers reject this division and argue that action research "leads to results tested in action and evaluated by professional social researchers and the relevant local stakeholder" (Levin & Greenwood, 2011, p. 29). As stated earlier, action research is research *with* people, not *on* (Heron & Reason, 2007) or *for* people (Levin & Greenwood, 2011). I therefore also sense a similarity between this way of understanding the role of the researcher and the role of the player engaged in social play. They contribute "playactions" (Jensen, 2013, p. 22), adjust the play frame, experiment, together with others, to find the flow of the process. Playing requires "co-ordinated attention" and the "establishment of common intentions" (Harvard, 2009, p. 140), and in the same way, the action researcher has to create this space for play together with the participants, just as children do when they play together. The aim was that staff would become co-researchers in a project that would develop both practical and theoretical knowledge. This would mean that the action research project would make a contribution to the field of playwork as well as the academic fields of child and youth studies and education.

The research/change process

The action research process often starts with identifying a problem, something that needs improving (Edwards-Groves, Olin, & Karlberg-Granlund, 2016; Elliot, 1991). At the time I started working with the Swedish group, the status of school-age childcare staff was threatened more than ever before, due to the introduction of a 'licence to teach' system in Sweden. All of a sudden, those staff who had achieved their qualification before it was part of the teacher training (introduced in 2000) were no longer considered qualified to take responsibility for the service they had worked in for a very long time, even though they had a university degree. Since then, this has been questioned and changed; yet, at that particular time, staff felt devalued. Equally, the situation in the English setting with part-time workers without resources to commit time to a research project of this type suggested that the staff were not valued by their employers. Due to this context, I felt that initiating the project with the usual starting point of action research, focusing on a problem (in the facilitation of play), may easily have been considered a weakness or even a fault in their practice and would not be conducive to the research project. Therefore, I turned to action research inspired by appreciative inquiry (Cooperrider & Srivastva, 1987). This type of action research might be considered influenced by social psychology and in Kemmis' (2009) terms be 'technical' and not at all 'critical'. However, I envisioned that this would be a conducive starting point for a first cycle of action and that we would move on to a more problem focused and critical action research method in a second cycle.

In the Swedish setting, which I will focus on from now on, we had an initial period of reading and coming to some sort of common agreement about what we meant when we talked about play. We needed to 'discover' a common base from which we could 'design' and 'dream' (Ludema et al., 2001, p. 192). At first, staff did not perceive that the children at their setting, called 'the club', were actually playing. Yet after reading, reflecting together and most importantly observing the children, they came to the conclusion that the children most certainly played, but that the playing did not take the form they had expected it to! What they had perceived to be going on, for example, playing computer and board games, turned out to be a backdrop to the playing that was going on between the children as they interacted with each other and the games. They discovered role-playing at the computers and possibly some sort of communication play and social play as the children tried to steal money from each other without getting discovered whilst playing a board game which included buying and selling with paper money.

As we continued on in the 'discovery step' in the cycle (Ludema et al., 2001, p. 192), I asked staff in the Swedish setting what they were already doing well in relation to facilitating play. They answered that there was friendly banter going on between staff and staff and children, which created a good atmosphere. What form this took and what staff actually said was then explored in this fact-finding stage (Smith, 2001; 2010). Staff wore microphones during a session (approximately a total of two hours per person), and then they listened to themselves and reflected on what they actually said and how. Staff had asked the children and their carers for written permission, and this had been given. The agreement was that only the individuals themselves would listen to the recording and that they would then write down their reflections in their log books. When we later explored their reflections together, they eventually concluded that they often used a technique of saying or doing the opposite of what could be generally expected from staff in a school. For example, one staff member had joined in stealing money from another player during the board game. Another example of banter was that they had often answered 'no' when the same question previously had been answered by 'yes'. Moving to the "dream step", "what could be" (Ludema et al., 2001, p. 192), I then asked the staff what it might look like if they transferred this way of working to the physical space. It did not take them long to come up with the idea to turn everything in their space up-side-down. This ended up being one of the play frames that they "designed" (Ludema et al., 2001, p. 192) and offered the children in the next step of the cycle. When the up-side-down day came, they had turned everything upside down – furniture, posters, flowerpots, computers and so on – and when the children arrived they were promptly greeted with: "It was nice to see you, bye bye!" as they were welcomed in by waving of hands and told to put their shoes on the hat rack and hats on the shoe rack. Some children engaged straight away with the play frame: one child took a book, sat down and promptly started 'reading' it up-side-down! Other children went on a hunt for things staff had forgotten to turn. One child with a diagnosis on the autistic spectrum was carefully watching and listening to what was going on. The child never strayed very far from the member of staff assigned to the child, but eventually smiled broadly and said: "I hope the snack today is disgusting!" There were, of course, children attending the club that day who did what they normally do, which was play computer games. They did so sitting on the floor with the laptops on the upturned tables. The play frame had been offered as a play cue (Bateson, 1976) by the adults, as a physical change as well as an alternative reality which some children engaged with and others not.

During reflection time afterwards, it became apparent that some staff had been disturbed by watching the children at the computers. The staff had always emphasised that the club belonged to the children, it was their club! Yet not a single child had questioned the setup that day: they had even sat down beside the upturned chairs and played the computers on the upturned tables, sitting extremely uncomfortably for an extensive period of time. What did that say about the club? This playing made the staff ask themselves what level of participation the children felt was possible in 'their' space. These reflections turned up a problem to focus the next part of the research project on. To sustain the change (the increased focus on play that opened up opportunities for more playing), they had to continue to disturb the space. I was taken by surprise by this turn of events. In my planning I had envisioned a first cycle of 'technical' action research and a second of 'critical action research' (Kemmis, 2009, pp. 464–470), but I had not thought that this would happen without a new start and a new focus. Instead the first cycle automatically had led to staff experiencing a problem they wanted to deal with. If we understand critical action research as a vehicle for challenging assumptions and asking questions about power and sustainability (Kemmis, 2009), then it seems that even the initial appreciative method led us there.

Play research from a playwork perspective

I started out in my research project with the idea that playwork is about supporting the child's play agenda. I wanted to explore that playwork practice together with staff and focus on how it may be possible to facilitate and enable children's play in a school-based setting. It was what staff did, their professional practice and how it could be developed that interested me. This led to my choice of an action research method where participants are active collaborators in initiating and controlling change in their setting. The design of research as a process that moves between observation, reflection/analysis and action is similar to that found in the reflective practice of playwork. The aim of action research is not to find out how things are, rather it strives towards finding out how things could be, "an inquiry into the not yet known" (Gale, 2014, p. 677). This may be considered a playwork approach similar to that which supports children in creating a space for play. When playworkers modify the space, add materials and respond to play cues, they explore what could be, imagine what could happen and what could become, just as children when they play (Lester, 2013).

Playwork defines play as a process (PPSG, 2005), which suggests that instead of being reactive, play points towards that which may become, rather than that which is already. It also suggests that play is in continuous transformation and movement. I had to try and understand action research and the staff's practice also from a theoretical perspective that focused on this continuous change. With the help of Deleuze and Guattari's (1980; 2004) philosophy, playing, rather than play, became the focus, since playing implied process, continuous change, flow and transformation. In their philosophy, 'becoming' does not imply not yet finished or "valued only for the future potential" (Haglund, 2015, p. 1557). Instead, it suggests that nothing and no-one are ever the same. Not only humans are seen as actors: both living and non-living matter are considered forces that effect change and are considered playing forces. For example, governing documents are forces of change, and the change they effect is not always that intended by those who developed them. In this way, we are continuously changing; in Deleuze and Guattari's (1980/2004) terms, we are continuously becoming. We become in the network of multitudes of histories and expectations, the forces of each moment in a continuous movement between order and chaos. The return of difference, even when seemingly the same, does not become the same. To an onlooker, it may seem like children play the same thing over and over again, yet it is not the same, it cannot be the same. The wind blows from another angle, the red block can no longer be found, the look on your face is different: it is not possible, nor may we want to, control all the forces. This is the playing of forces, and as such, playing may itself be a force of potentiality, pointing towards what we do not yet know and what might be (Massumi, 2002).

Then how is research possible? If nothing ever stays the same, how can we choose a method and 'capture' data? Those who try to 'capture' data in this continuous flow of forces, seem to suggest that we stay with the 'mess' (Cook, 2009) and recognise that our decisions made in the play of forces in our becoming-researchers are what construct the realities that end up being described (Law, 2004). In other words, we need to recognise that we choose what to see, document and describe out of all that happens and that sometimes, these choices are not obvious until we start to explore them. When this exploration starts, then other forces are at play and again we make choices about what to see and describe. This is the "mess" (Cook, 2009) we have to stay with. What we did was to put ourselves "in play" (Henricks, 2011, p. 9), and by focusing on playing, we opened ourselves up to the playing forces of children, equipment, governing documents, feelings, expectations and so forth and then tried to describe it.

I would argue that from a playwork perspective, second person critical action research, as a collective process that allows the voice of those not often listened to, may be the best fit to explore play facilitation. This is not to say that other forms of action research based on other theories may not also be effective, but I had the opportunity and made the choice to promote the voice of school-age childcare and playwork staff by engaging in second person critical action research. In both Sweden and England, this is not a voice often heard in the school community, nor in academia. The little research that has been published about school-age childcare in Sweden and UK all point in the same direction. School-age childcare staff and playworkers operating in school-based settings find it hard to resist the culture and discourse of the school (see, for example: Kane, 2015; Smith, 2010; Smith & Barker, 2000).

Critical research has a tendency to be reactive, to come after that which has already happened (Elfström, 2013; Hardt & Negri, 2001), just as playwork is reactive in its compensatory response to the diminishing space and time for children's own playing (Hughes, 2001; Play Wales, 2016). Yet to be critical, research focusing on playwork also needs to be open to critical inquiry into playwork's own assumptions and open up for the thought that playwork may be understood differently in different contexts. Such critical playwork research will question that which is taken-for-granted also within playwork itself.

Just as playwork may be considered a compensatory practice, action research when informed by critical theory is also reactive to unjust policy and practice and a vehicle for challenging assumptions and asking questions about power and sustainability (Kemmis, 2009). Since playworkers and school-age childcare staff can be considered having low-status jobs, I choose to engage in a type of action research that opened up possibilities for their voices to be heard both in their own contexts as well as in the academic field that I as a doctoral student was part of. Just as playwork works to the child's play agenda, I attempted to work to staff's playwork agenda within the constraints of an outcome-driven school.

Action research does not come with predefined methods to use when producing data, and therefore, we needed to remain open to using a variety of methods. Which methods to use had to evolve from the issues that staff decided to focus on, as well as the changes they wanted to try out. Another feature of action research is the dual audiences for knowledge developed. What we learned together was of interest both to the field of playwork/school-age childcare as well as the field of educational science. The process of developing relevant presentations and texts for both these audiences was difficult, and yet has proven to be rewarding. Initially, we did some presentations for school-age childcare staff together, but my main collaborators in the staff team became more independent speakers and writers over time.

Conclusion

How school-age childcare staff facilitate play can be studied from many different perspectives. The research project presented in this chapter was designed to align with some of the Playwork Principles (PPSG, 2005). Principle no. 2 states that the players control their play and Principle nos. 3 and 4 state that the child's play process is primary. The chosen research design was action research informed by critical theory. This was to allow for the focus of the research as well as the content of the research process to be controlled by the practitioners. In this collaborative project, trust was built to allow us to open ourselves up to challenges which we had taken for granted, whether in practice or in research. A playwork perspective allowed us to challenge an instrumental view of play by also attending to the child's view of playing as something you do for its own sake (Factor, 2009; Øksnes, 2013). Playwork may be considered an invitation to playing, with others, in a continuous process. That process, whether planned or unplanned, disturbs that which we take for granted, whatever view of play or practice we hold and as such can be a powerful force in research. Action research in combination with concepts from Deleuze and Guattari's (1980/2004) philosophy allowed us to discover playwork's inherent *and*, or as I put it in the introduction, 'more than'. This attention to *and* made it possible to research play from multiple perspectives and retain its complexity. We played together *and* put ourselves 'in play'.

References

Bateson, G. (1976). A theory of play and fantasy. In J. S. Bruner, A. Jolly, & K. Sylva (Eds.), *Play: Its role in development and evolution* (pp. 119–129). New York: Penguin books.

Beard, C. & Wilson, J. P. (2002). *The power of experiential learning: A handbook for trainers and educators.* London: Kogan Page.

Brown, F. (2009). *What is playwork? Factsheet No. 14.* London: NCB, Children's Play Information Service. Retrieved from www.ncb.org.uk/media/124806/no.14_what_is_playwork.pdf.

Brydon-Miller, M., Greenwood, D., & Maguire, P. (2003). Why action research? *Action Research, 1*(1), 9–28.

Chan, S. (2008). Community-based play projects: Somewhere to play, somewhere to grow. In F. Brown & C. Taylor (Eds.), *Foundations of playwork* (pp. 158–161). Maidenhead: Open University Press.

Cook, T. (2009). The purpose of mess in action research: Building rigour though a messy turn. *Education Action Research*, *17*(2), 277–291.

Cooperrider, D. L. & Srivastva, S. (1987). Appreciative inquiry. In *Organizational life research in organizational change and development* (Vol. 1, pp. 129–169). Retrieved from www.centerforappreciativeinquiry.net/wpcontent/uploads/2012/05/APPRECIATIVE_INQUIRY_IN_Orgnizational_life.pdf.

Cranwell, K. (2007). Adventure playgrounds and the community in London (1948–70): An appreciation of the ideas an actions that shaped the spirit of the 1960s play movement. In W. Russell, B. Handscomb, & J. Fitzpatrick (Eds.), *Playwork voices* (pp. 62–73). London: London centre for playwork education and training.

Deleuze, G. & Guattari, F. (1980/2004). *A thousand plateaus: Capitalism and schizophrenia* (trans. B. Massumi). London: Continuum.

Dewey, J. (1916). *Democracy and education*. Retrieved from www.gutenberg.org/files/852/852-h/852-h.htm.

Dewey, J. (1938). *Experience and education*. New York: The MacMillan Company.

Dick, B. (2006). Action research literature 2004–2006: Themes and trends. *Action Research*, *4*(4), 439–458.

Dick, B. (2015). Reflections on the Sage Encyclopedia of Action Research and what it says about action research and its methodologies. *Action Research*, *13*(4), 431–444.

Edwards-Groves, C., Olin, A., & Karlberg-Granlund, G. (2016). Partnership and recognition in action research: Understanding the practices and practice architectures for participation and change. *Educational Action Research*, *24*(3), 321–333.

Elfström, I. (2013). *Uppföljning och utvärdering för förändring: Pedagogisk dokumentation som grund för kontinuerlig verksamhetsutveckling och systematiskt kvalitetsarbete i förskolan* [Monitoring and evaluation for change: Pedagogical documentation as a base for continuous development and systematic quality work in pre-school]. Doctoral thesis. Stockholm: Stockholm University.

Elkjaer, B. (2009). Pragmatism: A learning theory for the future. In K. Illeris (Ed.), *Contemporary theories of learning: Learning theorists-in their own words* (pp. 74–89). London: Routledge.

Elliot, J. (1991). *Action research for educational change*. Buckingham: Open University Press.

Else, P. (2008). Playing: The space between. In F. Brown & C. Taylor (Eds.), *Foundations of playwork* (pp. 79–83). Maidenhead: Open University Press, McGraw Hill.

Factor, J. (2009). 'It's only play if you get to choose': Children's perceptions of play, and adult interventions. In C. D. Clark (Ed.), *Play & culture studies, volume 9: Transactions at play* (pp. 129–146). Lanham, MD: University Press of America.

Gale, K. (2014). Action research and the assemblage: Engaging Deleuzian pedagogy and inquiry beyond the constraints of the individual and the group in educational settings. *International Journal of Qualitative Studies in Education*, *27*(5), 667–681.

Greenwood, D. & Levin, M. (1998). *Introduction to action research: Social research for social change*. Thousand Oaks, CA: Sage.

Guilbaud, S. (2003). The essence of play. In F. Brown (Ed.), *Playwork: Theory and practice* (pp. 9–17). Buckingham: Open University Press.

Haglund, B. (2015). Pupil's opportunities to influence activities: A study of everyday practice at a Swedish leisure-time centre. *Early Child Development and Care*, *185*(10), 1556–1568.

Hardt, M. & Negri, A. (2001). *Empire*. Cambridge, MA: Harvard University Press.

Harvard, Å. (2009). Imitation och design för lek: Exempel från tre sandlådor [Imitation and design for play: Examples from three sandpits]. I M. Jensen & Å. Harvard (Eds.), *Leka för att lära. Utveckling, kognition och kultur* [Play to learn. Development, cognition and culture] (pp. 123–144). Lund: Studentlitteratur.
Henricks, T. S. (2011). Play as deconstruction. In C. Lobman & B. E. O'Neill (Eds.), Play and cultural studies: Play and performance (pp. 201–236). Lanham, MD: University Press of America.
Heron, J. & Reason, P. (2007). The practice of co-operative inquiry: Research 'with' rather than 'on' people. In P. Reason & H. Bradbury (Eds.), *Handbook of action research* (pp. 144–154). Thousand Oaks, CA: Sage.
Hughes, B. (2001). *Evolutionary playwork and reflective analytic practice*. London: Routledge.
Jensen, M. (2013). *Lekteorier* [Play theories]. Lund: Studentlitteratur.
Kane, E. (2003). *The development of professional competence in playwork in Northern Ireland: An evaluation of current practice.* Unpublished masters dissertation, Belfast: Queen's University Belfast.
Kane, E. (2015). *Playing practices in school-age childcare: An action research project in Sweden and England.* Unpublished doctoral dissertation, Stockholm: Stockholm University.
Kemmis, S. (2009). Action research as a practice-based practice. *Educational Action Research, 17*(3), 463–474. doi:10.1080/09650790903093284.
Kemmis, S. (2013). Critical theory and participatory action research. In P. Reason & H. Bradbury (Eds.), *The Sage handbook of action research: Participative inquiry and practice* (pp. 121–138). London: Sage.
Kemmis, S. & McTaggart, R. (2005). Participatory action research: Communicative action and the public sphere. In N. Denzin & Y. Lincoln (Eds.), *Handbook of qualitative research* (3rd ed., pp. 559–604). Thousand Oaks, CA: Sage.
King, P. (2015). The possible futures for playwork project: A thematic analysis. *Journal of Playwork Practice, 2*(2), 143–156.
Kolb, D. A. & Fry, R. (1975). Toward an applied theory of experiential learning. In C. Cooper (Ed.), *Theories of group process* (pp. 33–57). London: John Wiley. Retrieved from www.colorado.edu/ftep/sites/default/files/attached-files/kolb_-_experiential_learning.pdf.
Law, J. (2004). *After method: Mess in social science research.* Abingdon, UK: Routledge.
Lester, S. (2013). Playing in a Deleuzian playground. In E. Ryall, W. Russell, & M. Maclean (Eds.), *Philosophy of play* (pp. 130–140). London: Routledge.
Levin, M. & Greenwood, D. (2011). Revitalizing universities by reinventing the social sciences. Bildung and action research. In K. Denzin & Y. S. Lincoln (Eds.), *The Sage handbook of qualitative research* (4th ed., pp. 27–42). London: Sage.
Ludema, J. D., Cooperrider, D. L., & Barrett, F. J. (2001). Appreciative inquiry: The power of the unconditional positive question. In P. Reason & H. Bradbury (Eds.), *Handbook of action research: Participative inquiry and practice* (pp. 189–199). London: Sage Publications.
Massumi, B. (2002). *Parables for the virtual: Movement, affect, sensation.* Durham, NC: Duke University Press.
Office for Standards in Education (Ofsted). (2015). *The common inspections framework: Education, skills and early years* (Reference No: 150065). Manchester: Ofsted. Retrieved from www.gov.uk/government/uploads/system/uploads/attachment_data/file/461767/The_common_inspection_framework_education_skills_and_early_years.pdf.

Øksnes, M. (2013). 'We sneak off to play what we want!' Bakhtin's carnival and children's play. In E. Ryall, W. Russell, & M. MacLean (Eds.), *The philosophy of play* (pp. 130–140). London: Routledge.

Play Wales. (2016). *Playwork: What's so special?* Cardiff: Play Wales. Retrieved from www.playwales.org.uk/login/uploaded/documents/INFORMATION%20SHEETS/Playwork%20-%20whats%20so%20special.pdf.

Playwork Principles Scrutiny Group. (2005). *Playwork principles.* Retrieved from www.playwales.org.uk/login/uploaded/documents/Playwork%20Principles/playwork%20principles.pdf.

Polanyi, M. (1958/1974). *Personal knowledge: Towards a post-critical philosophy.* Chicago: University of Chicago Press.

Reason, P. & Bradbury, H. (2001). Inquiry and participation in search of a world worthy of human aspiration. In P. Reason & H. Bradbury (Eds.), *Handbook of action research: Participative inquiry and practice* (pp. 1–14). London: Sage.

Reason, P. & McArdle, K. (2004). Brief notes on the theory and practice of action research. In S. Becker & A. Bryman (Eds.), *Understanding research methods for social policy and practice.* London: The Polity Press. Retrieved from http://peterreason.eu/Papers/Brief_Notes_on_AR.pdf.

Smith, F. & Barker, J. (2000). 'Out of school' in school: A social geography of out of school childcare. In S. Holloway & G. Valentine (Eds.), *Children's geographies: Living, playing, learning* (pp. 245–256). London: Routledge.

Smith, H. H. (2010). *Children's empowerment, play and informal learning in two after school provisions.* Unpublished doctoral dissertation,London: Middlesex University.

Smith, M. K. (2001/2010). Kurt Lewin, groups, experiential learning and action research. *The encyclopedia of informal education.* Retrieved from www.infed.org/thinkers/et-lewin.htm.

St. Pierre, E. A. (2013). The posts continue: Becoming. *International Journal of Qualitative Studies in Education, 26*(6), 646–657.

Swedish National Agency for Education. (2014). *Leisure-time centre: Swedish national agency for education general advice and comments.* Stockholm: Skolverket. Retrieved from www.skolverket.se/publikationer?id=3301.

United Nations. (1989). *United Nations Convention on the Rights of the Child (UNCRC).* Geneva: United Nations.

Wenger, E. (1998). *Communities of practice: Learning, meaning, and identity.* New York: Cambridge University Press.

Conclusion

Pete King and Shelly Newstead

This book posed the question: "What is a playwork perspective when researching children's play?" From a brief introduction of what playwork is and how it has developed over the last 30+ years, different aspects of playwork and children's play have been discussed by the seven different authors who have reflected on how their playwork experience has informed their approach to research. Although the authors have all approached their doctoral research using theoretical and methodological frameworks from a range of different disciplines, this monograph offers some common themes which go some way to addressing the question which underpins the premise of this book. This concluding chapter considers what it means to research play from a playwork perspective by drawing together these common themes.

As Newstead points out, the practice and profession of playwork originated in a collaboration of people from different backgrounds and professions who worked in adventure playgrounds. Playwork has evolved over the last 70 years and, as Russell states in her chapter, has multiple perspectives, which she describes as *diffractive*, or spreading in different directions. The term 'playworker' still has multiple meanings and multiple understandings, as the playwork field, unlike other professions, such as teaching or youth work, does not have a regulatory body. This notion of diffraction in playwork can be applied to research design as well as to practice. The varied playwork backgrounds of the seven authors in relation to their professional playwork practice (adventure playgrounds; out of school provision; parks and open spaces), combined with their own knowledge and understanding of playwork as it evolves, have resulted in different approaches to research design.

The range of research designs in this monograph all focus on the playwork practitioner and their professional role in supporting children in a range of playwork environments, from the critical ethnographic studies of Russell's Cultural Historical Activity Theory (CHAT) and Smith Brennan's practitioner-researcher approaches, to Kane's second person action research and Newstead's historical approach. Water's narrative journey explored children's play in natural environments whilst King's critical realism approach used a combination of interviews, quasi-experiment and self-administered questionnaires. Both studies feature playfulness as a key element in their research design in collecting data and involved some form of active involvement of children in the research, but not necessarily as co-constructors of the research design. Children as co-constructors of research design were clearly evident in Shier's Transformative Research by Children and Adolescents (TRCA).

The different research designs outlined in each chapter also included both qualitative and quantitative research. Qualitative approaches included Smith Brennan's comparison of ethnographic research and playwork practice, using the term playworker-ethnographer, whilst Kane's research on professional practice involved both the researcher and participants in their second person action research. A quantitative approach was used in King's mixed-methods study where children became Play Detectives collecting data in their Play Detective Diary.

Doctoral research starts with a clear research question, which is often informed and shaped by a literature review and provides the 'hook' to develop the research design. Despite the diffractive influences of the authors' diverse playwork experiences on their approaches to researching play, they were united by the question of this book, "What is a playwork perspective when researching children's play?" Each author was asked to consider how their research design and methodology was influenced by their professional practice, and some common themes emerged. Using Newstead's 'Playwork Mirror Theory', four areas of playwork research appear to 'mirror' playwork practice from the seven chapters in this monograph:

1 Rights-based;
2 Playfulness;
3 Process;
4 Critical reflection.

1. Rights-based

When considering a playwork perspective on researching play, one theme that emerges is the rights of the child. Researching from a playwork perspective reflects the principles of the United Nations Convention on the Rights of the Child (UNCRC), where the need for the playworker (and, using Playwork Mirror Theory, also the researcher) is to both protect and promote children's rights to address issues of power, social justice, politics, ethics, inequality and tension, clearly indicated in Russell's chapter and that of Smith Brennan. A rights-based playwork perspective has been proposed by Wragg (2011), whose rights-based playwork perspective considers children as a minority group and the importance of voluntary involvement and non-coercion (which is, of course, an ethical issue for all research). This rights-based perspective is fully explored in Shier's chapter and also reflected in the chapters of both King and Smith Brennan. Many of the authors in this monograph alluded to the need to go beyond researching play from an objective 'outsider' perspective, summed up in Smith Brennan's chapter as the need to "penetrate different worldviews through the eyes of 'insiders'". As Newstead describes, in playwork children's knowledge is considered equal to adult knowledge. This means that when researching play from a playwork perspective, the children's perspective is as valid (if not more so) as the knowledge and perspective of the adult researcher. This epistemic equality provides a 'voice' for children and young people, with the adult's role (in both practice and research) as ensuring that children's perspectives are heard.

2. Playfulness

Playfulness is a particular state of being and is an approach and attitude to an activity (Howard & McInnes, 2014) and as such could be a beneficial approach to conducting research. Playfulness was used as an approach to research and considered in the chapters from Waters, King and Kane. Water's chapter focused on the use of playfulness as a method of research, where adults and children were co-players in the data collection, again reflecting the power balance between the two. The aspect of playfulness was considered as a disposition towards behaviour (experience). Whilst Waters outlined how playfulness was central to his research design of a narrative journey, King used playfulness with respect to the research tools used for data collection, and the practitioners in Kane's research playfully turned the play environment upside down. Playfulness within playwork practice (Wilson, 2010) appears to be 'mirrored' in playwork research.

3. Process

As indicated throughout this monograph, the Playwork Principles (PPSG, 2005) provide the ethical and professional framework for playwork practice. In particular, the focus is on the process of play for children, rather than the product of play in adult terms. Although each doctoral research project had an outcome (to gain the award of a Doctor in Philosophy), the importance of the research process for those undertaking research from a playwork perspective is also evident from the chapters in this monograph. Drawing on Vygotsky, Russell states that "phenomena should be studied as a process rather than fixed", whilst King's chapter outlined the incorporation into his research of Bronfenbrenner's (1995, 1999) process-person-context-time. Waters's use of playfulness as a research tool also developed a narrative process.

The play process often involves interaction between children and other people, which may sometimes involve playwork practitioners. The degree of interaction in playwork can range from being passive to actively involved (Sturrock & Else, 1998). This degree of involvement also applies to the research process in relation to how involved children are in the research. Children's involvement in research can be placed on a continuum from passive participants using observations, as indicated in Smith Brennan's chapter, or through interviews (see chapters from King and Kane) to active participants (Waters's chapter) to being co-constructors of the research process (see Shier's chapter).

4. Critical reflection

Since the publication of Sturrock and Else's (1998) 'Colorado Paper', the degree of adult intervention in the play process has raised much debate on how much involvement or influence playworkers should have on children's play. Sturrock (2003) discusses how playworkers need to consider their own subjectivity when working objectively with children in their play.

126 *Pete King and Shelly Newstead*

Researching play is also both an objective and subjective matter, for both the researcher and the participants. This subjective–objective intertwining was discussed in many of the chapters. King's chapter discusses inter-subjectivity (midway between objectivity and subjectivity), Waters makes reference to the 'inter-subjective adult' (the adult immersed in play) and Russell describes the use of intra-actions, where symbolic objects and knowledge emerge through entanglements. Newstead describes how the first playworkers inhibited their adultness as a way of preventing the adulteration (Sturrock & Else, 2005; Thomson, 2014) of children's perspectives. As with playwork practice, this subjective–objective interaction requires careful consideration when researching play, with the reflexive researcher acknowledging their own subjectivity–objectivity in the research process and employing both critical reflection (of the research process) and critical self-reflection (of themselves).

From diffraction to collection

The diffractive approach to researching play from a playwork perspective resulted in research designs which were grounded in the different playwork practice backgrounds and knowledge sets of the individual researchers, and the varied research design and methods within this monograph mirrored this initial diffractive approach. However, the four themes of children's rights, process, critical reflection and playfulness are common throughout the chapters in this monograph and can therefore be described as a playwork perspective to researching play, as summed up in Figure 8.1:

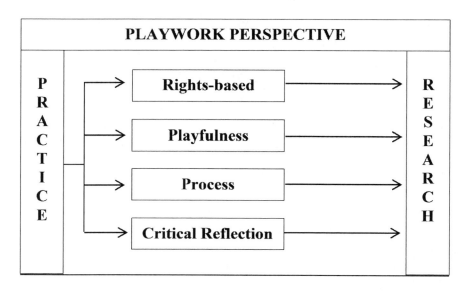

Figure 8.1 Researching play from a playwork perspective

Shier talks about a 'playworker's mind-set' and argues that our playwork experience enables us to take a different approach to research in children's play from other disciplines. Is this playworker mind-set evident in current playwork research? Playwork research has increased over the last ten years, culminating in playwork having its own journal, the *Journal of Playwork Practice*. The peer-reviewed papers reflect the playwork perspective, as suggested above. Waters, Waite and Frampton's (2014) use of cameras on children's physical play (where children were active participants in the research process in collecting data) from a first person's and third person's perspective (inter-subjectivity) makes reference to the power position of between researchers and participants (children's rights) and the need for critical reflection. The power position was a strong feature in Hurst's (2015) research on the views of play of children aged between nine and 12 years. The children were consulted on the proposed research methodology, making children "research partners" (p. 11). Children were also involved in taking photographs as data collection methods to use for the semi-structured interviews. This playful approach to researching play using cameras was also adopted in a collaborative study with children by Bell and Cartmel (2014). A playful approach to play was also undertaken by Wright, Goodenough, and Waite (2015) using art as data collection which involved a combination of observations and discussions. The use of discussions with participants they describe using Harrison and Harrison's conversational drift (Adcock, 1992) is very process orientated, as it is "allowed to go wherever it leads" (Wright et al., 2015, p. 29). This action research method also had a strong emphasis on the artist-researcher being reflective.

Playwork research is still very much in its infancy, and our analysis of common themes in the playwork research literature relies out of necessity on a very small sample size. Perhaps other themes and directions may emerge in future, as new literature on playwork research pursues both a diffractive and a collective approach to establishing what it means to do playwork from a playwork perspective. One of the biggest challenges that the playwork field will face over the next few years is the development of a discrete knowledge base (Newstead, 2016), and questions about the nature and purpose of playwork research will play a vital part in securing playwork not only as a unique discipline, but also as a unique profession in its own right. This monograph aims to play a part in that debate.

References

Adcock, C. (1992). Conversational drift: Helen Mayer Harrison and Newton Harrison. *Art Journal*, 51(2), 35–45.

Bell, K. & Cartmel, J. (2014). Stepping back in school age care. *Journal of Playwork Practice*, 1(1), 157–172.

Bronfenbrenner, U. (1995). Developmental ecology through space and time: A future perspective. In P. Moen, G. H. Elder Jr, & K Luscher (Eds.), *Examining lives in context: Perspectives on the ecology of human development* (pp. 619–647). Washington, DC: American Psychological Association.

Bronfenbrenner, U. (1999). Environments in developmental perspective: Theoretical and operational models. In S. L. Friedman & T. D. Wachs (Eds.), *Measuring environment across the life span: Emerging methods and concepts* (pp. 3–28). Washington, DC: American Psychological Association Press.

Howard, J. & McInnes, K. (2013). *The essence of play: A practice companion for professionals working with children and young people.* London: Routledge.

Hurst, B. (2015). Not always fun: Older children's play worlds in Australian outside school hours care. *Journal of Playwork Practice*, 2(1), 7–22.

Newstead, S. (2016). Editorial. *Journal of Playwork Practice*, 3(1), 3–5.

Playwork Principle Scrutiny Group. (2005). *Playwork principles.* Retrieved from www.playwales.org.uk/login/uploaded/documents/Playwork%20Principles/playwork%20principles.pdf.

Sturrock, G. (2003). Towards a psycholudic definition of playwork. In F. Brown (Ed.), *Playwork: Theory and practice* (pp. 81–97). Buckingham: Open University Press.

Sturrock, G. & Else, P. (1998). 'The Colorado Paper' – The playground as therapeutic space: Playwork as healing. In P. Else & G. Sturrock (Eds.) (2005), *Therapeutic playwork reader one 1995–2000* (pp. 73–104). Eastleigh: Common Threads Publications Ltd.

Thomson, S. (2014). 'Adulterated play': An empirical discussion surrounding adults' involvement with children's play in the primary school playground. *Journal of Playwork Practice*, 1(1), 5–21.

Waters, P., Waite, S., & Frampton, I. (2014). Play frames, or framed play? The use of film cameras in visual ethnographic research with children. *Journal of Playwork Practice*, 1(1), 23–38.

Wilson, P. (2010). *The playwork primer.* College Park, MD: Alliance for Childhood.

Wragg, M. (2011). The child's right to play: Rhetoric or reality? In P. Jones & G. Walker (Eds.), *Children's rights in practice* (pp. 71–81). London: SAGE.

Wright, N., Goodenough, A., & Waite, S. (2015). Gaining insights into young people's playful wellbeing in woodland through art-based action research. *Journal of Playwork Practice*, 2(1), 23–43.

Index

Abernethy, W. Drummond 2, 9, 22, 28, 30–2, 35
action research 5, 109, 111–19, 127, 118, 123–4
Adcock, Craig 127
adulteration xv, 19–21, 42, 48, 77, 126
adventure playground 2, 4, 9, 25–34, 44, 60, 77, 83, 91, 123
after (out of) school club 56–61, 68, 91, 98–9, 101–2, 109, 110, 115–16
Ailwood, Jo 59, 69
Aitken, Stuart 81–2, 85
Alcock, Sophie 75, 80–2, 85
Alderson, Priscilla 94, 102, 104
Alldred, Pam 62, 69
Allen, Marjory 25–6, 28–9, 31–2, 35–8
Anderson, Ceris 94, 105
Angen, Maureen 81, 85
Ansell, Nicola 63, 69
Armitage, Andrew 95, 104
Armitage, Marc 4–5
Atkinson, Paul 61–2, 65, 70
Axline, Virginia 58, 69

Babcock, Barbara A. 103–4
Back, Les 61, 69
Bagiati, Aikaterini 79, 85
Baines, Ed 58, 71
Bairaktarova, Diana 79, 85
Ball, David 58, 69
Balmforth, Nick 28, 35
Barad, Karen 39–40, 42, 46, 48–9, 52–3
Barbour, Ann C. 98–9, 104
Barclay, Mike 5
Barker, John 58, 62, 69, 118, 122
Barnett, Lynn 74, 85
Barrett, Frank J. 113, 121
Bascombe, Dominic 58, 69
Bateson, Gregory 113, 116, 119
Bateson, Patrick 75–6, 78, 85

Battram, Arthur 44, 52
Beard, Colin 111, 119
Beck, Ulrich 56, 69
Bell, Kevin 127
Bellin, Wynford 75, 86
Bengtsson, Arvid 25, 32, 35
Benjamin, Joe 25, 28–31, 32, 35–6
Bennett, Jane 48, 52
Bennett, John 57, 69
Bertelsen, John 28–9, 34–5
Beunderman, Joost 11, 22, 31, 35
Bhaskar, Roy 69, 104
Birks, Melanie 27, 36
Blades, Mark xv–xvi
Blaikie, Norman 62, 69
Blaise, Mindy 49, 55, 79, 85
Blatchford, Peter 58, 71
Bonel, Paul 3, 5, 58, 69, 97, 104
Boradhead, Pat 1, 5, 90, 104
Bourdieu, Pierre 62, 69
Brettell, Caroline 62, 69
Bradbury, Hilary 111–12, 122
Braidotti, Rosi 41, 48, 52–3
Brettell, Caroline 62, 69
Bronfenbrenner, Urie 5, 97–8, 104, 125, 127–8
Brooker, Liz 79, 85
Brophy, Sean 79, 85
Brown, Fraser 3–5, 20, 22, 25, 33, 36, 42–3, 53, 56, 58–9, 63–4, 69, 72, 76, 85, 111, 119
Bruner, Jerome S. xv, 44, 78, 81, 83, 85
Brydon-Miller, Mary 112, 119
Bryman, Alan 95–6, 105
Buck, Donne 30, 36
Bundy, Anita C. 74, 88
Burden, George 32, 36
Burghardt, Gordon M. 48–9, 53, 58, 69, 83, 85
Burke Johnson, Robert 95, 105
Butler, Judith 41, 53

Caillois, Roger 48, 53
Candler, Catherine 75, 88
Carey, Malcolm 41, 54
Carspecken, Phil F. 62–4, 69
Cartmel, Jennifer 4, 5, 127
Castillo, Jose 81, 85
Chan, Steve 112, 119
Cheesman, Brian 33, 36
childcare 5, 21, 57, 109, 110–11, 113, 115, 118–19
child friendly 4, 12, 15, 18, 97
childhood 3, 27–8, 34, 40–5, 48–9, 58, 64, 67–8, 78–80, 91, 93–6, 104
children's voices 67, 93, 95, 118
Chilton, Tony 77, 85
Christie, James 83, 88
Clarke, Tilean 5
Clifford, James 62, 70
Cockburn, Tom 56, 70
Cocken, Dorothy 28, 30, 36
Cohen, Louis 96, 105
Cole, Becky 94, 105
Cole, Doug 94, 105
Cole, Michael 47, 53
Cole-Hamilton, Isobel 3, 5
Connolly, Paul 61–2, 70
Conway, Mick 3, 6, 44, 53
Cook, Tina 118, 120
Cooperrider, David L. 113, 115, 120–1
Corbin, Juliet 27, 36
Corsaro, William 1, 6, 61–6, 70, 82, 85
Costabile, Angela xvi
Cowie, Helen xv–xvi
Cranwell, Keith 2, 6, 26, 36, 44, 53, 112, 120
critical: action research 112, 115–16, 118 (*see also* action research); ethnography 4, 41–2, 56–7, 60–1, 63–5, 67–8, 123 (*see also* ethnography); realism 5, 96, 98, 104, 123; reflection 4, 14, 21, 57, 67–8, 74, 102, 124–7; reflective practice 9, 67, 114 (*see also* reflective, in practice); theory 5, 63, 96, 98, 104, 114, 118–19
Crowley, Kevin 99, 106
Crowther, S. 32, 36

Dahlberg, Gunilla 40, 53
Dapretto, Mirella 27, 37
Darwin, Charles 1, 6
David, Tricia 94, 105
Davies, Charlotte A. 102–3, 105
Davy, Annie 31, 36

Deci, Edward L. 98–9, 105
Deleuze, Gilles 117, 119–20
Denzin, Norman K. 43, 53, 63, 70
Devine, Dympna 90, 105
Dewey, John 111, 120
Dick, Bob 111–12, 120
diffractive 4, 41–2, 45, 52, 123–4, 126–7
Ding, Sharon 91, 95, 97, 106
Dolphijn, Rick 42, 47, 53
Downward, Paul D. 96, 105
Duggan, Edward P. 32, 36
Duren, Gwendolyn J. 75, 87

Edmiston, Brian 81, 83–4, 86
Edwards, Rosalind 62, 71
Edwards, Susan 79, 85
Edwards-Groves, Christine 115, 120
Eide, Asbjørn 10, 22
Elfström, Ingela 118, 120
Elkjaer, Bente 111, 120
Elliot, John 115, 120
Ellis, Michael J. 9, 22
Elkind, David 79, 86
Else, Perry 3, 7, 10, 19–21, 24, 31–2, 36–7, 42–3, 48, 55, 59, 65, 68, 71–2, 75–7, 79–80, 83–4, 86, 88, 92, 94, 96, 103, 107, 113, 120, 125–6, 128
empowerment xv, 13, 56, 58, 60, 63–4, 93, 97
engagement 30, 41–2, 61, 74, 84
Engeström, Yrjö 41, 46, 53
epistemology 4, 8–9, 33–4, 41, 45, 47, 95–7, 104
ethics: nomadic 41; in playwork practice 3, 40, 42, 47, 49, 52, 60, 76, 124–5; in research xvi, 4, 39, 41, 49, 52, 81, 94, 104, 124
ethnography 4, 20, 40–4, 52, 56–7, 60–8, 82, 84, 123–4; *see also* critical, ethnography
Evangelou, Demetra 79, 85

Factor, June 119–20
Farell, Ann 94, 105
Faulkner, Dorothy 81, 89, 95–6, 102, 108
Fetterman, David 61–2, 70
fieldwork 17, 42–3, 51, 56, 61, 66
Fisher, Katherine 2, 6
Fischer, Michael J. 62, 71
Fitzpatrick, John 4–6
Fleer, Marilyn 79, 86
Flick, Ewe 66, 70

Index 131

Foucault, Michel 62, 70, 78, 86
Frampton, Ian 79, 86, 127–8
Francois, Pierre 25, 36
Freeman, Michael 58, 64, 70
Freire, Paulo 13, 22, 74, 86
Freud, Sigmund 58, 70
Frimberger, Katja 74, 80, 86
Fromberg, Doris 83, 86
Frost, Joe L. 1, 6
Fry, Ronald 110, 121

Gadda, Andressa 78, 86
Gale, Ken 117, 120
Garvey, Catherine 48, 53, 92, 105
Geertz, Clifford 62–3, 70
Gibson, James J. 101, 105
Gill, Tim 3, 5, 45, 51, 53, 56, 58, 69, 70
Golcher, W. J. 32, 36
Goodall, Deborah 74, 88, 90, 107
Goodenough, Alice 127–8
Gore, Neil 90, 107
Graue, M. Elizabeth 82, 86
Greenwood, Davyd J. 111–14, 119–21
Grieg, Anne 91, 105
Griffiths, Carol 74, 88, 90, 107
Groos, Karl 1, 6
Grover, Sonja 96, 105
Guattari, Felix 117, 119–20
Guba, Egon, G. 18, 22
Guilbaud, Sylwyn 113, 120
Gutkind, Peter Claus Wolfgang 29, 32, 36

Habermas, Jürgen 114
Haglund, Björn 117, 120
Hall, Granville S. 1, 6
Hammersley, Martyn 61–2, 65, 70
Handscomb, Bridget 4–6, 32–3, 36
Haraway, Donna J. 39–40, 48, 53
Hardman, Charlotte 64, 70
Hardt, Michael 118, 120
Harrison, Helen Mayer 117
Harrison, Newton 117
Harrop, Andy 3, 5
Hart, Roger xv–xvi, 91, 93, 95–6, 100, 104–5
Harvard, Åsa 114, 121
Hastrup, Kirsten 66, 70
Heidegger, Martin 75, 86
Hendrick, Harry 1, 6, 58, 70
Henricks, Thomas S. 118, 121
Herbert, Joan A. M. 32, 36
Heron, John 112, 114, 121
Heseltine, Peter 26–7, 33, 36
Hey, Valerie 61, 70

Hochschild, Arlie R. 41, 53
Hoedemækers, Casper 45, 53
Holme, Andrea 2, 6
Holt, John 44
Hood, Suzanne 95, 106
Horton, John 32, 37, 68, 71
Howard, Justine 1, 6, 75–6, 86, 92, 98–102, 105–6, 125, 128
Hughes, Bob xvi, 2–3, 6, 20, 22, 25–6, 31, 33, 36–7, 42–3, 48, 53–4, 56, 58–60, 64–5, 70, 76–7, 79–80, 86, 91–4, 104–5, 110, 112, 118, 121
Huizinga, Johan 48, 54, 58, 70
Hurst, Bruce 127–8
Hyvönen, Pirkko T. 101, 105

Iacoboni, Marco 27, 37
insider researcher 13, 44, 57, 61–3, 66–8, 94, 124
inter-subjective 4, 84, 126–7
intervention 10, 16, 26, 30, 48–9, 51, 61, 64, 67, 80–1, 84, 110, 125; *see also* playwork, intervention
interviews: by adults 43, 47, 56, 61, 64–6, 95–6, 99, 101–2, 123, 125, 127; by children 13, 17–19

Jackson, Anthony 66, 70
Jackson, Mary 30, 37
Jago, Leo 31, 34, 37
James, Allison 56, 58, 61–2, 71, 93, 95–6, 104, 106
Jeffs, Tony 56, 58, 71
Jenkin, Rebecca 79, 86
Jenks, Chris 56, 71
Jennings, Sue 1, 6
Jensen, Mikael 113–14, 121
Jolly, Alison 83, 85
Jones, Peter E. 46, 54
Jones, Phil 92, 106
Jones, Susan S. 27, 37
Juujärvi, Marjaana 101, 105

Kamberelis, George 44, 54
Kane, Eva 5, 109–10, 118, 121, 123–5
Kane, Liam 13, 23
Karlberg-Granlund, Gunilla 115, 120
Kato, Kentaro 58, 71
Katz, Cindi 41, 43, 54
Kellett, Mary 17, 23, 91, 97, 106
Kemmis, Stephen 112–18, 121
Kerstetter, Katie 94, 106
Kilvington, Jacky 3, 6, 25, 37, 43, 48, 54, 66, 71, 80, 86, 91, 94, 106

132 *Index*

Kincheloe, Joe L. 47, 54
King, Pete 3–4, 6, 76, 86, 92–3, 98, 100, 102, 105–6, 110, 121, 123–6
Kingston, Ben 33, 37
Kofoed, Jette xvi
Kohut, Heinz 27, 37
Kolb, David A. 94, 106, 110–11, 121
Kraftl, Peter 32, 37, 68, 71
Kuhaneck, Heather 98–9, 106
Kuhn, Thomas S. 95, 106
Kvale, Steinar 66, 71
Kyttä, Marketta 101, 106

Lahman, Maria 74, 87
Lambert, Jack 25, 28, 30–1, 37
Lansdown, Gerison 11, 23
Lather, Patti 44, 49, 54
Law, John 118, 121
Lazarus, Moritz 1, 6
learning: as experiential xv, 79, 81, 110–11; as formal 58, 74, 79; as informal 56, 58, 60, 64, 74, 110
Lees, Ray 9, 23
Lefebvre, Henri 41, 43, 45, 50–1, 54
Lenz-Taguchi, Hillevi 49, 54
Lester, Stuart 4, 6, 13, 23, 32, 37, 48–9, 54, 59–60, 68, 71, 75, 79, 83, 87, 97, 101, 106, 117, 121
Levin, Morten 111–14, 120–1
Levinas, Emmanuel 41, 54
Lewin, Kurt 111
Lieberman, J. Nina 75, 87
Lincoln, Yvonna S. 63, 70
Lindon, Jennie 3, 5, 58, 69, 97, 104
Lindqvist, Gunilla 77, 83, 87
Loacker, Bernadette 45, 53
Ludema, James D. 113, 115–16, 121
Lundy, Laura 17, 23

MacLure, Maggie 49, 54
Maegusuku-Hewett, Tracey 94, 105
Maguire, Patricia 112, 119
Manion, Lawrence 96, 105
Mannello, Marianne 4, 7
Manwaring, Beth 2, 4, 7, 51, 54
Marcus, George E. 62, 70–1
Martin, Adrian D. 44, 54
Martin, Paul 76, 78, 85
Mason, Jan 95, 106
Mason, Jennifer 66, 71
Massey, Doreen 40, 54
Massie, Peter 2, 6
Massumi, Brian 117, 121
Maudsley, Martin 4, 6, 101, 106

Mayall, Berry 93–4, 96, 106
Mayo, Marjorie 9, 23
Mays, John Barron 28, 30, 37
Mazziotta, John C. 27, 37
McArdle, Kate 113–14, 122
McGhee, Paul E. 74, 87
McInnes, Karen 1, 6, 98–9, 105–6, 125, 128
McIntosh, Jonathan 82, 87
McKendrick, John 32, 37, 68, 71
McTaggart, Robin 112, 121
Mello, Robin 81, 87
Merleau-Ponty, Maurice 75, 87
Mertens, Donna M. 14, 23
Meynell Games Group (Meynell, Walter) 32, 37
Mignolo, Walter D. 52, 54
Miles, Gareth 99, 106
Miller, Elissa 98–9, 106
Mills, Jane 27, 36
mixed-method 5, 6, 95–6, 98, 104, 124
Molinari, Luisa 82, 85
Montessori, Maria 1, 7
Moran, Dermot 74–5, 84, 87–8
Morrison, Keith 96, 105
Morrow, Virginia 91, 94, 102, 104
Moss, Peter 40, 53–4, 56, 71
Moyles, Janet R. 78, 87
Mygind, Annie 28, 30, 37

narrative 67, 77, 79, 84, 102, 113, 124; cues 79; framing 79; journey 4, 74, 78–81, 83–4, 123; style 43; thirding 83–4
Negri, Antonio 118, 120
Neisser, Ulric 81, 87
Nelson, Wendy 28, 35
Nettle, Daniel 75, 85
Neumann, Eva A. 92, 107
Newstead, Shelly 2, 4, 7, 25–8, 37, 76–7, 87, 123–4, 126–8
Nicholson, Mary 25, 27–8, 35
Nicholson, Simon 28, 37
Nicolini, Davide 83, 87
Nuttall, Eddie 25, 37, 43, 54

objective 44, 62, 67, 84, 94–6, 114, 124, 126
O'Brien, Jane C. 75, 87
observations 56, 61, 65–7, 76, 81, 94, 117, 125
Øksnes, Maria 119, 122
Olin, Anette 115, 120
ontology 4, 27–8, 31, 33–4, 94, 96–7

Onwuegbuzie, Anthony J. 95, 105
outsider researcher 44, 66–7, 94, 113, 124

Palermiti, Anna Lisa xvi
paradigm 10, 11, 14, 16, 31, 47, 80, 81, 95–6
Parten, Mildred B. 1, 7
participants 1, 13–14, 47, 56, 59, 61–3, 65–7, 74, 80, 90–1, 93–6, 100, 102, 104, 111, 114, 117, 124, 127; as active participants 4, 62, 91, 93, 95, 100, 103, 111, 125, 127; with children 91, 93, 95–6, 98, 100–1, 125, 127; in facilitating children's involvement 2–13, 19, 13, 17–18; non-participation 93; passive 4, 95–6, 101, 125; as young researchers 5, 13–15, 17–19
Patte, Michael 33, 36
Pedersen, Michael 45, 53
Pellegrini, Anthony D. 58, 71
Pence, Alan 40, 53
Petrie, Pat 56, 63, 71
Pfeifer, Jennifer H. 27, 37
Piaget, Jean 1, 7, 58, 71
Plato 1, 7
play: advocate 3, 48, 59, 61, 68, 75, 80, 93, 96, 103, 111; behaviour 74, 76, 90; and children's agenda 77, 111, 118; and children's right to xii, 3, 8, 10–13, 18–20, 64, 92–3, 103 (*see also* rights, in Article 31); choice scale 96, 99, 101–2; cue 10, 65, 76, 79, 117; cycle 77, 92, 96, 103; definition of 16, 40–1, 49, 92; Detective Diary (PDD) 98–100, 124; facilitation of 2, 9–10, 16, 60–1, 63, 109–11, 113–15, 117–19; frame 77, 79, 113–14, 116; and freely-chosen xv, 2, 40, 48–9, 60, 73, 76, 78, 90–2, 94, 97, 109; and intrinsically motivated 16, 40, 48, 60, 76, 109; and intrinsic nature 3, 45, 75, 79–80; policy 61, 92; process 3, 16, 20–1, 31, 48, 59, 61, 76, 91–4, 98, 103, 109, 111, 117, 119, 125; purpose 9, 79; return 76, 92; and self-directed 21; space 29, 59, 61, 67, 102; theory 1; types 2, 60, 76
playfulness: in adult-child interactions 74–5, 77, 80–4; in adults 74; in children 31, 74; as a mood state 74, 78, 82; in playwork 31, 65, 73–4, 76, 78–81, 83–4, 98, 125, 127; for

Index 133

playworkers 76–7, 98; in research 4–5, 73–4, 78–84, 98–101, 123–7; in research methodologies 4–5, 73–6, 78–84, 98–100, 123–7; in space 50–1, 83
playgrounds xvi, 11, 26, 98–9, 101–2
playwork: curriculum 10, 60; education 32, 41, 90; ethos 12, 40, 109; experience xv, 16, 26, 110, 123–4, 127; field 2, 4, 25, 27, 33–4, 123, 127; intervention 16, 26, 30, 48, 61, 64, 67, 80, 84, 110 (*see also* intervention); literature 4, 9, 11, 20, 26–7, 31, 33, 43, 56, 58; mind-set 8, 20–2, 127; mirror theory 4, 25, 27–32, 31–5, 124–6; perspective 2–5, 27, 31–4, 40–2, 52, 56–7, 59–60, 63–4, 67–8, 76, 78, 90, 103–4, 109, 113, 117–19, 123–7; politics 9, 20, 40, 45, 52, 56, 68, 92, 124; practice 3–5, 10, 15, 18–20, 26–7, 31, 33–4, 42, 57, 60, 64–5, 67–8, 78, 83, 90–8, 101, 103, 110, 117, 123–6; praxis 74; purpose 25–8, 31, 52; research 25, 32–4, 39, 49, 57, 68, 118, 124–5, 127; roots 2, 8–9, 12, 15–19, 22, 44; space 2–6, 18, 21, 28–30, 32, 40, 77, 83, 93; theory 3, 18, 26, 32, 40–4, 59, 64, 76–8, 110; training 9, 27, 32, 60, 92, 110; values and assumptions 3, 97
playwork principles 3, 12, 16–17, 20–1, 31, 33, 35, 40–1, 47–8, 50, 59–61, 63–4, 66, 68, 76–9, 92–3, 97, 102, 109, 112, 114, 117, 119, 125; Principle no. 1 16; Principle no. 2 16, 20, 40, 48, 76, 109, 119; Principle no. 3 16; Principle no. 4 20, 48, 59, 93; Principle no. 5 50, 112, 114; Principle no. 6 63, 66; Principle no. 8 16
Podyma, Ross 5
Polanyi, Michael 110, 122
Powell, Jason 41, 54
Powell, Sacha 94, 105
praxis: in culture 77; in practice 31, 73–4, 76–81, 83–4; in research 73–4, 76–81, 84
Prout, Alan 56, 62, 71, 93, 95, 104, 106
Proyer, René 74–5, 87
Punch, Samantha 82, 88, 97–8, 102, 107

Qian, Xinyi Lisa 74, 88
qualitative 4, 14, 43, 57, 68, 74, 80, 95–6, 100, 103, 124

quantitative xv, 4, 95–6, 98, 100–1, 103, 110, 124
quasi-experiment 96, 99, 101–2, 123
questionnaire 18, 93, 123

Rautio, Pauliina 75, 88
Ray, Larry 41, 55
Reason, Peter 111–14, 121–2
Reddy, Vasudevi 75, 83, 88
Rees, Val 75, 86
reflective: in practice 3, 9, 14, 61, 64, 66–7, 94, 117; in research 64, 66–7, 91, 102, 117, 127; *see also* critical, reflection
reflexivity 61, 94, 102–3, 126
Rennie, Stephen 32, 37
research method xv, 4, 8, 17, 34, 41, 45, 47, 56–7, 61–2, 73–4, 78–81, 84, 94–5, 97–8, 102, 111–13, 115, 117–18, 125–7; methodology 2, 8, 12, 14, 16, 19–20, 32–4, 39, 41–2, 45, 49, 75, 68, 78, 82, 97, 123–4, 127; politics 4, 39, 41, 43, 47–8, 50, 62–3, 68, 74, 96; process xv, xvi, 4, 15–18, 56, 63, 66, 68, 90–1, 94–100, 102–3, 112, 115, 117, 119, 125–7
Ribbens, Jane 62, 71
Rice, Louis 98, 107
rights: in Article 2 11; in Article 3 11; in Article 12 11, 19, 93, 96, 97, 103; in Article 13 93, 103; in Article 31 8, 10–11, 92–3, 103, 110; children's xv, xvi, 4, 8, 10–12, 18–20, 56, 63–5, 90–3, 103, 124, 126–7; human 8, 10, 13, 15–17; to play 3, 8, 10–13, 18–20, 64, 92–3, 103, 110; research 90–1, 103, 124, 126–7; in social construction 93, 95, 104; United Nations Convention on the Rights of the Child (UNCRC) 10–11, 13, 19, 22, 92–3, 96–7, 124; views on 19, 90, 92–3, 95–6
Robinson, Helja A. 63, 71
Rosa, E. Della 75, 83, 88
Rose, Nikolas 40, 42, 55
Roskos, Kathleen 83, 88
Rushing, Sara 41, 55
Russell, Wendy 3–4, 6, 7, 13, 20, 23, 25, 31–2, 37–8, 42–5, 48–9, 50–2, 55, 59–60, 68, 71, 75, 78–9, 82–3, 87–8, 97, 106, 123–6
Ryan, Richard M. 98–9, 105
Ryan-Bloomer, Katherine 74, 88

St. Pierre, Elizabeth Adams 44, 55, 114, 122
Sandlands, Chiquita 30, 38
Santer, Joan 74, 82, 88, 90, 107
Schmid, Christian 45, 55
Schön, Donald 94, 107
Schwartzman, Helen B. 1, 7
Scribner, Sylvia 47, 53
Shier, Harry 3–4, 8–14, 17, 19, 23–4, 35, 38, 93, 107, 123–5, 127
Siemens, George 81, 88
Silverman, David 62, 71
Skard, Geva 74, 88
Smilansky, Sara 1, 7
Smith, Chris 2
Smith, Fiona 58, 62–3, 69, 118, 122
Smith, Hannah Henry 68, 71, 118, 122; *see also* Smith Brennan, Hannah
Smith, M. 56, 58, 71
Smith, Peter K. xv–xvi, 1, 7, 90, 94, 107
Smith Brennan, Hannah 4, 123–5; *see also* Smith, Hannah Henry
Snowden, Dave 81, 88
Soames, Paul 29, 38
social construction 93, 95, 104; development 57, 59–60; justice 56, 63, 67–8, 112, 124; policy 22, 31, 34, 43–5, 50–1, 56, 60, 64, 118; in power relations 4, 5, 14, 48, 50, 59, 63–5, 67–8, 78, 82, 91, 114, 117–18, 124–5, 127
Sørensen, Carl Theodor 29–30, 38
Spears, Barbara A. xvi
Spencer, Herbert 1, 7, 58, 71
Spiegal, Bernard 58, 69
Springer, Simon 41, 55
Srivastva, Suresh 113, 115, 120
Statham, June 4, 7
Stein, Jane 60, 71
Strauss, Anselm 27, 36
Street, Cathy 3, 5
Sturrock, Gordon 3, 6–7, 10, 19–21, 24–5, 38, 42–3, 48, 55, 59, 65, 72, 76–7, 79–80, 83–4, 88, 92, 94, 96, 103, 107, 125–6, 128
subjective 62, 75, 91, 94–7, 103, 126
subjective–objective 101, 103–4, 126
Sutherland, Allan T. 29, 38
Sutton-Smith, Brian 48, 50–1, 55, 102–3, 107
Sylva, Kathy 44, 83, 85

Takhvar, Mehri 90, 107
Tashakkori, Abbas 95, 107

Tawil, Ben 5
Taylor, Affrica 49, 55
Taylor, Chris 2, 4–5, 7, 32, 38, 43, 51, 53–4, 56, 58–9, 63, 69
Taylor, Jayne 91, 105
Teddlie, Charles 95, 107
Tedlock, Barbara 62, 72
Tegano, Deborah W. 74, 84, 88
Thomson, Sarah 19–20, 24, 79, 88, 126, 128
Tonkin, Jo 94, 105
Torstenson-Ed, Tullie 95, 107
Treseder, Phil xv–xvi, 93, 107
Trew, Richard 94, 105
Turner, Herbert S. 30, 32, 38, 43, 55
Turner, Victor 83, 88

van der Tuin, Iris 42, 47, 53
Vannini, Phillip 44, 55
Virdi, Michelle 32–3, 36
Vollstedt, Ralph 90, 94, 107
Vygotsky, Lev S. xv, 45, 47, 55, 125

Waibel, Alexandra 3, 6
Waite, Sue J. 82, 89, 127–8
Walsh, Daniel J. 82, 86

Ward, Colin 44
Waters, Philip 4, 74, 79, 82–3, 86, 88–9, 125–8
Webb, Sophie 25, 36, 64, 69, 72
Welsh, Richard 25, 35
Wenger, Etienne 110, 122
Whatmore, Sarah 48, 55
Williams, Hank 33, 38
Wills, Ray 30, 38
Wilson, John P. 111, 119
Wilson, Penny 21, 24, 78, 89, 98, 108, 125, 128
Wolcott, Harry 66, 72
Wood, Ali 3, 6, 25, 37, 43, 48, 54, 66, 71, 80, 86, 91, 94, 106
Woodhead, Martin 81, 89, 95–6, 102, 108
Woods, Peter 61, 72
Wragg, Mike 3, 7, 11, 24, 79, 89, 124, 128
Wright, Naomi 127–8

Yarnal, Careen 74, 88
Yeung, Henry Wai-chung 96, 108
Yorke, John 79, 89
Youell, Biddy 74–5, 83, 89